The 1630s

Manchester University Press

Politics, culture and society in early modern Britain

General Editors
PROFESSOR ANN HUGHES
PROFESSOR ANTHONY MILTON
PROFESSOR PETER LAKE

This important series publishes monographs that take a fresh and challenging look at the interactions between politics, culture and society in Britain between 1500 and the mid-eighteenth century. It counteracts the fragmentation of current historiography through encouraging a variety of approaches which attempt to redefine the political, social and cultural worlds, and to explore their interconnection in a flexible and creative fashion. All the volumes in the series question and transcend traditional interdisciplinary boundaries, such as those between political history and literary studies, social history and divinity, urban history and anthropology. They thus contribute to a broader understanding of crucial developments in early modern Britain.

The 1630s

Interdisciplinary essays on culture and politics in the Caroline era

edited by
IAN ATHERTON AND JULIE SANDERS

Manchester
University Press
Manchester and New York

distributed exclusively in the USA by Palgrave

Copyright © Manchester University Press 2006

While copyright in the volume as a whole is vested in Manchester University Press, copyright in individual chapters belongs to their respective authors, and no chapter may be reproduced wholly or in part without the express permission in writing of both author and publisher.

Published by Manchester University Press
Oxford Road, Manchester M13 9NR, UK
and Room 400, 175 Fifth Avenue, New York, NY 10010, USA
www.manchesteruniversitypress.co.uk

Distributed in the United States exclusively by
Palgrave Macmillan, 175 Fifth Avenue,
New York, NY 10010, USA

Distributed in Canada exclusively by
UBC Press, University of British Columbia, 2029 West Mall,
Vancouver, BC, Canada V6T 1Z2

British Library Cataloguing-in-Publication Data is available

Library of Congress Cataloging-in-Publication Data is available

ISBN 978 0 7190 7159 1 paperback

First published by Manchester University Press in hardback 2006

This paperback edition first published 2013

The publisher has no responsibility for the persistence or accuracy of URLs for any external or third-party internet websites referred to in this book, and does not guarantee that any content on such websites is, or will remain, accurate or appropriate.

Printed by Lightning Source

To Ann Hughes

Contents

LIST OF FIGURES —viii
LIST OF CONTRIBUTORS—ix
PREFACE—xi
LIST OF ABBREVIATIONS—xii

1 Introducing *The 1630s*: questions of parliaments, peace and pressure points *Julie Sanders and Ian Atherton*   1

2 Force, love and authority in Caroline political culture *Malcolm Smuts*   28

3 The image of Charles I as a Roman emperor *John Peacock*   50

4 'From his Matie to me with his awin hand': the King's correspondence during the period of personal rule *Sarah Poynting*   74

5 Henrietta Maria in the 1630s: perspectives on the role of consort queens in *Ancien Régime* courts *Caroline Hibbard*   92

6 'The faction of the flesh': orientalism and the Caroline masque *James Knowles*   111

7 Buried alive: Thomas May's 1631 *Antigone* *Karen Britland*   138

8 Placing Caroline politics on the professional comic stage *Matthew Steggle*   154

9 Stigmatizing Prynne: seditious libel, political satire and the construction of opposition *Andrew McRae*   171

10 Coteries, complications and the question of female agency *Jerome de Groot*   189

INDEX—211

Figures

1 Anthony Van Dyck, *Charles I and M. de St Antoine*. The Royal Collection © 2004, Her Majesty Queen Elizabeth II. *page* 51
2 Inigo Jones, Oberon in *Oberon, the Fairy Prince*, 1611. Devonshire Collection, Chatsworth. Reproduced by permission of the Duke of Devonshire and the Chatsworth Settlement Trustees. 53
3 Antonio Tempesta, Caius Caesar (Caligula) from *The Twelve Caesars*, 1596. Photo: Warburg Institute. 54
4 Inigo Jones, St George's Portico in *Prince Henry's Barriers*, 1610. Devonshire Collection, Chatsworth. Reproduced by permission of the Duke of Devonshire and the Chatsworth Settlement Trustees. 56
5 Inigo Jones, Albanactus in *Albion's Triumph*, 1632. Devonshire Collection, Chatsworth. Reproduced by permission of the Duke of Devonshire and the Chatsworth Settlement Trustees. 57
6 Marcantonio Raimondi, *Trajan crowned by Victory* from the Arch of Constantine. Photo: Warburg Institute. 58
7 Inigo Jones, Sketch for 'a stately temple' in *Albion's Triumph*, 1632. Devonshire Collection, Chatsworth. Reproduced by permission of the Duke of Devonshire and the Chatsworth Settlement Trustees. 60
8 Jacques Androuet du Cerceau, *Basilica of Alexander Severus*, 1584. Photo: Victoria and Albert Museum. 61
9 Inigo Jones, A Roman atrium in *Albion's Triumph*, 1632. Devonshire Collection, Chatsworth. Reproduced by permission of the Duke of Devonshire and the Chatsworth Settlement Trustees. 63
10 Anthony Van Dyck, *William Feilding, 1st Earl of Denbigh*. National Gallery, London. © National Gallery, London. 116

Contributors

Ian Atherton is Senior Lecturer in History at Keele University. He is the author of *Ambition and Failure in Stuart England: The Career of John, First Viscount Scudamore* (Manchester University Press, 1999) and co-editor of *Norwich Cathedral: Church, City and Diocese, 1096–1996* (Hambledon, 1996), and has published several articles on religion and news in Stuart Britain.

Karen Britland is Lecturer in Renaissance Literature at Keele University, and an associate editor for the *Cambridge Edition of the Works of Ben Jonson*. Her main research interest is in Caroline drama, most particularly in the court entertainments sponsored by Queen Henrietta Maria. Her monograph on the subject, entitled *Drama at the Courts of Queen Henrietta Maria*, is soon to be published by Cambridge University Press.

Jerome de Groot lectures in English at the University of Manchester. He has held manuscript fellowships at Oxford, UCLA, Harvard and the Folger Memorial Shakespeare Library. He has published articles on subjects ranging from early modern court culture and national identity to Oscar Wilde. His book, *Royalist Identities*, was published by Palgrave in 2004.

Caroline Hibbard is Associate Professor of History at the University of Illinois at Urbana-Champaign. She is the author of *Charles I and the Popish Plot* (University of North Carolina Press, 1983) and a number of articles on early Stuart Catholicism and on her current research focus, the court of Henrietta Maria.

James Knowles is Professor of English Literature at Keele University. He edited *Shakespeare's Late Plays: New Essays* (with Jenny Richards, Edinburgh University Press, 1999), *The Roaring Girl and Other City Comedies* (with Eugene Giddens, Oxford World's Classics, 2001) and has written widely on the masque genre, especially on Jonson's *The Entertainment at Britain's Burse*. He is currently editing Jonson's complete entertainments, selected masques and *The Gypsies Metamorphosed* for the *Cambridge Edition of the Works of Ben Jonson*.

Andrew McRae is Professor of Renaissance Studies at the University of Exeter. His publications include *Literature, Satire and the Early Stuart State* (Cambridge University Press, 2004), *God Speed the Plough: The Representation of Agrarian England, 1500–1660* (Cambridge University Press, 1996) and, as co-editor, 'Early Stuart Libels: An Edition of Poetry from Manuscript Sources', *Early Modern Literary Studies*, Text Series, 1 (2005) <http://purl.oclc.org/emls/texts/libels/>

Contributors

John Peacock, who teaches English at Southampton University, is the author of *The Stage Designs of Inigo Jones* (Cambridge University Press, 1995), and of a recently completed book on Van Dyck's view of the art of painting: a complementary study of his portraits of the Caroline courtiers is in preparation.

Sarah Poynting is a Research Fellow in the Department of History at Keele University, where she is working on a scholarly edition of *The Writings of Charles I*, to be published in three volumes by Oxford University Press. Her edition of Walter Montagu's *The Shepherds' Paradise* was published by the Malone Society in 1998.

Julie Sanders is Professor of English Literature and Drama at the University of Nottingham. Her publications include *Caroline Drama* (Northcote House, 1999). She has recently edited *The New Inn* for the *Cambridge Edition of the Works of Ben Jonson* and James Shirley's *The Bird in a Cage* for *Three Seventeenth-Century Plays on Women and Performance* (Manchester University Press, forthcoming).

Malcolm Smuts is Professor of History at the University of Massachusetts, Boston and President of the North American Society for Court Studies. His publications include *Culture and Power in England* (Macmillan, 1998) and *Court Culture and the Origins of a Royalist Tradition in Early Stuart England* (University of Pennsylvania Press, 1987).

Matthew Steggle is Lecturer in English at Sheffield Hallam University. His publications include *Richard Brome: Place and Politics on the Caroline Stage* (Manchester University Press, 2004). He has also written the introductions and commentary on *Cynthia's Revels* for the forthcoming *Cambridge Edition of the Works of Ben Jonson*.

Preface

The idea for this book began with a conference at Keele University in May 2002, 'The 1630s: Interdisciplinary Approaches'. Many of the contributors were involved in that event, but there were many others whose contributions to the weekend of lively discussion and debate were crucial and we would like to thank all those who were involved on that occasion. Especial thanks to Martin Butler, David Como, Richard Cust, Kenneth Fincham, Tom Healy, Ann Hughes, James Loxley and Clare McManus. The conference was made possible by generous grants from Keele University and the Royal Historical Society, and the editors would like to record their gratitude for that support.

As editors, we have incurred many other debts – too many to remember or to mention, let alone discharge here. Among the most important, we would like to thank our contributors, for disproving the old adage that editing a collection such as this is the fastest way to sour old friendships; the series editors, Ann Hughes, Peter Lake and Anthony Milton, for their encouragement and helpful comments; Alison Welsby and Jonathan Bevan at Manchester University Press for supporting the project; colleagues at Keele (especially the Early Modernists' group) and Nottingham; friends and (not least) family, for their patience and forbearance while this book emerged. The volume is dedicated to an early modern historian whose work, example and friendship has been hugely important for both editors and we are glad of the opportunity to recognise her help in this way.

Chapter 9 appears in a slightly altered version in Andrew McRae, *Literature, Satire and the Early Stuart State* (Cambridge: Cambridge University Press, 2004), chapter 6, © Cambridge University Press, and is produced here with permission of the author and publisher.

All dates are old style except that the new year is taken as beginning on 1 January, not 25 March.

Abbreviations

BL British Library, London
Bodl. Bodleian Library, Oxford
NAS National Archives of Scotland, Edinburgh
O&S Stephen Orgel and Roy Strong, *Inigo Jones: The Theatre of the Stuart Court* (2 vols, Berkeley, Los Angeles and London: University of California Press and Sotheby Parke Bernet, 1973)
PRO National Archives (Public Record Office), Kew

Chapter 1

Introducing *The 1630s*: questions of parliaments, peace and pressure points

Julie Sanders and Ian Atherton

WHY THE 1630s?

Establishing the decade of the 1630s as a specific field of enquiry raises a host of important questions about scholarly motives and methodology.[1] Why, for example, select that particular decade for focus rather than the period of Caroline rule as a whole? Is there anything that can be described as intrinsic to this cultural and political moment? There is, of course, the pragmatic sense in which a decade provides a manageable sample of cultural, literary and political events and trends, a definable set of evidence, archival and otherwise, but, nevertheless, the 1630s constitute an identifiable 'moment' between the dissolution of parliament in March 1629 and the meeting of the Short Parliament in April 1640. Those eleven years have come to be known by such ideologically loaded titles as the 'King's peace', or the 'eleven years' tyranny'.[2] Cavalier poets, preachers and others regularly referred to them as the 'halcyon days',[3] but the most standardised form used to refer to this political and cultural era is the 'Personal Rule'.[4] That term, however, is not without its own complications or biases. It privileges the role of King Charles I and views all events from the perspective of the centre. While the courtly perspective is of undoubted importance in a personal monarchy, what this collection seeks to establish is the significance of other perspectives; these alternative viewpoints can be retrieved or located, for example, through analysis of the role of the Queen or coterie communities both in and beyond the parameters of the court, and by means of the cultivation of a regional understanding of the period.

In addition, a term such as 'Personal Rule' implies that Charles's refusal to call a parliament was *the* key issue throughout the period. Pressure for a parliament waxed and waned during the 1630s, growing in intensity from 1637 so that by 1640 it could be called 'the grievance of all grievances ... [the] mischiefe that makes all mischiefes irremediable',[5] but focusing on the absence of parliament from 1629 as a defining feature of the 1630s has a

1

number of limitations. First, although it helps to emphasise the often arcane forms of prerogative government favoured by Charles I at this time, it is an Anglocentric view. The period 1629–40 carries no special weight in Scottish or Irish parliamentary history: the Scottish parliament had not met since 1621 when it met briefly in 1633 and it sat again in 1639, while the Irish parliament met in 1634–35 for the first time since 1615.[6] Second, when Charles dissolved the English parliament in March 1629 it was with a public, albeit enigmatic, promise that he would 'bee more inclinable to meete in Parliament againe, when Our People shall see more cleerely into Our Intents and Actions'. John Reeve has suggested that Charles's private resolution never to call another parliament in England dates from the winter of 1631–32, not 1629.[7] Parliament's continuing absence did not define the difference of the 1630s to contemporaries, and attempts to define the period by the absence of parliament are as a result only partially successful.[8] There is a danger of according the parliamentary absences of the 1630s a falsely unique status: James VI and I had called no English parliament for seven years between 1614 and 1621, and from the end of the last session of parliament in 1610 until the beginning of the parliament of 1621 the two Houses were in session for only two months in 1614.[9] Only with hindsight, then, and only to the English, did the 1630s appear as a uniquely non-parliamentary decade. Finally, to define the period in this way is to suggest that the Houses of Lords and Commons had a fixed place in the English constitution; this was a claim that some contemporaries sought to establish but it did not command universal support. Parliament was not a permanent institution in England at this time: in Conrad Russell's phrase, 'there is no such subject as "parliament in the early seventeenth century": there are irregularly recurring events called Parliaments'.[10] Hence our preference in this collection for the more neutral term 'the 1630s' to describe the period.

In opting to focus on this decade we need to ask what, if anything, was distinctive about the 1630s? Historians and literary and cultural scholars alike have certainly registered a perceptible cultural shift in this period. One possible reason for this change in the cultural and political climate was the assassination of George Villiers, Duke of Buckingham in August 1628. No new favourite replaced Buckingham, and as a result access to the King, which had been increasingly monopolised by the Duke in recent times, became relatively more open. For this reason, a number of scholars regard Felton's knife as beginning the Personal Rule.[11] With Buckingham's death, Charles I also appeared to find greater accommodation with his French queen consort, Henrietta Maria. Critics debate the extent to which this marital harmony can be directly attributed to the demise of Buckingham, but, as Caroline Hibbard's essay here (Chapter 5) indicates, the Queen's influence on Caroline politics and culture is certainly more discernible in the 1630s than in the years immediately following her 1625 marriage.[12]

Introducing The 1630s

A further reason for the shift in the climate at the beginning of the 1630s was the change from war to peace. War with France, begun in 1627, was ended with the Treaty of Susa in April 1629; peace with Spain came with the Treaty of Madrid in November 1630. The former owed much to the demise of Buckingham and Charles's new-found uxoriousness: the Queen's first pregnancy, it was said at the beginning of 1629, assuaged the King's anger with France and made him more inclinable towards a peace with his wife's brother.[13] Peace was, then, a defining characteristic of the 1630s, at least until the conflict between England and Scotland in the latter part of the decade, not just in comparison to the wars against France and Spain that marked the first years of Charles's reign, but particularly in contrast to the Thirty Years' War, in which most of continental Europe was then embroiled. It was a peace much remarked upon at the time – 'the benefit / Of peace and plenty, which the blessed hand / Of our good King gives this obdurate Land' praised by Thomas Carew – and perhaps even more so retrospectively from the perspective of the bloodshed of the 1640s: 'so excellent a composure throughout the whole kingdom that the like peace and plenty and universal tranquillity for ten years was never enjoyed by any nation' elegised Clarendon later.[14] Peace identifies and defines the 1630s not least because, where James I had been *Rex Pacificus*, Charles was (in Michael Young's phrase) *Rex Bellicosus* who spent all of his reign bar the 1630s at war.[15]

England's peace in the 1630s was, however, contested, controversial and fragile, owing as much to the force of contingency and circumstance as it did to the wishes of King, Queen or privy councillors. Where Clarendon espied peace and plenty, others privileged prerogative, popery and prelacy; such is the view of the 1641 Grand Remonstrance.[16] Charles I meanwhile was apt to espy puritanism and popularity wherever he looked.[17] And the King did not absent himself entirely from military operations in the 1630s, actively seeking engagement in the European conflict after 1630 in order to see the restoration of the Palatinate (albeit engagement on his own, limited and unrealistic terms). The year 1637 came close to witnessing naval operations against the Habsburgs.[18] The Queen herself and many in her circle, particularly puritans such as the Earl of Northumberland, were often the most vociferous for English engagement in the war, indication in itself that there was no easy division along ideological lines over many issues in the 1630s.[19]

In identifying peace as a defining feature of the 1630s, then, it is all too easy to fall prone to exaggeration, in particular through a concentration on the royal cult of peace that ran through much of the cultural production of the Caroline court. One of the key themes of that culture was the way that the Queen had soothed the King's martial ardour and their love had induced harmony throughout the kingdom.[20] We need to beware of believing too readily the image management this involved. While the focus of many contemporaries and historians has been on the pacific elements of Caroline culture, a number of indicators suggest that Charles's military passions had only been cooled, not cured. Henrik Langelüddecke's study of the county militias demonstrates that they were kept at a similar pitch of training and readiness during the peace of 1630–38 as during the war of 1625–30.[21] Charles took an especially close interest in naval affairs, commissioning what was probably the largest warship in the world, the *Sovereign of the Seas*, parts of which he designed himself.[22] As Malcolm Smuts's essay in this volume (Chapter 2) indicates, war and peace were not simple opposites in Caroline political culture; instead, the themes of force, love and authority were bound together in a triangular relationship throughout the 1630s.

Moreover, despite Charles's attempts to impose peace, or at least silence, on religious polemic over predestination, there was little peace in the religious sphere in the 1630s. Laudianism or Arminianism – prelacy to its enemies – is seen as one of the hallmarks of the decade. The grip of the anti-Calvinist faction on church and king was made manifest by three acts in 1628–29: the translation of Laud to London in July 1628; the royal declaration for the peace of the church composed in December 1628; and the proclamation of the following January. The last two actions forbade the debate of predestination and were used quite effectively to clamp down on Calvinism.[23] The Laudian triumph seemed complete by the beginning of the 1630s – Peter Heylyn ended his account of the rise of 'Anti-Calvinians' in 1629 for by then they had become 'considerable both for power and number'.[24]

Historians are still debating what that triumph meant. In Nicholas Tyacke's version, Laudians were committed to a theological revolution, overthrowing the Calvinism that had dominated the English church since Elizabeth's day and replacing it with an Arminian, anti-predestinarian soteriology that emphasised sacrament over word.[25] Such a view has received backing from studies focusing on the material culture of Laudianism: the physical manifestations of the 'beauty of holiness' witnessed in the restoration of St Paul's Cathedral and other building programmes in the 1630s.[26] In an alternative version of events, Laud was obsessed not with theology but order and discipline and the church policy of the 1630s is best thought of as intensified conformity and vigour.[27] These are not just debates about theology and church discipline; they penetrate to the heart of questions about the nature of Charles's rule in the 1630s and the causes of the English civil wars. For some, Laud headed an unrepresentative and novel yet radical and destabilising element within the English polity in the 1630s that contributed directly to the wars.[28] As argued throughout this introduction, we need a dynamic understanding of the 1630s which, in the field of religion, as well as in other areas, offers a view (as in Anthony Milton's recent account) of Laudianism as a 'process through which English Protestants singly and collectively moved'.[29]

George Herbert's collection of poems, *The Temple*, for example, embodies Laud's concept of the 'beauty of holiness' within both its poetic themes (music, prayer, altars) and the quasi-architectural structure of the collection. The poet appears, then, to celebrate many of the structures and rituals that caused such anxiety for those of a puritan mindset. And yet, as Graham Parry has stressed, Herbert's 'sense of the formal harmonies of the Anglican Church' are not necessarily a direct endorsement of 1630s Laudianism.[30] His rejection of a courtly life and values in the early part of the decade suggests that high Anglicanism took many forms and directions in the Caroline period.

In the literary domain more widely, the 1630s offers an equally diverse picture of professional and amateur writing, often influenced by coteries or networks shaped by a complex web of family relations, political sympathies, geography or religion. Poetry circulated ever more widely via these groups and the period saw a concomitant rise in the assembly of miscellanies and commonplace books. In the theatrical domain, there was a vivid interplay between the professional playhouses and writers for the public stage such as Richard Brome, James Shirley, and John Ford, and courtly drama, in particular masque. While neither a sense of literature as merely endorsing the Caroline court ethic nor as wholly oppositional offers a satisfactory account of the agency of literature in the 1630s, the politicisation of both genre and practice is inescapable in any reading of cultural production at this time.

John Adamson has suggested that 'the accession of Charles I marked a major change in the cultural forms by which monarchy was represented', noting a 'classicizing, cosmopolitan aesthetic', in part indicated by the increasing Flemish influence on artistic tastes at court, and the dominance of Anthony Van Dyck's court portraiture.[31] The taste in poetry was predominantly for lyric over epic, leading to the emergence of the so-called Cavalier poets including Robert Herrick, Thomas Carew and Sir John Suckling, and the courtly theatrical preference for drama and masques of a Neo-Platonist and pastoral flavour began to seep out onto the public theatre stages, albeit in occasionally parodic vein.[32] While these courtly shapings of literary genre and fashion cannot be underestimated, there are additional ways of thinking about Caroline cultural production in the 1630s. The decade can usefully be explored from a regional perspective to reveal how particular areas responded or reacted to the period of personal rule, and the specific concerns it threw up, including the increased raising of prerogative taxes, not least the controversial Ship Money. These taxation policies placed particular stress on *local* administrative structures and officials and, since they often went hand in hand with the reactivation of ancient prerogative laws relating to royal claims on so-called common land in forests and fenlands, an intensification of regional identity often resulted from local responses to these policies.[33]

Julie Sanders and Ian Atherton

1632–34 AND 1637: FORCE FIELDS, FIELDS OF ENQUIRY AND INTERDISCIPLINARY STUDIES

The discussion of the cultural geography of the 1630s later in this introduction is just one example of how a regional angle on the decade might be pursued. The danger remains, however, that the Caroline period will be read from an entirely different vantage point: the hindsight of the civil wars. The risk involved in reading either the political debate or literary productions of this period from such a perspective is that it appears as if all 1630s roads necessarily led this way. Thinking in terms of a 'field of enquiry', as this introduction has already proposed we might do, shifts us away from a linear reading that subjects all events and texts to a teleological interpretation pointing towards 1642, or even 1649 and the execution of Charles I. The work of John Peacock in this volume is illuminating in this respect. He speaks of the need to examine the paintings and portraits of the Caroline era not as 'narratives' – as something we read *through* to reach a particular outcome, event or interpretation – but as 'visual fields' which we must read *around*, or read the environs of (see below, pp. 52–5). Extending this notion further, we might apply it to political and literary analyses of the period as well. Malcolm Smuts's linguistic analysis of the ethical and political debates of the 1630s is a further example of this widening of the field of enquiry, revealing as it does the continental European intellectual influences on the Caroline court.

In mobilising this idea of 'fields', however, we are conscious as editors of the need to avoid any simplistic homogenisation of the 1630s. In interrogating a particular decade in this way, it is helpful, rather than dealing always in continuities and generalisms, to acknowledge particular moments of crisis or disjuncture. As in any period there are certain months, even years, when debates around certain issues were particularly pressing or forceful. Focusing in on these particular moments enables us to identify specific issues of concern or particular contingencies in operation at a given time. It seems incontrovertible in a study of the 1630s that crisis moments or 'fields of force' emerge in the two periods between late 1632 and early 1634, and in 1637. Pausing to consider these in detail helps to identify issues of shared concern for literary and historical scholars of the period.

Late 1632 and 1633 saw the publication of two texts whose impact and effect were to ricochet out across England and over the ensuing years. Late in 1632, William Prynne saw into print his one-thousand-page *Histriomastix*, a text which John Creaser has memorably described as a 'massive compilation of puritanical extremity'.[34] *Histriomastix* had at its heart a wide-ranging debate about Catholic cultural influences in England but it has become perhaps best known in literary circles for the debate it galvanised in the 1630s about female theatricals, and in particular Henrietta Maria's experimentations in the form.

Prynne was prosecuted over the publication and much was made of the index in which 'women actors' are equated to 'notorious whores'. Despite Prynne's protestations to the contrary, his comments were taken to be a direct reference to the rehearsals under way in late 1632 for Walter Montagu's court pastoral *The Shepherds' Paradise* and the Queen's participation in this production, which countenanced women actors speaking and cross-dressing in performance. The numerous responses to Prynne in performed and printed drama produced in the years immediately following the release of *Histriomastix* are a marker of the cultural significance of the debate and a further indication of Henrietta Maria's importance as a cultural influence in the 1630s.[35] This last point is pursued in several of the essays in this collection, including those by Karen Britland and Jerome de Groot (Chapters 7 and 10).

The year 1633 was a significant date for Charles I in a number of respects. This was the year in which he made his own belated coronation trip to the kingdom of Scotland, a 'pilgrimage' designed as direct echo of that made by James VI and I in 1617, even deploying parallel routes and a similar retinue of accompanying courtiers.[36] The journey both to and from Scotland was marked by elaborate feasting at significant estates, including those of the Cavendish family in the East Midlands. Ben Jonson composed two entertainments for these events, the *King's Entertainment at Welbeck* (1633) and *Love's Welcome at Bolsover* (1634). The texts for these occasions demonstrate important interventions in contemporary debates about Neo-Platonism and popular festivity.

In 1633 Charles I oversaw another significant publication, or more accurately republication. Responding to a dispute over church ales in Somerset, he reissued what was popularly known as the *Book of Sports*, his father's 1618 declaration defending holiday pastimes and sabbath festivities against the encroachments and prohibitions of regionally based puritan officials.[37] Julian Davies and others have traced the enforcement of the 'king's book' in the dioceses and have found a wide variety of responses but not one minister suspended solely for refusing to read the declaration. While the book's opponents (who were by no means all puritans) could usually avoid censure, they were not spared what Davies calls 'a profound dilemma of conscience'.[38] Leah Marcus has traced at length the various responses made to this reissue in the form of poetry, masques and theatre for a range of venues, stretching from the provincial household to the metropolitan public playhouses.[39] As well as Herrick's poems, collected in 1648 under the title *Hesperides* but largely written during the 1630s, and which by his own admission 'sing of Maypoles, hock-carts, wassails, wakes / Of bridegrooms, brides, and of their bridal cakes',[40] plays such as Jonson's 1633 *A Tale of a Tub* self-consciously located themselves at bride-ales and in rural communities. Carew's *Coelum Britannicum*, performed at court on Shrovetide in 1634 is, according to Marcus's account, a masque that defends traditional pastimes, and therefore the prevailing court ideology of the time. A more complicated stance both on courtly ideology and rural pastimes can be found in another masque of that year: John Milton's commissioned entertainment for the installation of the Earl of Bridgewater as Lord President of the Council of the Marches and Wales, the *Masque Presented at Ludlow Castle*, better known as *Comus*. In Milton's 'vice-regal ceremony',[41] it is the dubious community of Comus and his 'crew' who participate in the wassails and morris dances defended by the *Book of Sports*. Diverse political views were, then, expressed on the hot issues of the day, and genre alone is rarely a clear indicator of political allegiance.

As the reissue of the *Book of Sports* suggests, 1633 was a crucial turning point in the King's religious policy not so much for the making of new policy, but for the making public of already established trends and ideas. In June Charles's coronation in Edinburgh was carried out with the use of English vestments, ceremonies and ornaments, some of which were then enforced upon the whole of the Scottish church, to the consternation of many.[42] That same year the first copies of the Scottish prayer book (modelled on the English one and a project set in train by Laud in 1629) were printed.[43] In August 1633 William Laud was elevated to the archbishopric of Canterbury, the King making good a private promise made to him in 1626.[44] Three months later Charles (presumably at Laud's behest) personally determined the case of the communion table of St Gregory's church, next to St Paul's Cathedral in London, giving public royal backing to the policy of placing communion tables altarwise that had already begun earlier that year in the province of York.[45] By the end of 1633 there could be no doubts over the direction of royal religious policy in either England or Scotland.

If 1632–34 represented one important set of debates and concerns in the 1630s, then 1637 can surely be registered as another crisis point, or moment of identifiable dissonance. Prynne is once again a significant player in these events. As explored in detail in Andrew McRae's essay (Chapter 9), Prynne found himself on trial once again, along with John Bastwick and Henry Burton, for libel and seditious publication, undergoing a brutal public ear-cropping as his sentence. This was, as McRae indicates, a time of heightened paranoia about popish plots and Catholic conspiracies and the high-profile trial of these scapegoat puritans must be considered in this context. A potential revolution in foreign affairs also provides a background to the trial of Burton, Bastwick and Prynne in the spring and summer of 1637: at that time Charles I nearly brought off a revolution in his foreign policy by securing a treaty with France for the restoration of the Palatinate. Many observers expected that Charles would enter the Thirty Years' War in the spring of 1637; writing from court, the Earl of Dorset noted 'Here are warrs and rumors of warrs'.[46] Others were less certain; despite the 'great rumors of warres',

Viscount Conway forecast in April 'that there will be noe warre but that between the Bishops and the Puritans whitch growes very hot by bookes written by Bastweeke and Burton and some other namelesse men'.[47]

Intriguingly, 1637 was also the year in which the text of *Comus* was published. This was not a straightforward record of the 1634 Ludlow performance, but a revised version, the revisions indicating an increase in anti-Catholic references and concerns.[48] In political terms, 1637 has often been regarded as a watershed moment, the 'high-water mark' of the Personal Rule,[49] 'a turn of the tide' and 'the dawn of its collapse'.[50] Increasing tensions in relationships with the Scottish kirk have led many to suggest this is the year that sounded the death-knell of the 'King's peace', if such a thing ever existed. Moreover, 1637 witnessed the judges' declaration of the legality of Ship Money (in February), the beginning of the legal process against John Hampden for refusal to pay (August) and the opening of his trial (December). Sarah Poynting's valuable survey (Chapter 4) of the King's epistolary output during the decade provides some crucial indicators and markers of these changes of emphasis within his government during the period of the Personal Rule.

Sarah Poynting's extensive editorial and interpretative work on the writings of Charles I – which will eventually culminate in a much-needed edition for Oxford University Press – is representative of a wider academic movement in the field of early modern studies, one that has been labelled by many – scholars and research councils alike – as interdisciplinary, but which is perhaps best described as an intellectual encounter between the interests and approaches of different disciplines. The disciplines most noticeably evoked and in dialogue with each other in the essays collected here – and reflected in the interests of the editors, who themselves hail from different disciplinary backgrounds – are history, literature, geography, art history and cultural studies. Alternative versions of the 1630s would look to musicology, architecture or perhaps science for additional encounters.

'Multidisciplinarity' perhaps best describes the interactive and sometimes conflicting approaches represented here. As the preceding survey of existing analyses of the 1630s suggested, the approaches of historians and literary historians often produce markedly different accounts of the same material. While the former might question the centrality of parliamentary absence as a theme, the latter find in the alternative talking shops of the London theatres or the country estates of aristocrats an intriguing alternative to the temporarily silenced debates of the Houses of Lords and Commons. The study of material culture which rewrites understandings of Laudianism for a historian of religion might enable for the scholar of the household masque a welcome recovery of female agency in the domestic theatrical domain. If linguistic analysis mobilises for the court historian a more nuanced, and Eurocentric, version of Caroline culture (see, for example, Malcolm Smuts's essay, Chapter 2), a consideration of high politics can in turn enhance understanding of the deployment of theatrical space and setting for a literary scholar (see Matthew Steggle's essay, Chapter 8). The aim is not simply to harmonise or even consolidate approaches but to find intellectual stimulus and challenge emerging and evolving from the differences. The value is in the encounter, rather than some false process of continuity of practice.

Raymond Williams's subtle understanding of the operations of communities, the 'structures of feeling' that create a sense of shared knowledge or experience and the existence or otherwise in societies of 'knowable communities', proves invaluable for thinking about cultural activities and political identities during the 1630s.[51] Historians have undoubtedly expanded the parameters of their concerns recently when examining the cultural poetics of the political and religious groupings who dominate in the period.[52] In literary studies the investigation of communities of readers, writers, performers and audiences, sometimes within public institutions such as the theatre and sometimes within the more domestic setting of the estate or household, has in turn benefited from various turns in historical approach. This collection and the multidisciplinary work it celebrates, then, does not constitute an attempt to erase or flatten disciplinary differences or integrity.[53] Neither do the editors wish to imply that inter- or multidisciplinarity is the only route possible through the complex domain of Caroline culture. Nevertheless, in the conversations held in and between the essays collected here, and between the approaches and techniques of the scholars involved, we believe that potentially beneficial means and methodologies for reinvestigating a cultural moment from a range of angles and vantage points are unlocked.

'THE SCENE IS VARIED ...':[54] A CULTURAL GEOGRAPHY OF THE 1630s

Given Ronald Hutton's recent account of 'the new framework for early Stuart studies',[55] which places the 'British problem' centre stage – the analysis of the interaction between the three kingdoms of England, Ireland and Scotland (or four, or even five nations, if the Welsh and the Cornish are included)[56] – our focus on the 1630s may strike some readers as surprising. For the 'three-kingdom approach' has served to deflect attention away from the 1630s and the Personal Rule, with that decade assumed to have less meaning for England's 'Celtic fringe'. A new periodisation has been stressed, where 1603, 1637, 1638 or 1641 rank more highly in an 'archipelagic view of the period' than 1629 and 1640. The 'new British history' has also been used to suggest that any argument based on the English experience can be trumped by evidence from Scotland or Ireland.[57]

Introducing The 1630s

Cultural approaches are not blind to the Atlantic archipelago and the rival kingdoms, nationhoods and principalities of Wales, Scotland and Ireland must figure in any account of the complexities of Caroline culture. The presentation of arguments about the Union of England and Scotland on the stage and writings about British identities have both recently been analysed.[58] If Milton's *Comus* interacts with localised tensions in the Forest of Dean, as several critics have argued, then it is also crucial as a text that negotiates the slippery border country between England and Wales.[59] In Ireland, as Alan Fletcher has shown, as well as witnessing the tense political negotiations between long-term residents and the King's representative, the Lord Deputy, Sir Thomas Wentworth, later Earl of Strafford, the 1630s saw the establishment of Ireland's first purpose-built public theatre in Werburgh Street, Dublin.[60] It was here that James Shirley found employment in the late 1630s when plague temporarily closed the London playhouses. As well as directing plays including Jonson's *The Alchemist* at Werburgh Street, Shirley wrote several dramas, such as *St Patrick for Ireland* (1639), with explicitly Irish subject matter.

Yet there are significant differences within such approaches to the multiple kingdoms. Many English historians have adopted a three-kingdom approach in seeking the origins of civil war. Since the revisionism of the 1970s dispensed with all instabilities and conflicts (save only religion) in England in the 1630s, many have been forced to look to Scotland and Ireland to explain how such an apparently consensual and pacific polity could collapse into civil war.[61] Inter- or multidisciplinary work has not needed such a spur to look beyond England and such approaches offer alternative avenues of exploration.

Multi- or interdisciplinary approaches allow for more inflected readings of texts and events; conflict and disharmony as a result become more apparent, along with the polyvalence of Stuart culture in the 1630s. The news diary of William Davenport, a minor Cheshire squire, is full of gossip and tittle-tattle, including the details of the trial of the Earl of Castlehaven in 1631 for rape and sodomy. John Morrill, noting the absence of news of 'serious constitutional clashes' such as the Petition of Right, decided that it revealed a localist mentality uninterested in real politics and hence likely to seek refuge in neutralism in the 1640s. Alastair Bellany, however, analyses this and similar material with the literary critic's techniques of scrutinising the cultural productions in which court scandal was disseminated in what he calls an 'ethnography of early Stuart political culture [that] demands above all a broad definition of the political, a willingness to read new sources in multiple ways, an openness to the possibility that serious, meaningful politics happened in surprising places, in curious forms and unfamiliar languages'.[62] A shift from high politics to a much wider understanding of the political, including the politics of culture and the culture of politics, has been achieved through the influence of feminist scholars and social theorists, among others. The 'notion of the political' is now 'extended ... into all the ways in which contemporaries endeavoured to construct values and represent themselves'.[63]

Many of the most fruitful approaches use the techniques of the literary scholar. Treating primary sources as texts rather than simply documents allows a more nuanced, closer reading.[64] Reading against the grain permits the exploration of textual silences: where historians once looked simply for what a document said or what an author meant, scholars are now also interested in what they do not say or did not intend to proclaim. The techniques of manuscript studies facilitate consideration of the publication, circulation, consumption, collection and preservation of texts other than the printed word and hence the afterlife, the memory, reputation and retelling of events. They also enable the investigation, as undertaken here by Jerome de Groot (Chapter 10), of coteries and the groups in which such texts circulated, revealing a greater degree of female agency than other studies allow.

The turn to a British context in much recent historical scholarship has generally entailed an abandonment of the English regions and the imposition of a monolithic and metropolitan view of England. Early revisionist work in the 1960s and 1970s sought to focus on the English counties, but with the undermining of the localist case in the 1980s[65] many historians lost interest in the particularities of the English provinces, preferring to emphasise national differences between Scotland and England, or reducing the English experience to that of Westminster, Whitehall and London. As set out later, we wish to re-assert the importance of a regional perspective in the 1630s, but one entirely divorced from previous, localist claims about the primacy of the county, attempts to privilege local preoccupations at the expense of national concerns or assertions about fissures between court and country.

Just as the 'British problem' has diverted attention away from the English regions, so it has been accused of ignoring the European dimension, and recent controversy has focused on the extent to which England's (or Britain's) troubles should be considered a part of wider, European developments. Until the outbreak of the Scottish crisis in 1637–38 the English looked far more to Europe than they ever did to Ireland or Scotland. Contemporaries saw their worlds in sub- and supra-national terms as well as in a national context,[66] and, as the case of William Cavendish discussed below suggests, there is no simple choice between such dichotomies. A consideration of political and cultural space in the 1630s must focus on a variety of shifting locales including: London and Westminster (though without homogenising either); the multifarious courts of Charles, Henrietta Maria and the Elector Palatine; the many sub- and para-courtly spaces including the fringes of the royal courts, the councils of Wales and of the North and the households of the nobility and greater gentry; the English regions; the Stuarts' multiple kingdoms; and continental Europe. Moreover, as James Knowles's essay (Chapter 6) indicates, readings of cultural production and political attitudes must be sensitive to extra-European influences, nor should they attempt to collapse cultures beyond Europe into one 'other'.

As readers and historians, we need to move beyond the geographical boundaries of the British Isles if we are to avoid the insularity so knowingly performed by Thomas Carew, when in his forestalled poetic effort to write an elegy on the death in battle of Gustavus Adolphus (Gustavus II of Sweden) he declared:

> Alas! how may
> My lyric feet, that of the smooth soft way
> Of love, and beauty, only know the tread,
> In dancing paces celebrate the dead
> Victorious king ...

adding:

> ... these are subjects proper to our clime:
> Tourneys, masques, theatres, better become
> Our halcyon days. What though the German drum
> Bellow for freedom and revenge? The noise
> Concerns not us, nor should divert our joys!
> ('In Answer of an Elegiacal Letter ...', lines 5–9; 95–9)[67]

Carew's confident assertion that the continental European context of the Thirty Years' War was a distant drumbeat in 1630s England may have held some truth, but, as already stressed, the 1630s cannot be dismissed as mere 'halcyon days' removed from any zone or sphere of outside influence.[68] Even those cultural forms which Carew accepts as indicative of his age – theatre, masques, public spectacle – clearly embody political ambivalences and cultural uncertainty. As well as indicating the need to give full weight to the European influences and inflections to Caroline rule (the essays by Smuts, Hibbard and Peacock all emphasise this fact), essays in this collection look to spaces beyond Europe, recording and exploring the effects and impact of trade and adventure in the East Indies and elsewhere on 1630s culture and practice. Knowles's essay explores the complex significations of Anthony Van Dyck's exquisite painting of William Feilding, 1st Earl of Denbigh, (figure 10, p. 116) which 'shows the Earl after his return from Persia and India with his Indian page striding through a jungle landscape'.[69] Knowles argues that we need to re-examine the nuances and complexities of 1630s 'orientalism' in which this portrait and several Caroline masques, such as Aurelian Townshend's *Tempe Restored*, participate.[70] One of the purposes behind the multidisciplinary approach of this volume is, then, to expand the range of theoretical and methodological approaches to the 1630s. Recent developments in the field of cultural geography, for example, assist us in thinking about the 1630s as a field of cultural production.⁷¹ We need to consider the environments, habitats, communities and ecologies that people found themselves in, and found themselves responding to, as well as thinking about specific political or historical 'events' which might have shaped their understandings of the world.⁷²

Recent attempts to explore cultural conflict in the early Stuart south-west provide one set of regional approaches to such questions. While many scholars have noted the connections between Cavalier poets and traditional rural rituals, David Underdown and Mark Stoyle explore the geographical distribution of traditional festive culture in Devon, Dorset, Somerset and Wiltshire. Underdown has attempted to produce a political ecology by seeing settlement and farming patterns as underlying local festive, religious and political culture, while Stoyle's explanations rest on a mixture of religion and race, identifying in the geography of civil war allegiance elements of ethnicity, with a Celtic fringe in England and Wales remaining more loyal to the Crown. As this last comment suggests, both scholars' investigation of regional patterns is still principally motivated by the long-standing desire among historians to explain the civil wars.⁷³

Underdown's work rests on an understanding of culture that is principally derived from the cultural ethnography of Clifford Geertz and Victor Turner, and is also heavily indebted to the traditions of local history and agrarian history typified in the work of Joan Thirsk in identifying settlement patterns and farming types.⁷⁴ Moreover, both he and Stoyle are more interested in 'popular' than 'high' culture. Their sense of place differs, therefore, from the analyses of those historians and geographers who have taken a linguistic turn, but their insights are an important corrective to any view of the 1630s that wishes simply to pit court against country, or ignores England and Wales outside London altogether. Tom Cogswell's study of 1630s Leicestershire is a conscious attempt 'to return the prominence and lustre to local studies' – in his case to analyse prerogative taxation and the growth of the state.⁷⁵ The sense of place missing from many empirical or high political accounts of the early Stuart period is, therefore, slowly being restored by multidisciplinary approaches.⁷⁶

Architectural and horticultural histories can also prove illuminating in any regional approach to the 1630s. The garden history of Roy Strong and others contributes to our understanding of the symbolism of specific places and communities in this period; in the 1630s, formal Italianate gardens at Wilton House near Salisbury, Wiltshire, and at Arundel House in London, demonstrated both the continental and masquing interests of their respective aristocratic patrons, the Pembroke family and the Earl and Countess of Arundel.⁷⁷ In a related vein, specific architectural studies such as Mark Girouard's detailed considerations of the Smythson family's impact on the

Introducing The 1630s

building culture of the East Midlands in the seventeenth century shed light on the significance of coterie groupings and their specific operations, artistic as much as political, in certain geographically defined areas.[78]

As Matthew Steggle's essay in Chapter 8 of this volume indicates, coterie ecologies and economies in the 1630s might just as likely be urban as rural. Many of the self-proclaimed 'city comedies' of James Shirley, Richard Brome, Thomas Nabbes and others take as their setting and inspiration emerging urban spaces and communities in this period. The Earl of Bedford's residential and civic development in the Covent Garden area is a prime example. Malcolm Smuts and Martin Butler have both explored this locale's significance as a marker of changing social demographics in the 1630s, not least, in Smuts's account, the emergence of the 'Town' as a genuine topographical entity.[79] Public theatre plays such as Brome's *The Weeding of Covent Garden* refer to specific architectural innovations in the area, including the introduction of Italianate balconies, as well as interrogating some of the Crown policies attached to it.[80]

One remarkable cultural production for Covent Garden at this time was Sir Francis Kynaston's 1635 masque *Corona Minervae*. Written to celebrate the opening of his school for elite young boys, the College of the Museum Minervae, it was published, along with the constitution for the academy, the following year. Kynaston's masque is a remarkable town-based version of the extravagant, emblematic Caroline court masques of Jonson, Townshend and others.[81] In its development of a tradition of child performers – appearing in this instance in the roles of emblematic books – the production undoubtedly connects with contemporary interest in the public theatres in children's companies and child-authors such as Thomas Jordan.[82] Yet these traditions also had strong provenance in provincial household masques and entertainments, where the performance of child-members of the participating families, including females, was quite common. Milton's *Comus* is another example of this complex blend of family entertainment (the Bridgewater children and their music tutor performed the main roles in the 1634 Ludlow production) and geopolitical occasion. Kynaston's masque is a helpful mediator in the respect that it charges us to consider the metropolitan concerns of his school and its situation, but also gestures towards the powerful networks of performance and political interaction that existed in the regions. Metropolitan concerns are important, then, to any account of the 1630s, and yet there remains a need to register important shifts of balance away from the centre to the provinces. Simple binary demarcations are rarely sufficient in accounting for the cultural dynamics of early Stuart culture. We need to track a complex matrix of interplay and influence between metropolitan and provincial domains, and beyond that with literary tradition and generic convention.

One intriguing example of this approach in practice can be offered by the analysis of the phenomenon of school plays in this period. As well as texts written for their London schools by authors including Abraham Cowley and Richard Lovelace, several such dramas were staged in the provinces. One such was *Love Crownes the End*, written by John Tatham (*fl.* 1632–64) who, subsequently at least, had professional London connections, writing for the lord mayoral shows. *Love Crownes* is a fairly conventional pastoral, performed, as its printed title page tells us, by 'the schollees of Bingham in the county of *Notingham* in the yeare 1632'.[83] The play opens in a grove and exhibits throughout an awareness of the classical and literary aesthetics of pastoral. We have the familiar domains of valleys, groves, thickets and woods as the site for romantic play and love melancholy, but also, in a reference to Friar Tuck (sig. K7v), a pattern of local allusion and reference. The reference to Friar Tuck brings into the frame of the performance an all-too-real forest locale close to Bingham (which remains today a small market town to the east of the city of Nottingham), that of Sherwood Forest. This is in part a simple appeal to the local audience, but Sherwood Forest was not without precise literary and political significance in the 1630s. Just one year after the Bingham performance, Jonson would author the previously mentioned Welbeck entertainment, the first of his two Midlands-specific masque commissions for the Scottish coronation trip. Both entertainments were commissioned by the then Sheriff of Sherwood Forest, local magnate, literary patron, and author, William Cavendish, Earl of Newcastle. That Jonson would go on to begin two unfinished dramas with a Nottingham connection, *The Sad Shepherd* and *Mortimer, His Fall* (*c.* 1637), suggests that the resonance of a Nottinghamshire locale in a 1630s text was far from slight.[84]

Cavendish and his family form one of the most active provincial networks of political and intellectual exchange in the 1630s. Their Nottinghamshire and Derbyshire estates, at Welbeck Abbey and Bolsover Castle respectively, became a nucleus of architectural innovation, scientific debate, and literary exchange, both in print and manuscript form.[85] William Cavendish took a notoriously sceptical stand on Crown policy during the Personal Rule, and his assertion of his self-assigned role as a 'prince of the northern quarter', or as Cedric Brown puts it, 'chief man in the North Midlands' gives edge and significance to the cultural productions of his coterie.[86] While analysis of the Cavendish circle provides a good example of the benefits of exploring the 1630s through multidisciplinary approaches – cultural geography, literature, architecture and other cultural production, and politics – it is also a reminder that regional groupings were not limited by a provincial outlook. Cavendish's passion for the art of horsemanship had been fostered by his French riding master, Monsieur de St Antoine, who also taught Prince Henry and Charles I (as John Peacock notes in his essay here). Cavendish constructed riding houses at Welbeck in the 1620s, at Bolsover in the 1630s, and in Antwerp (where, in exile, he rented the *Rubenshuis*) in the 1650s.[87] His treatise on horsemanship, like the daily training of horses in his riding school, was intended for a European audience: the book was published in English in London and in French in Antwerp and London. The art of the *manège* had strong political overtones, not only as a controlled display of ceremony, discipline and order, but also because the taming of a horse was analogous to the rider's taming of the bestial passions within not just himself but the common rabble also.

Echoing suggestions made by Jerome de Groot in his essay here, the Cavendish network offers a clear example of elite female cultural activity in the period. Several of the Cavendish women went on to author texts or patronise artists, including Alathea Talbot in her position as Countess of Arundel at Arundel House, a space which has already been cited here as a major focus for coterie activity in the Caroline period.[88] Significant female participation in coterie networks can also be traced in the 1630s in literary and familial groupings such as the 'Tixall circle', a grouping predominantly made up of members of the Aston and Thimelby families in Catholic-tolerant Staffordshire, though on occasion drawing significant literary figures such as Michael Drayton and Sir Richard Fanshawe into its literary orbit.[89] At Apethorpe Hall in Northamptonshire, a teenage Rachel Fane produced dramatic juvenilia for performance by her theatre-literate relatives.[90]

There are further discussions to be had as to the extent to which such activities were facilitated, even fostered, by the innovative and provocative operations of the coterie surrounding Henrietta Maria at Whitehall. As outlined by Caroline Hibbard's essay (Chapter 5), the queen consort's artistic patronage in the spheres of theatre, painting and music is considerable and its effect on wider aristocratic circles cannot be underestimated. The impact of her interests in particular dramatic modes, including Neo-Platonism and pastoral, filtered out into the public theatre repertories as well as shaping the generic interests of provincial plays, including the schoolboy dramas described above. Karen Britland's essay (Chapter 7) considers the specific example of Thomas May's 1631 play *Antigone* in the context of the politics and ideas promulgated by the Queen's feminocentric coterie and the debates engaged in by other contemporary playtexts, including those by Jonson and Shirley, that both adopted and contested the vogues of the day.

The significance of networks (often but not exclusively familial) and regional coteries in the 1630s is a defining feature of the period's political exchanges and its literary practice. One such regional network in the 1630s was the '"parliamentary-puritan" connexion' of the godly Warwickshire schoolmaster Thomas Dugard uncovered by Ann Hughes through Dugard's diary. Dugard and his fellow godly ministers exchanged verse, preached to and for each other, edited one another's works for publication and socialised together.

Significantly, they sheltered under the patronage of Lord Brooke, they discussed opposition to the 1633 *Book of Sports*, and in the later 1630s they read Covenanting propaganda.[91]

Considering the 1630s in terms of specific regional cultures and outputs can be fruitful. As well as the growing body of evidence already advanced for a Midlands masquing culture, several other regions appear to enjoy particular concentrations of dramatic interest and innovation at this time. Due to the ongoing discoveries of the Records in Early English Drama (REED) project based in Toronto, we now have a clear picture emerging of theatrical practice in several regions. Yorkshire provides us with another intriguing case-study. York itself was the residence of the Lord President of the North, according the city a distinct political voice and identity. The city also possessed an emergent print and bookselling culture. As with the significance of the Ludlow setting for Milton's *Comus*, the political voice claimed by texts performed in these vice-regal capitals deserves note. These regions seem to have developed a clear sense of themselves not merely as extensions of the Crown, but as competing communities and cultural centres.

The significant landholding family in Yorkshire was the Cliffords. Like the Cavendishes, they had a considerable reputation by the time of the 1630s for sponsoring the arts and for autonomous political thinking. Francis Clifford, 4th Earl of Cumberland had commissioned masques, such as that staged at Brougham Castle to greet James VI and I on his return from Scotland in 1617, and was a major patron to composer William Byrd and musician and masque-writer Thomas Campion. His son, Henry, Lord Clifford, who was by the decade of the 1630s in charge of the family's indebted estates, continued this tradition, staging plays at Skipton Castle, including revivals of Francis Beaumont's *The Knight of the Burning Pestle* and Philip Massinger's *A New Way To Pay Old Debts* in 1636. He jointly sponsored a local troupe of players at this time, and, as is indicated by a set of account books held in the Chatsworth archive, he also appears to have staged a masque which enacted a version of the Comus story. Chatsworth Bolton MS 175 records a payment to 'Tho: Bleasdell for tayler worke for Comus and his Companye'.[92] Since the text of the occasion remains unidentified, it cannot be known whether this masque reworked Jonson's 1618 Comus-masque *Pleasure Reconciled to Virtue* or Milton's Ludlow entertainment, unpublished as yet in 1636 but already circulating in manuscript, or whether it reworked the story for a new performative context. The sense of an active regional culture in the north of England is, however, indisputable.

The emerging multidisciplinary area of cultural geography can then aid us in establishing the 1630s as a field of enquiry that benefits from the textual turn in historical studies, and from the historical and spatial turn in the humanities and the social sciences more generally. We can also learn much as scholars and students from the artistic technique of one of the definitive exponents of Caroline aesthetic culture. Malcolm Rogers has observed how often Anthony Van Dyck's sitters are not static but 'move through the landscape.'[93] The examples Rogers offers of this include several images of Charles I on horseback, depicted as a Roman emperor (these portraits are explored in greater detail in John Peacock's essay) and the portrait of Olivia Boteler, the wife of Endymion Porter, who is depicted as a nymph moving on foot across a bare terrain. Many of Van Dyck's sitters people the landscape of our own collection and the painter's capacity to create a sense of movement and action in his work provides in turn a model for the dynamic version of the 1630s that we wish to offer. Returning to John Peacock's helpful notion of reading the 'visual field' in this period, it is this wider sense of how the politics and literature of the Caroline era operate in complicated landscapes that we aim to capture and explore.

In summary, it occurs to us as editors that an inter- or multidisciplinary approach is the one that has the greatest capacity to release the aesthetic, cultural and political complexities of this period. The disciplines of history, art history, literary criticism, and musicology, among others, brought into relationship with one another, inform and challenge the findings of each in turn. The *rapprochement* between these disciplines enables an encounter between archival and textual scholarship and theoretical analysis that can be equally productive. By juxtaposing considerations of the cultural and political operations of artefacts, genres and arenas as diverse the public theatre, aristocratic households, letters, masques, music, poetry, material and economic culture, architecture, art, political and religious debate, the law and many other topics and issues which are covered in the essays in this collection, we hope to establish the 1630s as a justifiable and revealing focus for contained multidisciplinary study, as well as emphasising the richness and variation of the decade under scrutiny.

NOTES

1   For a theoretical exploration of the deployment of the term 'field' in this way, see Pierre Bordieu, *The Field of Cultural Production* (Cambridge: Polity Press, 1993).

2   See, for example, C. V. Wedgwood, *The King's Peace, 1637–1641* (London: Fontana, 1970; first published London: Collins, 1955); H. F. Kearney, *The Eleven Years' Tyranny of Charles I* (Historical Association, Aids for Teachers, 9, 1962).

3   See Thomas Carew's 'In Answer of an Elegiacall Letter, upon the Death of the King of Sweden ...', in his *Poems* (London, 1640), p. 130 (line 97), in which he suggests that the poetic subjects that best suit 'Our halcyon days' include 'tourneys, masques, theaters' (line 96). See also Giles Fleming, *Magnificence Exemplified* (London, 1634), p. 45; Richard Brathwaite, *The English Gentleman* (London, 1630), p. 298.

4 The standard history of this period is Kevin Sharpe, *The Personal Rule of Charles I* (New Haven and London: Yale University Press, 1992), although this study has its controversies and dissenters. For an earlier but still valuable account see S. R. Gardiner, *History of England from the Accession of James I to the Outbreak of the Civil War, 1603–42* (10 vols, London, 1883–84), vols vii–ix.

5 Henry Parker, *The Case of Shipmony* (London, 1640), p. 39.

6 David L. Smith, *A History of the Modern British Isles, 1603–1707: The Double Crown* (Oxford: Blackwell, 1998), pp. 410, 412. It would be misleading, however, to imply that Scottish historians have not paid considerable attention to the impact of English policies on affairs in Scotland; see, for example, Allan I. Macinnes, *Charles I and the Making of the Covenanting Movement, 1625–41* (Edinburgh: John Donald, 1991).

7 *A Proclamation for Suppressing of False Rumours Touching Parliament* (London, 1629); L. J. Reeve, *Charles I and the Road to Personal Rule* (Cambridge: Cambridge University Press, 1989), pp. 279–82.

8 For example E. S. Cope, *Politics without Parliaments 1629–1640* (London: Allen & Unwin, 1987).

9 Dates of parliamentary sessions are in David L. Smith, *The Stuart Parliaments, 1603–1689* (London: Arnold, 1999), p. 236. For suggestions that James VI and I had his own periods of 'personal rule', see Conrad Russell, 'Parliamentary history in perspective, 1604–1629', *History*, 61 (1976), 6 n. 18 and Andrew Thrush, 'The personal rule of James I, 1611–1620', in Tom Cogswell, Richard Cust and Peter Lake (eds), *Politics, Religion and Popularity: Early Stuart Essays in Honour of Conrad Russell* (Cambridge: Cambridge University Press, 2002), pp. 84–102.

10 Pauline Croft, 'Annual parliaments and the Long Parliament', *Bulletin of the Institute of Historical Research*, 59 (1986), pp. 155–71; Conrad Russell, 'The nature of a parliament in early Stuart England', in Howard Tomlinson (ed.), *Before the English Civil War* (London: Macmillan, 1983), pp. 123–50 (quotation at pp. 124–5).

11 See, for example, Sharpe, *Personal Rule of Charles I*, pp. 49–50. Compare Reeve, *Charles I and the Road to Personal Rule*, however, especially pp. 289, 292, for the argument that 1632, not 1629, was the key turning point.

12 Karen Britland, *Drama at the Courts of Queen Henrietta Maria* (Cambridge University Press, forthcoming). On Henrietta Maria's cultural influences, see Erica Veevers, *Images of Love and Religion: Queen Henrietta Maria and Court Entertainments* (Cambridge: Cambridge University Press, 1989).

13 Historical Manuscripts Commission, 23, *Twelfth Report, Appendix, Parts I–III. The Manuscripts of the Earl Cowper* (3 vols, London, 1888–89), i, p. 378.

14 Carew, 'In Answer of an Elegiacall Letter', lines 46–8; E. Hyde, Earl of Clarendon, *The History of the Rebellion and Civil Wars in England*, ed. W. D. Macray (6 vols, Oxford, 1888), i, p. 84 (book I sect. 146). See R. A. Anselment, 'Clarendon and the Caroline myth of peace', *Journal of British Studies*, 23 (1984), 37–54 for the hindsight and literary convention blended in such a view.

15 M. B. Young, *Charles I* (Basingstoke: Macmillan, 1997), p. 17.

16 Peter Lake, 'Anti-popery: the structure of a prejudice', in Richard Cust and Ann Hughes (eds), *Conflict in Early Stuart England* (London: Longman, 1989), pp. 72–106; Caroline Hibbard, *Charles I and the Popish Plot* (Chapel Hill: University of North Carolina Press,

Introducing The 1630s

1983). The Grand Remonstrance is printed in S. R. Gardiner (ed.), *The Constitutional Documents of the Puritan Revolution 1625–1660* (Oxford, 1899), pp. 202–32.

17 Richard Cust, 'Charles I and popularity', in Cogswell, Cust and Lake (eds), *Politics, Religion and Popularity*, pp. 235–58; R. Malcolm Smuts, *Court Culture and the Origins of a Royalist Tradition in Early Stuart England* (Philadelphia: University of Philadelphia Press, 1987), pp. 253–62. Cf. Bodl., MS Eng. Hist. e. 28, pp. 577, 581, 584.

18 For a consideration of Caroline foreign policy in the 1630s see Sharpe, *Personal Rule of Charles I*, pp. 70–97, 509–36, 825–34, and Ian Atherton, *Ambition and Failure in Stuart England: The Career of John, First Viscount Scudamore* (Manchester: Manchester University Press, 1999), pp. 171–219.

19 R. Malcolm Smuts, 'The puritan followers of Henrietta Maria in the 1630s', *English Historical Review*, 93 (1978), 26–45.

20 Smuts, *Court Culture*, pp. 247–50.

21 H. Langelüddecke, '"The chiefest strength and glory of this kingdom": arming and training the "perfect militia" in the 1630s', *English Historical Review*, 118 (2003), 1265–303.

22 B. Quintrell, 'Charles I and the navy in the 1630s', *The Seventeenth Century*, 3 (1988), 159–79.

23 K. Fincham (ed.), *Visitation Articles and Injunctions of the Early Stuart Church* (2 vols, Church of England Record Society, 1, 5, 1994–98), ii, pp. 33–4; J. F. Larkin and P. L. Hughes (eds), *Stuart Royal Proclamations* (2 vols, Oxford: Clarendon Press, 1973–83), ii, pp. 218–20. For an account which stresses the importance of these royal declarations in shutting down Calvinism, see D. R. Como, 'Predestination and political conflict in Laud's London', *Historical Journal*, 46 (2003), 263–94.

24 P. Heylyn, *Historia Quinqu-Articularis* (London, 1660), iii, pp. 102–10.

25 Most fully expressed in N. Tyacke, *Anti-Calvinists: The Rise of English Arminianism*, c. 1590–1640 (Oxford: Clarendon Press, 1990).

26 Atherton, *Ambition and Failure*, pp. 58–79, 110–19; Peter Lake, 'The Laudian style: order, uniformity and the pursuit of the beauty of holiness in the 1630s', in Kenneth Fincham (ed.), *The Early Stuart Church, 1603–1642* (Basingstoke: Macmillan, 1993), pp. 161–85; John Hoffman, 'The puritan revolution and the "beauty of holiness" at Cambridge', *Proceedings of the Cambridge Antiquarian Society*, 72 (1982–83), 94–105.

27 Sharpe, *Personal Rule of Charles I*, pp. 275–92; Peter White, 'The via media in the early Stuart church', in Fincham (ed.), *Early Stuart Church*, esp. p. 229.

28 Patrick Collinson, *The Religion of Protestants* (Oxford: Clarendon Press, 1982), p. 90; Conrad Russell, *The Causes of the English Civil War* (Oxford: Clarendon Press, 1990), ch. 8 and esp. p. 207; John Morrill, *The Nature of the English Revolution* (Harlow: Longman, 1993), part 1, esp. p. 52.

29 Anthony Milton, 'The creation of Laudianism: a new approach', in Cogswell, Cust and Lake (eds), *Politics, Religion and Popularity*, pp. 176, 183.

30 Graham Parry, *The Golden Age Restor'd: The Culture of the Stuart Court, 1603–42* (Manchester: Manchester University Press, 1981), p. 244.

31 J. S. A. Adamson, 'Chivalry and political culture in Caroline England', in Kevin Sharpe and Peter Lake (eds), *Culture and Politics in Early Stuart England* (Basingstoke: Macmillan, 1994), p. 161.

32 Sukanta Chaudhuri, *Renaissance Pastoral and its English Developments* (Oxford: Clarendon Press, 1989).

33 See, for example, Julie Sanders, 'Ecocritical readings and the seventeenth-century woodland: Milton's *Comus* and the Forest of Dean', *English*, 50 (2001), 1–18.

34 John Creaser, '"The present aid of this occasion": the setting of *Comus*', in David Lindley (ed.), *The Court Masque* (Manchester: Manchester University Press, 1984), p. 119.

35 James Shirley was commissioned by the Inns of Court to devise the special masque *The Triumph of Peace* which was in part performed as a progress through the City of London in 1634. The masque constituted public reparation for the actions of Prynne, who was an Inn member. Other dramatists, including Shirley and Ford, made scathing references to Prynne in their plays for the public theatres. The debate is discussed in more detail in the introduction to Hero Chalmers, Julie Sanders and Sophie Tomlinson (eds), *Three Seventeenth-Century Plays on Women and Performance* (forthcoming Manchester University Press, 2006).

36 Leah S. Marcus, *The Politics of Mirth: Jonson, Herrick, Milton, Marvell, and the Defense of Old Holiday Pastimes* (Chicago: University of Chicago Press, 1986), pp. 128–9.

37 T. G. Barnes, 'County politics and a puritan *cause célèbre*: Somerset church ales, 1633', *Transactions of the Royal Historical Society*, 5th series, 9 (1959), 103–22; Kenneth Parker, *The English Sabbath: A Study of Doctrine and Discipline from the Reformation to the Civil War* (Cambridge: Cambridge University Press, 1988).

38 Julian Davies, *The Caroline Captivity of the Church: Charles I and the Remoulding of Anglicanism* (Oxford: Clarendon Press, 1992), pp. 172–204; Sharpe, *Personal Rule of Charles I*, pp. 351–9.

39 Marcus, *Politics of Mirth*.

40 Robert Herrick, 'The Argument to his Book', lines 3–4, in his *Hesperides* (London, 1648), p. 1.

41 Creaser, 'The setting of *Comus*', p. 113.

42 Peter Donald, *An Uncounselled King: Charles I and the Scottish Troubles, 1637–1641* (Cambridge: Cambridge University Press, 1990), pp. 33–5; Sharpe, *Personal Rule of Charles I*, pp. 780–3; *The Grievances given in by the Ministers before the Parliament holden in June 1633* (n.p., 1635); Dougal Shaw, 'St. Giles' church and Charles I's coronation visit to Scotland', *Historical Research*, 77:198 (2004), 496–8.

43 Donald, *Uncounselled King*, pp. 34–5; G. Donaldson, *The Making of the Scottish Prayer Book of 1637* (Edinburgh: Edinburgh University Press, 1954), pp. 40–5.

44 H. R. Trevor-Roper, *Archbishop Laud 1573–1645* (London: Macmillan, 1940), pp. 79, 144.

45 Tyacke, *Anti-Calvinists*, pp. 199–200; Andrew Foster, 'Church policies of the 1630s', in Cust and Hughes (eds), *Conflict in Early Stuart England*, p. 204.

46 Atherton, *Ambition and Failure*, pp. 193–7.

47 BL, Additional MS 70002, fol. 139r.

48 The editors are indebted to James Knowles's unpublished paper '"Our concealed solemnity": *A Maske at Ludlow* and the popish plot', delivered at the North American Conference on British Studies in Pasadena, October 2000, as part of our panel on 'The cultural geography of the 1630s'.

49 Young, *Charles I*, p. 106.

50 Sharpe, *Personal Rule of Charles I*, pp. xix, 953–4; see also pp. 769–78.

51 See, for example, Raymond Williams, *Keywords: A Vocabulary of Culture and Society* (London: Fontana, 1988); *Marxism and Literature* (Oxford: Oxford University Press, 1987); and for his concept of 'knowable communities', see *The English Novel from Dickens to Lawrence* (London: Chatto and Windus, 1970).

52 An influential attempt to engage in this form of multidisciplinary encounter between scholars in these varying fields is Sharpe and Lake (eds), *Culture and Politics in Early Stuart England*. Examples of attempts to read political culture through its textual manifestations have been most successful in the civil war period; examples include Nigel Smith, *Literature and Revolution in England, 1640–1660* (New Haven: Yale University Press, 1994); David Norbrook, *Writing the English Revolution: Poetry, Rhetoric and Politics, 1627–1660* (Cambridge: Cambridge University Press, 1999) – this volume's chapter on 'The king's peace and the people's war, 1630–1643', pp. 63–92, is especially pertinent for this collection; and Ann Hughes, *'Gangraena' and the Struggle for the English Revolution* (Oxford: Oxford University Press, 2004).

53 For a recent claim that cultural studies has 'failed', see Kevin Sharpe and Steven Zwicker, 'Introduction: Refiguring Revolutions', in K. Sharpe and S. Zwicker (eds), *Refiguring Revolutions: Aesthetics and Politics from the English Revolution to the Romantic Revolution* (London and Berkeley: University of California Press, 1998), p. 2.

54 The quotation is from the stage directions to Aurelian Townshend's *Albion's Triumph* (London, 1632): see O&S, ii, p. 457, line 338.

55 Ronald Hutton, *Debates in Stuart History* (Basingstoke: Palgrave Macmillan, 2004), pp. 59–92. Compare Kevin Sharpe's celebration of the 'revolutionary new cultural turn' taken in early modern studies: Sharpe, *Remapping Early Modern England* (Cambridge: Cambridge University Press, 2000), p. 414.

56 See most notably Conrad Russell, *The Fall of the British Monarchies, 1637–1642* (Oxford: Clarendon Press, 1991); Brendan Bradshaw and John Morrill (eds), *The British Problem, c. 1534–1707* (Basingstoke: Macmillan, 1996); Steven Ellis and Sarah Barber (eds), *Conquest and Union: Fashioning a British State 1485–1707* (Harlow: Longman, 1995). For the argument that the Cornish should be considered as the fifth nation in the British Isles see Mark Stoyle, *West Britons: Cornish Identities and the Early Modern British State* (Exeter: Exeter University Press, 2002).

57 For example Martyn Bennett, *The Civil Wars in Britain and Ireland, 1638–1651* (Oxford: Blackwell, 1997), pp. 5–6.

58 T. Marshall, *Theatre and Empire: Great Britain on the London Stages under James VI and I* (Manchester: Manchester University Press, 2000); D. Baker and W. Maley (eds), *British Identities and English Renaissance Literature* (Cambridge: Cambridge University Press, 2002).

59 On the Forest of Dean context, see Marcus, *Politics of Mirth*, pp. 169–212, and Sanders, 'Ecocritical readings'. On the Welsh significances in the text, see Philip Schwyzer, 'Purity and danger on the west bank of the Severn: the cultural geography of *A Masque Presented at Ludlow Castle, 1634*', *Representations*, 60 (1997), 22–48.

60 Alan J. Fletcher, *Drama, Performance, and Polity in Pre-Cromwellian Ireland* (Toronto: University of Toronto Press, 2000).

61 Peter Lake, 'Retrospective: Wentworth's political world in revisionist and post-revisionist perspective', in J. F. Merritt (ed.), *The Political World of Thomas Wentworth, Earl of Strafford, 1621–1641* (Cambridge: Cambridge University Press, 1996), p. 279.

62 John Morrill, 'William Davenport and the "silent majority" of early Stuart England', *Journal of the Chester Archaeological Society*, 58 (1975), 115–29; Alastair Bellany, *The Politics of Court Scandal in Early Modern England: News Culture and the Overbury Affair, 1603–1660* (Cambridge: Cambridge University Press, 2002), especially pp. 10–14, 23. For more on the ambiguous meanings in early Stuart news, compare Richard Cust, 'News and politics in early seventeenth-century England', *Past and Present*, 112 (August 1986), 60–90, and Ian Atherton, 'The itch grown a disease: manuscript transmission of news in the seventeenth century', in Joad Raymond (ed.), *News, Newspapers, and Society in Early Modern Britain* (London: Frank Cass, 1999), pp. 39–65.

63 Sharpe, *Remapping Early Modern England*, p. 413.

64 For the difference between documents which furnish evidence and so allow the scholar to see more clearly, and texts that are constructed, see Kevin Sharpe, *Reading Revolutions: The Politics of Reading in Early Modern England* (New Haven and London: Yale University Press, 2000), pp. 5, 25–7.

65 Principally by Clive Holmes, 'The county community in early Stuart historiography', *Journal of British Studies*, 19 (1980), 54–73, and Ann Hughes, 'Warwickshire on the eve of the civil war: a county community?', *Midland History*, 7 (1982), 42–72.

66 Jonathan Scott, *England's Troubles: Seventeenth-Century English Political Instability in European Context* (Cambridge, Cambridge University Press, 2000); John Reeve, 'Britain or Europe? The context of early modern English history: political and cultural, economic and social, naval and military', in Glenn Burgess (ed.), *The New British History: Founding a Modern State, 1603–1715* (London: Tauris, 1999), pp. 287–312; Allan Macinnes and Jane Ohlmeyer (eds), *The Stuart Kingdoms in the Seventeenth Century* (Dublin: Four Courts Press, 2002).

67 See Kevin Sharpe, *Criticism and Compliment: The Politics of Literature in the England of Charles I* (Cambridge: Cambridge University Press, 1987) for insightful readings of this and other poems from the 1630s.

68 See R. Malcolm Smuts (ed.), *The Stuart Court and Europe: Essays in Politics and Political Culture* (Cambridge: Cambridge University Press, 1996).

69 Malcolm Rogers, 'Van Dyck in England', in Christopher Brown and Hans Vlieghe (eds), *Van Dyck 1599–1641* (New York: Rizzoli, 1999), p. 89.

70 In addition, William Davenant's 1638 poem 'Madagascar' could be considered here, since it was written as part of a campaign from 1636 promoted by Endymion Porter and the Earl of Arundel to settle Madagascar under Prince Rupert as viceroy. Charles withdrew his support for the scheme early in 1640 in the face of opposition from the East India Company (which did not wish to see a rival English company in the Indian Ocean) and the project collapsed. An English expedition did attempt to settle the island in 1645–6, but it failed. W. Foster, 'An English settlement in Madagascar in 1645–6', *English Historical Review*, 27 (1912), 239–50; R. Boothby, *A Breife Discovery or Description of the Most Famous Island of Madagascar* (London, 1646), pp. 2, 9–10, 69–70; E. B. Sainsbury, *A Calendar of the Court Minutes etc. of the East India Company, 1635–1679* (11 vols, Oxford: Clarendon Press, 1907–38), i, pp. 244–5, 322–3, 336; ii, p. 25; F. S. Hervey, *The Life, Correspondence and Collections of Thomas Howard, Earl of Arundel* (Cambridge: Cambridge University Press, 1921), pp. 417–19, 506–8.

71 Some examples of practice in this field include: Dennis E. Cosgrove, *The Palladian Landscape: Geographical Change and its Cultural Representations in Sixteenth-Century Italy* (Philadelphia: Pennsylvania State University Press, 1993); Dennis Cosgrove and Stephen Daniels (eds), *The Iconography of Landscape: Essays on the Symbolic Representation, Design, and Use of Past Environments* (Cambridge: Cambridge University Press, 1988); and Ian Cook et al. (eds), *Cultural Turns/Geographical Turns: Perspectives on Cultural Geography* (Harlow: Prentice-Hall, 2000). See also Mike Crang, *Cultural Geography* (London: Routledge, 1998) and Don Mitchell, *Cultural Geography: A Critical Introduction* (Oxford: Blackwell, 2000) for overviews of the field.

72 Alexandra Shepherd and Phil Withington (eds), *Communities in Early Modern England* (Manchester: Manchester University Press, 2000).

73 David Underdown, *Revel, Riot and Rebellion* (Oxford: Oxford University Press, 1985); M. Stoyle, *Loyalty and Locality: Popular Allegiance in Devon during the English Civil War* (Exeter: Exeter University Press, 1994); Stoyle, *West Britons*. For an assessment of their work see the debate between Underdown and Morrill in *Journal of British Studies*, 26 (1987), partly reproduced in Morrill, *Nature of the English Revolution*, pp. 224–41, and Ann Hughes, *The Causes of the English Civil War* (2nd edn, Basingstoke: Macmillan, 1998), pp. 133–40.

74 Clifford Geertz, *The Interpretation of Cultures* (New York: Basic Books, 1973); V. W. Turner, *Dramas, Fields, and Metaphors: Symbolic Action in Human Society* (Ithaca: Cornell University Press, 1974); J. Thirsk (ed.), *The Agrarian History of England and Wales. Vol. V: 1640–1750. 1: Regional Farming Systems* (Cambridge: Cambridge University Press, 1984).

75 Tom Cogswell, *Home Divisions: Aristocracy, the State and Provincial Conflict* (Manchester: Manchester University Press, 1998), p. 8.

76 In Sharpe, *Remapping Early Modern England*, the geographical metaphor is carried through in attempts to 'journey through the political culture of early modern England' to 'see the terrain': see esp. p. 20.

77 Roy Strong, *The Renaissance Garden in England* (London: Thames and Hudson, 1998 [1979]), pp. 147–61, 170–5. Strong goes so far as to suggest that we need to view Wilton in the 'context of Caroline civilization, as a symbol of the halcyon years of the King's Peace' (p. 161).

78 Mark Girouard, *Robert Smythson and the English Country House* (New Haven: Yale University Press, 1983); Timothy Raylor, '"Pleasure reconciled to virtue": William Cavendish, Ben Jonson, and the decorative scheme of Bolsover Castle', *Renaissance Quarterly*, 53 (1999), 402–39.

79 See Malcolm Smuts, 'The court and its neighbourhood: royal policy and urban growth in the early Stuart West End', *Journal of British Studies*, 30 (1991), 136–45; and Martin Butler, *Theatre and Crisis, 1632–42* (Cambridge: Cambridge University Press, 1984), pp. 141–80.

80 See Julie Sanders, *Caroline Drama* (Plymouth: Northcote House, 1999), pp. 43–55; and Matthew Steggle, *Richard Brome: Place and Politics on the Caroline Stage* (Manchester: Manchester University Press, 2004).

81 The inaugural masque was attended on 27 February 1635 by Prince Charles, Prince James, and Princess Mary. Thanks to Lauren Shohet and James Knowles for ongoing discussions of this text and its occasion.

82 The year 1629 had seen the establishment of the Children of the Revels, initially intended to provide trained boy actors for the King's Men. Jordan was a member of that company, and his first play, *Money is an Ass* (c. 1631–32) was written before he was fifteen. These details and their significance for 1630s culture were discussed in papers by Martin Butler and Lucy Munro for the Shakespeare Association of America seminar on 'Localizing Caroline drama', New Orleans, 2004.

83 The text was published, along with Tatham's pastoral poetry, under the title *The Fancies Theater* (London, 1640). Links are worth pursuing to other school drama in this period, including William Hawkins, *Apollo Shroving*, which was performed at the free grammar school of Hadleigh in Suffolk, on Shrove Tuesday 1627, and also to Kynaston's masque and Jordan's theatre work. That Kynaston's masque, *Apollo Shroving* and *Love Crownes the End* were all published in the 1630s indicates considerable public interest in variants of this form. Abraham Cowley's *Love's Riddle*, published in 1638, was said to have been composed at Westminster School and Richard Lovelace's *The Scholars* is also deemed to have been the production of a schoolboy dramatist. See G. E. Bentley, *The Jacobean and Caroline Stage* (7 vols, Oxford: Clarendon Press, 1941–68), iii, pp. 172–3, 179–80; iv, pp. 720–4. The editors are indebted to Lucy Munro for these details.

84 See Julie Sanders, 'Jonson, *The Sad Shepherd* and the North Midlands', *Ben Jonson Journal*, 6 (1999), 49–68; and Steggle, *Richard Brome*, pp. 165–7.

85 Timothy Raylor's work has been groundbreaking in establishing the significance, cultural and political, of William and Charles's building works at Bolsover, in particular the construction of the Little Castle with its internal imagery and symbolic layout. See, for example, his '"Pleasure reconciled to virtue"'. See also Raylor's special edition of *The Seventeenth Century* on 'The Cavendish family', 9 (1994). In addition to Jonson, William Cavendish patronised the work of John Ford, James Shirley and Richard Brome, as well as writing playtexts of his own.

86 Cedric Brown, 'Courtesies of place and arts of diplomacy in Ben Jonson's last two entertainments for royalty', *The Seventeenth Century*, 9 (1994), 150. Timothy Raylor has recently argued the case for viewing Cavendish's 'circle' as a series of overlapping networks rather than a cohesive coterie; see his 'Newcastle's ghosts: Robert Payne, Ben Jonson, and the "Cavendish circle"', in Claude J. Summers and Ted-Larry Pebworth (eds), *Literary Circles and Cultural Communities in Renaissance England* (Columbia: Missouri University Press, 2000), pp. 92–114.

87 Lucy Worsley and Tom Addyman, 'Riding houses and horses: William Cavendish's architecture for the art of horsemanship', *Architectural History*, 45 (2002), 194–229; Lucy Worsley, 'Reining Cavaliers', *History Today*, 54:9 (September 2004), 9–15.

88 See Julie Sanders, 'A sense of place in the writings of the Cavendish women', in Lynn Hulse and James Knowles (eds), *Prince of the Northern Quarter* (forthcoming).

89 See Julie Sanders, 'Tixall revisited: the coterie writings of the Astons and the Thimelbys in seventeenth-century Staffordshire', *Staffordshire Studies* 12 (2000), 75–93; and Victoria Burke, 'Women and early seventeenth-century manuscript culture: four miscellanies', *The Seventeenth Century*, 12 (1997), 135–50.

90 Mildmay Fane, Earl of Westmorland, authored and staged several theatrical productions at Apethorpe in the 1640s.

91 Ann Hughes, 'Thomas Dugard and his circle in the 1630s – a "parliamentary-puritan" connexion?', *Historical Journal*, 29:4 (1986), 771–93.

92 Transcripts of the entries are provided by Martin Butler in his pioneering account of this occasion: 'A provincial masque of *Comus*', *Renaissance Drama*, 17 (1986), 163–8. Chatsworth Bolton MS 175 is a book of receipts and disbursements in the hand of Robert Robotham, secretary and purse-bearer to Francis Clifford, the 4th Earl, and later Henry, Lord Clifford in 1636.

93 Rogers, 'Van Dyck in England', p. 89.

Chapter 2

Force, love and authority in Caroline political culture

Malcolm Smuts

This essay examines how the governing circle around Charles I perceived the challenge of ruling Britain in the 1630s. In particular it asks how this group's responses to practical issues reflected deeper ideas about statecraft. It thereby seeks to discover better ways of connecting detailed political history to studies of political thought. Perspectives on this problem have long been clouded by an uncritical assumption that the 1630s saw a failed experiment in absolutism. The term absolutism is a nineteenth-century neologism, originally a product of liberal journalism.[1] As a historical concept it glosses over important differences between European monarchies, while implying that administrative practices flowed in a fairly straightforward manner from an ideology of royal divine right. By doing so it begs all the questions we need to ask to arrive at a more precise understanding of the goals and characteristics of the Caroline state. But if we discard the absolutist label what do we put in its place? Can we develop alternative perspectives that provide a less anachronistic understanding of seventeenth-century political outlooks?

The boldest recent attempt to meet this challenge, Jonathan Scott's *England's Troubles*,[2] furnishes several useful insights. Scott rightly calls attention to the importance of the Thirty Years' War as a crucial European context for British politics. He correctly sees Charles I as a king intent on remedying the financial poverty that weakened the Stuart monarchy in Europe and the 'disease of disobedience' that compromised royal authority at home. But he ultimately provides no detailed discussion of the goals and methods of the 'state building' in which he insists Charles was engaged. Instead he portrays Caroline government as a weak reactionary holding action – a pallid British reflection of more robust continental programmes of political and religious repression – vainly trying to contain powerful forces of religious reformation that eventually overwhelmed it. This view is connected to another prominent feature of Scott's analysis, his claim that the seventeenth century witnessed a contest between weak institutions and powerful ideas generated by the Reformation. English puritans, he argues, absorbed from radical continental Protestants a profound anti-formalism – an instinctive mistrust of all external structures of religious and political authority that might impede the operation of the inner spirit. Scott sees this attitude as a powerful revolutionary force, whose impact he compares to an eruption of molten lava from a volcano.

Although this interpretation helps in recovering the perspectives of seventeenth-century republicans at the centre of Scott's analysis, it obscures other features of the period. He fails to explain the aggressive institution building of the Long Parliament and its successor regimes, whose puritan scruples did not prevent them from erecting new structures of coercive authority. He also fails to notice powerful intellectual and cultural traditions that reinforced attachments to traditional forms of government and worship instead of undermining them, such as John Pocock's common law mind, widespread loyalty to the Prayer Book liturgy and the devotion to the King and monarchy underlying royalism.[3] To understand seventeenth-century political culture from within, we need to give as much sympathetic attention to contemporary efforts at strengthening external forms of authority as to the ideas Scott emphasises. I hope to contribute to this goal by showing that Caroline state building was never the intellectually sterile holding action he portrays. Although the regime certainly wanted to combat puritan disobedience, it was never *simply* a question of coercing outward submission. Charles's councillors knew they had to restore his ability to lead and unify his subjects, as Elizabeth and other successful monarchs were thought to have done in the past, thereby strengthening the kingdom's internal peace while restoring its international reputation. Moreover they possessed a conceptual vocabulary for thinking about this task.

The words in my title – force, authority and love – derive from a major European treatise on statecraft, *The Six Books of Politics* of Justus Lipsius.[4] While I will not argue that Lipsius *directly* influenced Caroline political attitudes, I will contend that his ideas resembled those of Charles's circle sufficiently to provide a useful starting point for analysis. Lipsius regarded conflict and instability as intrinsic features of political life that can only be contained through some combination of the two qualities of 'force' and 'virtue'.[5] He equated force with soldiers, including a strong royal guard that would lend majesty to the prince and garrisons in fortified strongholds.[6] Lipsian virtue is not a quality of the prince alone, like the *virtu* of Machiavelli, but something that resides in the *relationship* between a ruler and his subjects. Arising from the prince's actions it lives in the hearts of his people, as a disposition that binds the state together.[7] Lipsius divided it into the two qualities of love, or 'a ready inclination and liking of the subjects towards the king and his estate' and authority, or 'a reverent opinion of the King and his estate, imprinted as well in his own subjects as in strangers', consisting of 'admiration and fear'.[8]

The best way to inspire love, he argues, is through leniency, indulgence and bounty, whereas authority requires 'severity' in punishing offenders and the capacity to conserve resources for emergencies. Since these prescriptions are somewhat contradictory, a ruler must balance them against each other, avoiding excesses in either direction. Too much indulgence will breed 'contempt', the deadly enemy of authority, whereas too much severity will engender a hatred that destroys love. The prince must also pay careful attention to the character of his subjects, since nations differ in temperament, some requiring greater severity while others respond more readily to gentler methods. Lipsius's equivocation sets him apart from Machiavelli, who famously advised princes to rule through fear instead of love. The difference reflects not only Lipsius's discomfort with Machiavelli's ruthlessness but his greater scepticism. He simply did not think rulers capable of mastering fortune in the way that Machiavelli sought, since political causation is too complicated and too obscure to allow total human control. God alone ultimately determines the fate of kingdoms. The best we can achieve is limited insights that provide some guidance, without guaranteeing success.

If we attempt to apply this analysis it immediately calls attention to the paucity of force at the British Crown's disposal, in comparison to the other major monarchies of Europe. Armies were normally important instruments of seventeenth-century statecraft: one thinks, for example, of the Spanish troops occupying the southern Netherlands, the establishment of military garrisons in strategic locations in France, by minister-favourites like Concini and Richelieu, and the Thirty Years' War.[9] Soldiers not only crushed rebellions but intimidated potential opponents into acquiescing in unpopular measures. There had been considerable anxiety in 1627 that Charles was about to introduce these methods, as he collected the Forced Loan while raising an army for service against France. The Earl of Dorset remarked to the Venetian ambassador that the absence of fortified towns in England left the people at the King's mercy should he attempt to govern by the sword.[10] But this was essentially bluster. More than any other major European state England was, in Glenn Burgess's phrase, a 'pacified monarchy', in which military coercion had ceased to be a significant instrument of domestic governance.[11] In the 1620s Charles had no intention of overturning this system.

Force remained important in two other contexts, however. One was Ireland, where the Crown did maintain a small army, which most Englishmen regarded as essential to government. When the commander of that army, Lord Wilmot, heard about the appointment of Thomas Wentworth as Lord Deputy in 1632, he wrote to London warning: 'beware how you disarm him at his first coming ... By a small force he may perhaps get some small things ... but by a force of some show you may not doubt but to do what you please .'[12] Although Wentworth disliked Wilmot, he agreed about the need for soldiers to govern this 'criminous ... lewdly affected people', with their 'habitual hatred to the English Government ... inciting all they can to blood and rebellion'.[13] He also appreciated Lipsius's point about palace guards adding majesty to government: 'I have three score horse in my [stable] ... and a guard of fifty foot waiting on ... [me] every Sunday', he boasted.[14] The Stuarts also adopted a second policy that Lipsius discussed under the rubric of force, the planting of colonies in conquered territories prone to rebellion. Lipsius reasoned that since colonists would always feel outnumbered by a hostile native population, they would remain loyal to their prince and furnish him with soldiers. As Tacitus had remarked, colonies are 'the very mansion places of bondage'.[15] Wentworth was a particularly energetic proponent of plantations, as Nicholas Canny has shown.[16]

To be sure, even in Ireland Stuart rule never relied *only* on soldiers and planters. The Crown and its agents attempted to instil habits of obedience and civility by introducing the common law, supporting the official Protestant church and 'improving' Irish agriculture, 'to bring this people in manners and matter to a conformity with England as much as possibly may be'.[17] The policy rested on good classical precedents, especially a well-known passage from the *Agricola* of Tacitus, explaining how the Romans had subdued Britain by gathering its 'rude and dispersed' people into towns and encouraging them to raise their sons 'in the liberal sciences', until they became thoroughly romanised, even adopting vices like an excessive fondness for banquets and baths. Although Tacitus described this cultural imperialism as a form of corruption and 'bondage'[18] writers associated with the Stuart court usually regarded it with approval.[19]

Everyone assumed, however, that the army had to remain in place while the slow process of anglicising the Irish proceeded. Moreover Wentworth's determination to pay for that army from Irish revenues meant that even the loyal English population needed to be bullied and manipulated into putting the interests of the Crown's soldiers before their own concerns. 'I find myself in the society of a strange people', he complained, 'their own privates altogether their study, without any regard to the public'.[20] 'It will be impossible to gain from them unless it be not only against their wills but before they be aware of what is intended.'[21] Although these policies built an enormous charge of resentment that exploded in the 1640s, for a time they seemed to work. Ireland in the 1630s provides a classic example of an attempt to erect a civil polity through autocratic government backed by an army. It was a place where the promotion of virtue depended on force. Indeed Wentworth wanted it to become the Crown's military reservoir. Since 'it is necessary that his

Majesty breed up and have a seminary of soldiers in some part or other of his dominions', he argued, Ireland should be used for this purpose, so that at any moment the King might deploy 'an army of twenty thousand men in any part of Christendom'.[22] He may have been thinking of the decisive intervention of the Spanish army of Flanders in Germany in the 1620s.

For the second context in which the Crown needed force was the international arena. But to sustain that force the Stuarts required parliamentary supply, which in turn depended on political goodwill. In England force therefore depended on virtue and especially on love. There is considerable evidence that people saw things in more or less this way. An endlessly repeated commonplace held that English kings have no greater source of strength than their people's love, which opens the way to supply. Some writers also saw a direct relationship between the quality of royal leadership and the military vigour of the population. They normally employed a slightly different terminology from Lipsius, involving words like honour, reputation, action and valour rather than authority and force, but the meanings were very similar. The second Earl of Essex had insisted that valorous acts by nobly born commanders like himself were essential to maintaining people's willingness to sacrifice blood and treasure in support of war.[23] He also regarded English valour as essential to maintaining 'the public cause' elsewhere in Europe, especially in the Netherlands. Without English support, he predicted, Dutch patriotism would collapse, allowing Spain to recover through duplicity and corruption what she had failed to gain by war.[24] Like Lipsius, Essex saw virtue as a quality that originated from effective leadership but ultimately invigorated an entire people – indeed several allied peoples – allowing them to resist tyranny. People widely criticised James I for undermining the valour of his subjects through his excessive desire for peace and the venality of his court. But even during his reign royal councillors remained acutely aware of the need to maintain England's international reputation by demonstrating that the King enjoyed enough public goodwill to raise money. As Sir Thomas Lake put it in 1615, 'all states subsist by two principal ways, by means and reputation ... and in reputation nothing more honourable or more available than is the opinion of the love of his people'.[25] Lake went on to say explicitly that broken parliaments hurt the King's reputation by suggesting that an absence of 'love' might hamstring military initiatives, a point also urged by James's ambassador in Madrid, John Digby.[26]

The rhetoric of Charles and his spokesmen, during the war parliaments of the 1620s, repeatedly stressed the connection between prompt parliamentary supply, the King's international reputation, and the success or failure of the 'public cause' in which Britain was engaged. Even acknowledged disasters, like Mansfeld's expedition, were justified on the grounds that England's efforts had encouraged German princes, the Dutch and the King of Denmark to enter the struggle.²⁷ If parliament wavered in its support after a few setbacks, the King's spokesmen insisted, other states would defect from the anti-Habsburg coalition, with disastrous results. Well-publicised attempts at retrenchment of expenses in the royal household were simultaneously hailed as examples of sacrifice and discipline at the top of society that set an example for the kingdom. In 1627 Roger Maynwaring repeated arguments that Essex had made a generation earlier that Englishmen's refusal to sacrifice domestic luxuries in support of war indicated a loss of virtue. This was not simply rhetoric for public consumption. Private communications between Crown servants also stressed that England's failure to unite behind its King led to reverses in Europe. 'I will be bold to tell you with grief of an English heart', a correspondent lamented to Henry Vane the elder in October of 1630: 'it is the want of an English fleet at sea, of moneys and union at home that gives no reputation to his Majesty's treaties abroad'.²⁸ Vane himself, Charles's ambassador to The Hague in 1629, repeatedly made similar points in his dispatches: the Crown's poverty and failure to honour its commitments, due to broken parliaments, played into the hands of groups in the Netherlands who wanted to abandon their English alliance and the cause of Charles's nephew, the Elector Palatine, and conclude a peace favourable to narrow Dutch interests.

Precisely because people viewed the wars of the 1620s as a test of whether the young King and his subjects could overcome the jealousies of his father's reign and renew England's virtue, the debacles of the period proved especially painful. Parliament's efforts to blame the Duke of Buckingham only further aggravated Charles, who saw attacks on his chief minister as slights on his own abilities. Court iconography represented Buckingham's critics as incarnations of Envy, the traditional enemy of honour and virtue.²⁹ Above all the court blamed malcontents who spread malicious accusations and stirred popular discontents, 'practising persons, who by scattering rumours and other devices seek to harden men's hearts even to their own hurt', as Viscount Dorchester described them.³⁰ The discontents appeared to have rendered the English state, in Bishop Harsnet's phrase, 'like a body without blood and sinews', incapable of defending itself. In 1630 the Venetian ambassador described England as a country 'enfeebled' by a 'King ... out of sympathy with his people, unequal to governing by himself and his councils distracted by private interests'.³¹ This perception of weakness further undermined Charles's position, by tempting foreign states and his own subjects to think they could defy him with impunity. There were even dark murmurs that he might not succeed in leaving the Crown to his as yet unborn children. The French ambassador reported in 1626 that the Earl of Arundel believed that the King's 'necessity was such' that even if he broke a parliament he would have to reassemble another session in two months or risk seeing not only 'his affairs perish ... but his house overturned'.³²

In short, Charles confronted a growing spirit of contempt. The nadir came during the 1629 session of parliament, when a strike by London merchants against paying tonnage and poundage threatened to bankrupt the Crown during time of war, as a means of compelling him to submit to parliament's demands. Faced with this attempt at blackmail the Council decided that it needed once and for all to demonstrate the King's ability to enforce his commands, by postponing further meetings of parliament indefinitely, and through the classic remedy of 'severity' against the Commons' ringleaders, who were promptly incarcerated in the Tower. This is precisely how Dorchester described the situation in a letter to Henry Vane, responding to a Dutch proposal for a joint West India Company. After promising that the Council would give the idea serious consideration, Dorchester added that the King

> is like to be better enabled than when you left us by the settling of the disquiet of men's minds after the first heats kindled by ... the last Parliament ... by sentences in the chief judicial courts against such as were the chief authors of those disorders ... Now the world sees that Parliament men must be responsible for their words and actions in other courts, they will be more moderate and circumspect.[33]

In another letter to his nephew, Dudley Carleton the younger, Dorchester expressed confidence that once the King 'established a settled course of proceeding in the conduct of affairs here at home ... there is no doubt his service abroad will fare the better and consequently his ministers appear more considerable in the eye of the world'.[34] A concerted effort at restoring Charles's damaged authority had begun.

The most immediate challenge, once the opposition ringleaders had been dealt with, was to demonstrate the Crown's capacity to raise significant military forces without parliamentary supply. The Council especially wanted to support the navy, as the one effective bargaining tool Charles had left in international affairs. Dorchester instructed Vane in February of 1630 to impress upon the Dutch that 'expedients' were being 'found for putting his Majesty's fleet in good order ... not only for the present but the future'. Ship Money was an extension and culmination of earlier initiatives, a means of upholding the English state's international reputation by displaying its capacity to employ significant military force. Even if the King's ships did nothing, Thomas Wentworth assured Viscount Conway in 1635, 'when other princes see his Majesty provided to set such a strength at sea it shall make him so considerable as they will court him on all sides ... nothing in reason of state [can] concern him more'.[35] Although over sanguine he was not fundamentally wrong: foreign powers did recognise that Charles's navy might alter the European balance of power, especially after the French annexation of Lorraine closed the overland route between southern Europe and Flanders.[36] One of only two English engravings of the period that seem to have enjoyed official sponsorship showed the *Sovereign of the Seas*, the great flagship built with Ship Money. Another print of 1638, sold by the Strand bookseller responsible for publishing the Caroline masques, featured a small portrait of the fleet's commander, the Earl of Northumberland, and a list of the royal ships sent out that year. The navy had become a symbol of the British state's recovered vigour.

By contrast, the regime showed little inclination to develop significant new instruments of coercive power within England. It expanded the use of proclamations, while engaging in somewhat sporadic efforts to infuse greater vigour into county magistracies and greater efficiency into the county militias.[37] But this amounted to little more than tinkering around the edges of the traditional system. The Council appears to have assumed – correctly – that once the most vociferous dissidents had been punished and the expectation of future parliaments dampened, normal procedures would suffice to restore royal authority. Within the international context of the 1630s this restraint is significant. The one domestic area where the regime did attempt to bring about fundamental change was religion. As historians have always recognised and as Julian Davies in particular has stressed, Caroline reforms in the church were also intended to reinforce the King's secular authority, by combating puritan dissidence and fostering obedience.[38] Although this point is too familiar to need emphasis, it does merit closer examination. Too many historians still treat the divine right of kings as a constitutional dogma, rather than an argument about political theology, whose precise meaning depended on how it was integrated within broader patterns of religious thought. Most discussions of divine right concerned religious duties at least as much as rights. They were exercises in political casuistry, treating the obligations that kings and subjects owed to each other as well as to God, and the dangers caused when false claims of conscience shaped political behaviour. Jacobean divine right arguments usually depended on interpretations of ancient Jewish monarchy that were implicitly double-edged, since the Bible provided numerous examples of sinful kings punished by God with rebellion, deposition and regicide. In their sources and style of argumentation, if not in their conclusions, they closely resembled the Calvinist resistance tracts they were intended to refute. Arguing from Old Testament sources also easily gave rise to prophetic and apocalyptic discourses with potentially unsettling implications. Arthur Williamson has shown that many Scottish clergy associated Stuart divine right with expectations that God had chosen the British monarchy to play a pivotal role in a climactic struggle between the reformed states of Europe and the Roman Antichrist.[39] Peter McCullough has uncovered similar emphases in some Jacobean court sermons, especially in the households of Henry and Charles himself while Prince of Wales.[40] Apocalyptic speculation among German Calvinists also shaped views of the King's sister, Elizabeth, and her husband Friedrich V of the Palatinate.[41]

By 1630 Charles had spectacularly failed to meet the expectations this theological tradition aroused. He lost his battles, he had a Catholic and therefore idolatrous wife and his court was accused of promoting heresy and popery. He needed, not simply to reassert divine right arguments, but to shift the ground on which they rested, to disarm suggestions that he risked a withdrawal of divine favour. Fortunately arguments already existed that helped point the way. Since the 1590s conformist clergy had attempted to link divine right arguments to a liturgical emphasis characteristic of anti-puritan theology. Not content simply to emphasise analogies between modern and ancient Jewish kings, they sought in addition to show that Christianity's sacred texts and rituals were suffused with royalist symbols, indicating that submission to kings was fundamental to Christian piety.[42] James's last published treatise, which he dedicated to Charles, turned away from the Old Testament analogies employed in his earlier Scottish tracts, focusing instead on Matthew's description of the mocking of Christ. James argued that the centurions unconsciously followed the exact procedures used to crown a Roman emperor and therefore unconsciously proclaimed his royal status with every gesture intended to humiliate him. The King went on to describe objects employed by the centurions as symbols for particular aspects of kingship: the sceptre of reed represents the responsibility to administer gentle chastisement to erring subjects, while the crown of plaited thorns stands for the interwoven 'stinging cares' that rulers must endure for the sake of their people.[43] Monarchy and Christianity depend on a shared symbolic system, reflecting their fundamental homology.

This Christocentric version of divine right developed alongside polemical attacks on puritans as people who worship their own pride under a guise of conscience, making them intrinsically factious and disobedient.[44] This abuse required correction by strong constraints on the will, through set forms of worship and hierarchical controls over wayward preaching. In Caroline sermons these attitudes expand into a claim that obedience to kings plays a key role in Christian salvation.[45] God 'establisheth scepters on earth as a ready means to help to reduce us to the perfection of our first rule, subduing our will to a man on earth that so he may the better subdue us to his own will in heaven', one royal chaplain argued.[46] Roger Maynwaring quoted Gregory the Great: 'no sooner are we rendered to the paths of our obedience, but we are set upon the borders of eternal life.'[47] This argument had a certain plausibility, since the Messiah was a royal figure, a king of the last days. Lancelot Andrewes once pointed out that of thirty-six scriptural uses of the term, *Christi dominus*, thirty referred to Jewish kings.[48] The conflation of Christian and royal symbolism found architectural expression in the Whitehall Banqueting

House, a modified basilica in which the royal throne – or occasionally a masque stage – occupied the position at the east end normally taken by the altar in Catholic and Laudian churches. Since basilicas had originated as secular law courts, Jones's design merely restored the form to its original purpose, in a way no doubt intended to suggest that Christian architecture derived historically from Roman courts and ultimately from buildings where ancient kings had sat in judgement.[49] The Rubens ceiling, depicting James I as a British Solomon, drove the point home. In the 1630s London's chief Christian basilica, St Paul's Cathedral, received a new 'royal' portico paid for by the Crown and topped by statues of Charles and his father during a restoration that some clergy compared to Solomon's re-edification of the Temple of Jerusalem.

Ultimately Caroline reforms sought not only to establish a pattern of royalist arguments and imagery but to reshape aesthetic sensibilities and physical comportment. People had to be made to kneel at the altar and behave decorously in church because 'the body is a part, and an essential part of the man'.[50] Slovenly worship will engender irreverence, toward God and other superiors. This attitude was related to the growing concern with 'civil' behaviour recently traced by Anna Bryson,[51] as a sermon by one of Charles's favourite chaplains illustrates with particular clarity. 'Good carriage is as well a point of religion as of civility and must be learned no less in the temple than in the court', he preached: 'Godliness is good manners.'[52] The concept of a 'reformation of manners' mattered as much to the Caroline church as it did to the godly, although it took different forms, involving ritualised expressions of reverence toward superiors and charity to neighbours, rather than strict observance of the Sabbath and the suppression of 'ungodly' sports.

If we turn from sermons to other discourses produced by the court – especially poetry and masques – we find a similar ideal associated less with concepts of obedience and authority than the second Lipsian virtue of love. This emphasis on love has been persistently noted by literary scholars and just as persistently ignored by most historians.[53] Partly this may reflect the bad press Charles's rule has long received but it also stems from the fact that in modern culture love has become a private emotion that seems essentially irrelevant to politics. We have already seen that this was not true in the seventeenth century and we therefore need to ask what the concept of a 'rule of love' meant to Charles's circle.

At the simplest level it meant that by the standards of the period, England remained a peaceful country where governance depended more on an ethos of service to the King than coercive force and draconian punishments. Royal love also had a dynastic significance, since it led to the engendering of royal offspring. This was one sphere in which Charles decisively outperformed his main European rivals, Louis XIII and Philip IV, who both had trouble siring heirs, a fact that helps explain the marked emphasis on the King's marriage and children in court poetry and painting. The only royal portrait by Van Dyck engraved by an artist connected to the court showed the King and Queen as a married pair, with an iconography celebrating their fertility.[54] At the same time a number of much cruder prints, produced for London stationers, indicates the existence of a market for images of the royal family extending well beyond sophisticated court circles.[55] Devotion to Charles's sister, Elizabeth of Bohemia, also shaped attitudes toward the great German war. So long as power was defined dynastically, the emotional and sexual relationships of royalty remained politically important.

At a deeper level, love served as the central metaphor for a concept of governance as a process of regulating passions and appetites. Love arises from basic physical sensations but produces more complex responses, ranging from selfless devotion to jealousy and anger. It lies at the core of the human family, as an erotic bond between husbands and wives and an asexual attachment between parents and children. If the family is the basic political form, as Aristotle had argued, love must therefore be humanity's most fundamental political instinct. For all these reasons love became an apt metaphor for the sentient desires and emotional forces activating social and political life, while virtuous love, represented above all by royal monogamy, stood for a well-ordered polity:

> The Stoic, who all easy passion flies,
> Could he but hear the language of their eyes,
> As heresies would from his faith remove
> The Tenets of his sect and practice love.
> The barbarous nations which supply the earth
> With a promiscuous and ignoble birth
> Would by this precedent correct their life
> Each wisely choose and chastely love a wife.
>   Princes example is law. Then we
> If loyal subjects must true lovers be.[56]

The point here is not simply that Charles sets a good example by confining his amorous attentions to his wife but that a properly governed society will regulate passion without suppressing it, by apportioning goods and teaching people to 'love' only what properly belongs to them. The proscenium arch to the last court masque, *Salmacida Spolia*, conveyed this idea through a figure representing 'deliberative appetite', who looked up to another personification of 'right reason'.

Because political life is driven by appetites rooted in sensation it must be regulated through forms the senses can apprehend. Decorum, ceremony and visible splendour are therefore essential to governance. This meant preventing the promiscuous building of cheap housing near the court, to preserve a more dignified environment. It meant driving the gentry away from London – to which they were attracted by an excessive appetite for urban consumer goods and court offices – back to the shires, where their hospitality and participation in local government assured prosperity and good order. For all subjects must remain within their proper spheres, limiting their appetites in ways determined by birth and occupation, unless the King specifically summoned them to a higher calling. Finally it was also crucial that the King and his entourage must set good examples, since the people will naturally imitate behaviour they *see* in their rulers.[57]

As Caroline Hibbard has shown, the King's belief in the personal and dynastic nature of political authority led him to arrange marriages between the great noble families of his realm.[58] He believed his dominions were held together by the paternalistic influence of major landed families over the localities, and the personal ties of loyalty and obligation that connected those families to himself. These values find expression in court culture through evocative descriptions of hospitality in country houses and other rituals associated with peaceful, hierarchically structured communities, including courtship rituals and peasant marriages. Court culture represented Charles's rule essentially as a system of affective bonds, cemented through social rituals and sensual activities like feasting and dancing, which extended from the court through provincial landed society down to simple villagers. This view is diametrically opposite to the modern concept of the State, as a system of *impersonal* laws and institutions.[59] It equates state authority with the King's person and the royal blood, and therefore places greater emphasis on duty, loyalty and affection than laws and institutional structures. Given the importance of kinship, friendship and patronage at all levels of early modern society this was not an altogether unreasonable view.[60] However exaggerated and idealised the vision of England projected by court literature may have been, it reflected attitudes and practices that had real political resonance in a world where public institutions had not yet become wholly separated from the domestic affairs of the court and other great households, the networks of friendship and alliance uniting the landed elite and a culture placing enormous emphasis on ideals of personal service and loyalty.[61]

By the mid-1630s efforts to restore the King's authority and recapture the love of his subjects appeared to be working. The British kingdoms had experienced several years of domestic peace, the Crown was closer to achieving solvency than for more than a generation and Ship Money had begun to restore British naval power. After failed negotiations with the Emperor over the restoration of the Palatinate, Charles even felt secure enough to contemplate some kind of military retaliation. Over the next several years these achievements dissolved, leaving him even more exposed than in 1629. As this happened the triangular relationship between force, authority and love continued to provide a framework within which his counsellors argued over the policies he should follow.

Even before the outbreak of conflict in Scotland, one royal servant felt uneasy about the solidity of the regime's achievements. Upon hearing of schemes to lend royal ships to a privately financed campaign to attack Spain's Atlantic commerce, under the command of the Elector Palatine, Thomas Wentworth grew seriously alarmed. Although wealthy and influential peers and London merchants had offered to lend support, Wentworth seriously doubted the depth of their affection for the King's German relatives. 'The men that were ever seen to wed that cause most were never observed to signal themselves very far by works of charity,' he warned; 'Lord deliver me from seeking an alms from the hands of a puritan.'[62] If charity is the fruit of love, he seems to have reasoned, puritan charity will never provide a secure basis for royal wars. Wentworth also feared that resistance to prerogative taxation might increase during a war: 'Believe me I was always so fearful of Ship Moneys as I could never advise any great action to have been raised from so uncertain a foundation. If there be not a straight hand held upon it and the refusers roundly proceeded against it will to the ground again.'[63] Love and respect for the King remained too fragile to risk foreign entanglements.

Wentworth's correspondence also betrays a growing alarm over attacks on the church hierarchy, by William Prynne and others, which he attributed less to religious scruples than a spirit of contempt. The problem 'grows from an universal distemper of this age', he warned the King, 'where the subject nestles itself too near the sovereignty, where we are more apt wantonly to dispute the powers which are over us than in former times.'[64] The disease had spread, he thought, through a 'universal easiness which is observed nowadays in all punishments and toward all sorts of delinquents ... the depraved disposition of men being such that the generality of us are to be governed by fear. They that endeavour by that nobler way of love many times fall into neglect.' Unlike some of his colleagues at Whitehall, the Lord Deputy never doubted that severity must take precedence over the gentler methods used to nurture affection. 'A prince that loseth the force and example of his punishments loseth withal the greatest part of his dominion', he flatly asserted.[65]

This attitude shaped his responses to the conflict in Scotland. He welcomed the new Scottish liturgy, sarcastically remarking to Laud that it promised to cure the Scots of their religion.[66] At the first sign of resistance he suspected English complicity, perhaps even from within the royal court, and feared the contagion would spread.[67] But he remained confident that a display of severity backed by force would prevail. 'Those bold Scots [are] easy enough to be brought to reason, if the right way be taken with them.'[68] He advocated placing strong garrisons in Berwick and Carlisle, 'which had it been early done, perchance the Covenanters ... would never have wound themselves up to that insolence they are now come unto'.⁶⁹ In retrospect, he commented, James I had made a mistake in dissolving those garrisons, instead of keeping them as 'seminaries for soldiers, whence they might have been drawn for the service of the public upon all occasions, a most necessary consideration for any king that looks to preserve for himself respect and fair quarter as well at home as abroad'.⁷⁰ But it was still not too late to repair the damage since, he believed, most Englishmen would remain loyal, displaying 'no other humour than a just indignation' toward the rebels.⁷¹ He suggested that the King lead his army in person, both to 'make the officers more careful' and to provide 'a noble recreation to himself.'⁷²

This emphasis on severity and force was consistent with Wentworth's personal interest in the arts of war. Almost alone among Charles's courtiers, he had himself painted by Van Dyck wearing armour and commanding an army. His friend, Viscount Conway, sent him a copy of the Duke of Rohan's *Le Parfait Capitaine*, 'wherein I find many observations of good note', Wentworth commented.⁷³ He scathingly dismissed the military abilities of the Earl of Arundel, whom Charles placed in command of his army in 1639, the Earl of Holland, who commanded the horse, and the Catholic Earl of Antrim, who returned to Ireland in 1639 to mobilise his Ulster clansmen to attack the territories of the Covenanter Earl of Argyll.⁷⁴ 'For let the great wits believe as they please, we of mean capacity comprehend not that men are born great captains and generals, nor yet like to become so on a day's warning', he sarcastically remarked.⁷⁵ He urged summoning experienced English soldiers from the Dutch wars to exercise the trained bands during the winter, before the campaigning season began.⁷⁶ After the English defeat by the Scots army in 1640, Wentworth alone among the English commanders wished to continue aggressive fighting. He not only believed in the use of force but felt confident that he knew how to command it more effectively than most of his colleagues.

By contrast, councillors who doubted the wisdom of war against Scotland tended to stress the importance of keeping the love of the King's people and the danger that military intervention might fail, with disastrous consequences. A speech attributed to the Duke of Lennox warned Charles that 'affections are like crystal glasses, which being once broken no art can solder and cement again' and that a king 'that commits once error in war, especially in his own kingdom, seldom lives to commit a second', as the examples of Richard II and Edward II showed.⁷⁷ Another sceptic was Algernon Percy, Earl of Northumberland. Like Wentworth, who was for a time a close ally, Northumberland was a man with a taste for military action and a vigorous administrator, who shared the Lord Deputy's impatience with the vacillations, inefficiency and petty corruption that hampered warlike preparations. But whereas the Lord Deputy directed his wrath at other Crown servants, Northumberland sometimes also blamed the King. When Charles failed to give sufficient backing to his proposed reforms of the navy he threatened to give up in disgust, grumbling that 'I am an ill solicitor of other men's business when they themselves will not countenance me in it.'[78] He happily accepted command of the navy but complained when it failed to see action that 'if the King hath not more use of this fleet than is yet known he may well save one half the charge and give me leave to stay at home'.[79] If Wentworth was chary of foreign wars but ready to use force within Britain, Northumberland's attitude was the reverse. At the outset of the conflict in Scotland he expressed three misgivings: the treasury was nearly empty; the kingdom lacked arms, ammunition and able commanders and – most crucially – 'the people [of England] ... are generally so discontented, by reason of the multitude of projects daily imposed upon them, as I think there is reason to fear that a great part of them will be readier to join with the Scots than to draw their swords in the King's service.'[80]

Northumberland also saw no reason to engage his own estate deeply to help Charles since, as he explained to Leicester, his 'house hath in these latter ages received little or no advantage from the Crown'.[81] Lipsius had argued that kings must nurture love by giving rewards. Northumberland stood the advice on its head: a king who failed to reward his great nobles should not expect extraordinary loyalty. By 1640 he had concluded that Charles's entanglement in Scotland made him incapable of paying his debts to his own servants, much less of earning devotion by raising subjects to great fortunes.[82] Although this did not lead him to abandon the King's service it did persuade him that the only way to rescue the kingdom, while advancing his own career and those of his allies, was to force Charles to govern in ways contrary to his own inclinations. In December of 1640 he was attempting to procure Leicester's appointment as Wentworth's successor in Ireland. He wrote to his brother-in-law that the King continued to regard him with 'coldness' but that he should not be discouraged, 'for within a few months I am confident that [the King] will be necessitated to change many of his present opinions, and I am persuaded [I] will be able to get [you] recommended to [Ireland] by Parliament, if by no other means.'[83] Charles once again appeared so weak that others – including members of his Council – thought they could blackmail him.

For many councillors the choice between policies of conciliation and force depended less on ideological conviction than pragmatic calculations of how best to restore stable governance. The Earl of Hamilton, whom Charles sent north to settle the Scots rebellion, wanted to suppress the Covenanters by force,[84] but he also insisted that the force must be sufficient to 'light upon them soundly and make them really smart'.[85] Half-measures that irritated the rebels without subduing them, he warned, would only provoke violent retaliation against the few open friends Charles had left in Scotland. As the crisis deepened, Hamilton worried that royal authority would collapse entirely, taking down with it the power and influence of noblemen like himself.⁸⁶ When Charles finally appeared to acknowledge defeat by conciliating the Covenanters in the summer of 1641, he quickly tried to salvage his own position by contracting a marriage alliance with the rebel leader Argyll, whom he pointedly began to address as 'brother'. This step reflected both self-interest and his belief in the urgent need to reunite the Scots nobility after the recent upheavals.

Henry Vane the elder provides an example of a councillor who evolved from a hardliner into a sceptic as he became increasingly alarmed at the effect the King's Scottish policy was having on English sentiment. Vane had always believed that Englishmen should unite among themselves to uphold their country's honour abroad. His diplomatic missions to the Netherlands in 1620–30 and to Gustavus Adolphus in 1631 had convinced him of the damage that broken parliaments and financial poverty inflicted on Britain's international reputation. He therefore warmly supported Ship Money and at the outset of the conflict in Scotland he helped organise the war effort. Like Wentworth, he urged Charles to lead his army in person, since 'his generals and officers loves his person so well that they will not be absent from him at their charges'.⁸⁷ But he was more eager than the Lord Deputy to end the war in a way that would heal divisions and more concerned that its prolongation might weaken English government. He welcomed the negotiated truce that ended the 1639 campaign and worried that Ship Money collections might collapse amidst the distractions of the northern campaign. In early 1640 he expressed the hope that the parliament scheduled for April would produce good results, 'notwithstanding what rumours soever are or may be spread abroad by ill-affected persons'.⁸⁸ He served as the King's chief spokesman in the Commons during the Short Parliament, contributing to its unhappy outcome by setting the financial demands too high. His position owed more to fiscal realism, however, than any aversion toward parliamentary courses.

Although for a time thereafter Vane remained cautiously optimistic that Charles would prevail against the Scots if it came to a battle,⁸⁹ he continually fretted about the lack of money and the alarming reports of sympathy for the Scots and disaffection toward the King within England. He also began nervously looking over his shoulder at the situation on the continent, where he feared the great Catholic powers were about to conclude a peace that would free them to exploit Britain's internal divisions.⁹⁰ By late summer Vane favoured a negotiated settlement and a new English parliament, 'to settle men's hearts and minds'.⁹¹ From this point his letters repeatedly express his desire to settle the quarrel with Scotland and regain public affection in England, 'so that king and people may go close together' and restore 'the honour of our nation … upon such principles as in the famous times of [Charles's] predecessors … made them glorious'.⁹² The King's journey to Scotland in the summer of 1641 and concessions to the Covenanters momentarily restored his optimism. 'His Majesty takes infinite pains ... and will certainly part fair with this people. Thus you see God's goodness to this island, to settle peace amongst us, which is past man's understanding.'[93] But the debates on the Grand Remonstrance and outbreak of the Irish rebellion then brought him close to despair. 'It is high time to give over talking of party, and that King and people should heartily unite. Three kingdoms in this condition, no money and little affection, should be well thought of, and the Catholic Romish princes abroad all drawing to a peace ... We cannot be happy if we change not our counsels.'[94]

'No money and little affection' sums up the fundamental problem that Charles and his Council never managed to solve. Broken parliaments were less the cause of that problem than its most painful outward symptom. They made visible to the world the lack of respect and affection the English felt for their kings and the resulting weakness of the Stuart state. For most of the 1630s the King and his Council believed they could solve the problem by punishing the kingdom's most vociferous malcontents, enlarging the navy with the proceeds of a non-parliamentary tax and gradually transforming the political climate. Charles and some of his ministers, like Laud and Wentworth, regarded religion as key. Associating disrespect for the King with puritanism, they believed that by breaking the back of non-conformity in both British kingdoms and promoting a religious ethic of obedience and civility they might gradually subdue the factious humours of the age. By resisting this project with force the Scots dramatically raised the stakes. The King had to back down and risk encouraging further defiance in England as well as Scotland, or else embark on a campaign of military compulsion, gambling that he was strong enough to prevail and that the English would remain loyal until he did. By failing on both counts Charles produced a major crisis in British governance.[95]

This outcome can be described, in Lipsian terms, as a collapse of virtue that opened the door to a rule of force. Much of the history of the years 1640–60 can be read as a series of failed attempts to escape this conundrum, initially through negotiations aimed at restoring a workable basis for cooperation between the contending parties and ultimately through the creation of an alternative system of puritan and republican virtues, to replace the old values of love and reverence for the King. It will be noticed, I hope, that describing the outbreak of civil war in terms of a dialectic of force and virtue also anticipates the neo-machiavellian political vocabulary that emerged in the 1650s. One of the implications of my analysis is that royalist and republican thought had more in common than historians have usually supposed. We have missed the similarities partly because we have taken partisan rhetoric at face value but also because, in our preoccupation with institutional structures, we have paid insufficient attention to the blend of moral and pragmatic discourses that characterises much early modern political thought. In important respects Justus Lipsius, Charles I, Thomas Wentworth and John Milton belonged to the same intellectual universe. They believed that good government depends not only on effective institutions but ethical dispositions that promote unity and service to the common good. They associated virtue with military strength, while assuming that its absence meant weakness, division and vulnerability to foreign conquest. They differed primarily in how they defined political virtue, especially on the fundamental issue of whether *personal* devotion to a crowned head of state was essential or inimical to the public good. England's troubles continued for as long as they did because neither side succeeded in winning this argument. In the absence of consensus about the moral foundations of governance, armed coercion remained the ultimate source of authority, as Lipsius had foreseen.

NOTES

1 The *Oxford English Dictionary* finds no earlier example of absolutism as a political term than 1830; it had been used as a theological label (for Calvinism) as early as 1753 and in French polemics of the 1790s. In English the word absolutist also dates from 1830. For discussions see Nicholas Henshall, 'The myth of absolutism', *History Today*, 42 (1992), 42–7 and John Miller (ed.), *Absolutism in Seventeenth Century Europe* (London: Macmillan, 1990), esp. J. H. Burns, 'The idea of absolutism', p. 22. Contemporaries did have a concept of absolute monarchy but this had subtly different connotations from the later historical usage, for which, in addition to the above, see J. Daly, 'The idea of absolute monarchy in seventeenth-century England', *Historical Journal*, 12 (1978).

2 Jonathan Scott, *England's Troubles: Seventeenth-Century English Political Instability in European Context* (Cambridge: Cambridge University Press, 2000).

3 See, e.g., J. G. A. Pocock, *The Ancient Constitution and the Feudal Law: A Reissue with a Retrospect* (Cambridge: Cambridge University Press, 1957, reissue 1987); John Morrill, 'The Church of England 1642–1649', in John Morrill, *The Nature of the English Revolution* (London: Longman, 1993), pp. 148–76; R. Malcolm Smuts, *Court Culture and the Origins of a Royalist Tradition in Early Stuart England* (Philadelphia: University of Philadelphia Press, 1987); Lois Potter, *Secret Rites and Secret Writing: Royalist Literature, 1641–1660* (Cambridge: Cambridge University Press, 1989).

4 Justus Lipsius, *Six Bookes of Politickes or Civil Doctrine* (London, 1591).

5 *Ibid.*, p. 72.

6 *Ibid.*, p. 73.

7 *Ibid.*, pp. 74–5.

8 *Ibid.*, pp. 75, 79.

9 See, esp., J. F. Dubost, 'Between *mignons* and principal ministers: Concini, 1610–1617', in J. H. Elliott and L. W. B. Brockliss (eds), *The World of the Favourite* (New Haven and London: Yale University Press, 1999), pp. 71–8.

10 *Calendar of State Papers Venetian*, xix, p. 528.

11 Glenn Burgess, *Absolute Monarchy and the Stuart Constitution* (New Haven and London: Yale University Press, 1996), p. 2 and *passim*.
12 Sheffield Library, Wentworth Woodhouse Muniments (hereafter Wentworth Papers) StrP12/271.
13 Wentworth Papers StrP10(a)/9–10.
14 Wentworth Papers StrP3/21.
15 *Ibid.*, 74.
16 Nicholas Canny, *Making Ireland British* (Oxford: Oxford University Press, 2000).
17 Wentworth Papers StrP8/131.
18 Henry Savile, *The End of Nero and Beginning of Galba* (1592), p. 251.
19 e.g. Edmund Bolton, *Nero Caesar* (London, 1624), pp. 93–4.
20 Wentworth Papers StrP8/11.
21 *Ibid.*, 95.
22 William Knowler (ed.), *The Earl of Strafforde's Letters and Dispatches* (2 vols, London, 1739), ii, p. 198.
23 Folger Shakespeare Library, MS Vb 142, fol. 38.
24 See esp. Robert Devereux, Earl of Essex, *An Apologie of the Earle of Essex* (London, 1603), sigs C2–3.
25 PRO, SP 14/81/115. Lake was a privy councillor, soon to be made Secretary.
26 PRO, SP 94/21, dispatch of 7 September 1615.
27 Maija Jansson and William Bidwell (eds), *Proceedings in Parliament 1625* (New Haven and London: Yale University Press, 1987), p. 135.
28 PRO, SP 84/142–4.
29 Thomas Birch (ed.), *The Court and Times of Charles I* (2 vols, London, 1848), i, p. 226.
30 PRO, SP 84/139/99.
31 *Calendar of State Papers Venetian*, xxii, p. 289.
32 PRO, PRO 31/3/63.
33 PRO, SP 84/141/98–9.
34 PRO, SP 84/139/77.
35 PRO, SP 84/141/99 and 172; Wentworth Papers Str9/330.
36 See Thea Lindquist, 'The Politics of Diplomacy: The Palatinate and Anglo-Imperial Relations in the Thirty Years' War' (unpublished University of Wisconsin PhD thesis, 2001).
37 Kevin Sharpe, *The Personal Rule of Charles I* (New Haven and London: Yale University Press, 1992), ch. 7.
38 Julian Davies, *The Caroline Captivity of the Church* (Cambridge: Cambridge University Press, 1992).
39 Arthur Williamson, 'Patterns of British identity: Britain and its rivals in the sixteenth and seventeenth centuries', in Glenn Burgess (ed.), *The New British History: Founding a Modern State 1603–1715* (London: I. B. Tauris, 1995), pp. 138–74, esp. pp. 143–52.

40 Peter McCullough, *Sermons at Court: Politics and Religion in Elizabethan and Jacobean Preaching* (Cambridge: Cambridge University Press, 1998).

41 Howard Hotson, *Johann Heinrich Alsted 1588–1638* (Oxford: Oxford University Press, 2000), ch. 5.

42 An especially clear early example is Thomas Bilson, *A Sermon Preached at Westminster before the King and Queenes Maiesties, at their Coronations* (London, 1603), sigs Aiv–v. Cf. William Barlow, *A Sermon at Paul's Cross* (London, 1601).

43 J. P. Sommerville (ed.), *Political Works of James VI and I* (Cambridge: Cambridge University Press, 1994).

44 e.g. James I, *A Meditation upon the Lord's Prayer* (London, 1619), pp. 18–19: 'Trusting to the private spirit of Reformation, according to our Puritans' doctrine, it is easy to fall and slide by degrees into chaos.'

45 Isaac Bargrave, *A Sermon Preached before King Charles* (London, 1627), pp. 6–7.

46 *Ibid.*, p. 2.

47 *Religion and Alegiance* (London, 1627), part ii, p. 12.

48 Lancelot Andrewes, *Ninety-Six Sermons* (Oxford, 1851), p. 49.

49 The term basilica is a form of the Greek adjective meaning 'royal'.

50 Foulke Robarts, *God's Holy House and Service* (London, 1639), sig. 3r.

51 Anna Bryson, *From Courtesy to Civility: Changing Codes of Conduct in Early Modern England* (Oxford: Oxford University Press, 1998).

52 Richard Stuart, *Three Sermons* (London, 1657), pp. 1–2.

53 The main exceptions have been historians studying court culture, e.g. Kevin Sharpe, *The Literature of Compliment: The Politics of Literature in the England of Charles I* (Cambridge: Cambridge University Press, 1987); Smuts, *Court Culture*, ch. 9. For discussions by literary scholars see, e.g., D. J. Gordon, '*Hymenaei*, Ben Jonson's masque of union', in Stephen Orgel (ed.), *The Renaissance Imagination: Essays and Lectures by D. J. Gordon* (Berkeley: University of California Press, 1975), pp. 157–84; Earl Miner, *The Cavalier Mode from Jonson to Cotton* (Princeton: Princeton University Press, 1971), ch. 5; Stephen Orgel, 'Platonic politics' in O&S, i, pp. 49–75, and Arthur Marotti, *Manuscript, Print and the English Lyric* (Ithaca: Cornell University Press, 1995).

54 See Margery Corbett and Michael Norton, *Engraving in England in the Sixteenth and Seventeenth Centuries: A Descriptive Catalogue. Part III. The Reign of Charles I* (Cambridge: Cambridge University Press, 1964), p. 203 and plate 99.

55 *Ibid.*, plates 54–6, 112–13, 179 and 184.

56 William Habbington, 'To Castara Upon the Mutual Love of their Majesties', *Poems*, ed. K. Allot (Liverpool: University of Liverpool Press, 1948), p. 57.

57 Kevin Sharpe, 'The image of virtue: the court and household of Charles I, 1625–1642', in David Starkey *et al.* (eds), *The English Court from the Wars of the Roses until the Civil War* (London: Longman, 1987), pp. 226–60.

58 Caroline Hibbard, 'The theatre of dynasty', in R. Malcolm Smuts (ed.), *The Stuart Court and Europe: Essays in Politics and Political Culture* (Cambridge: Cambridge University Press, 1996), pp. 156–77.

59 The degree to which this modern concept continued to shape historical scholarship is

illustrated by Michael Braddick's fine study, *State Formation in Early Modern England c. 1550–1700* (Cambridge: Cambridge University Press, 2000).

60 On this see Catherine Patterson, *Urban Patronage in Early Modern England: Corporate Boroughs, the Landed Elite and the Crown, 1580–1640* (Stanford: Stanford University Press, 1999).

61 For a European study stressing the degree to which bureaucratic institutions of governance remained embedded in the domestic sphere of royal courts, see Jeroen Dunindam, *Vienna and Versailles: The Courts of Europe's Dynastic Rivals, 1550–1780* (Cambridge: Cambridge University Press, 2003).

62 Knowler (ed.), *Strafforde's Letters*, ii, p. 54.

63 Wentworth Papers StrP7/54.

64 Knowler (ed.), *Strafforde's Letters*, ii, p. 161.

65 *Ibid.*, p. 119.

66 Wentworth Papers StrP7/56.

67 *Ibid.*, 66.

68 Wentworth Papers StrP10a/193.

69 Wentworth Papers StrP10b/55v.

70 Wentworth Papers StrP7/132.

71 Wentworth Papers StrP10a/184.

72 Wentworth Papers StrP10b/57v.

73 Wentworth Papers StrP9/426.

74 e.g. NAS, GD 406/1/1162.

75 Wentworth Papers StrP10b/33.

76 *Ibid.*, 10.

77 BL, Additional MS 72432, fol. 85 (notes of Lennox's speech before the King concerning war with Scotland in the papers of Rudolph Weckherlin). For the probably spurious character of this speech see Peter Donald, *An Uncounselled King: Charles I and the Scottish Troubles, 1637–1641* (Cambridge: Cambridge University Press, 1990), p. 89, n. 47.

78 Wentworth Papers StrP9/421.

79 Wentworth Papers StrP10a/18.

80 Knowler (ed.), *Strafforde's Letters*, ii, p. 186.

81 Alnwick Castle (Northumberland) MS 15/1v.

82 Alnwick Castle MS 15/28v, 29.

83 Alnwick Castle MS 15/141v. The words in brackets are in cipher in the original.

84 NAS, GD 406/1/566.

85 *Ibid.*

86 e.g. NAS, GD 406/1/552 and 553.

87 NAS, GD 406/1/1207.

88 *Calendar of State Papers Domestic, 1639–40*, p. 477.
89 *Ibid.*, pp. 586–7.
90 *Calendar of State Papers Domestic, 1640–41*, p. 80.
91 *Ibid.*, p. 47.
92 G. F. Warner (ed.), *The Nicholas Papers. Vol. I. 1641–1652* (Camden Society, 2nd series, 40, 1886), p. 9.
93 *Ibid.*, p. 25.
94 *Ibid.*, p. 149.
95 This is not to imply that the gamble was doomed to fail; with better luck or better generalship it might well have established the King's authority more firmly. I wish to thank David Scott for a discussion of this point.

Chapter 3

The image of Charles I as a Roman emperor

John Peacock

The portraits of King Charles I painted by Van Dyck in the 1630s cover a range of types and settings. Several show the King in armour and, of these, three have imperial Roman associations, which, however, are not always obvious at first sight. Jeremy Wood has shown that the half-length of Charles in armour holding a baton (Phoenix Art Museum, Arizona) is based on a portrait of the Emperor Otho, one of Titian's *Twelve Caesars* which were in the royal collection;[1] and in the image of *Charles I on horseback* (National Gallery) the implicit presence of the antique equestrian statue of Marcus Aurelius has been discussed by Roy Strong.[2] By contrast, in *Charles I and M. de St Antoine* (Royal Collection) the imperial allusion is obvious, as the King rides through a recreation of a Roman triumphal arch, against which leans a shield with the arms of the modern 'empire' of Great Britain surmounted by an imperial crown (figure 1).[3] The evocation of a Roman emperor is appropriate to the picture's original environment in St James's Palace: this large canvas was hung at one end of the Gallery, while along the walls were displayed Titian's portraits, with Giulio Romano's smaller equestrian images, of the *Twelve Caesars*. Van Dyck's imposing picture closed off the vista and formed a climax to this imperial succession.

It is worth asking whether Van Dyck's major 'imperial' image of the King, designed to complement and complete the work of two acknowledged masters of the High Renaissance (for one of whom, Titian, he had a consuming fascination), makes more than a generalised reference to the notion of an antique Roman ruler. Titian's *Caesars* were all vigorously characterised,[4] some of them showing the marks of historical turmoil or the traits of autocratic wilfulness to an unsympathetic degree. It seems clear that when Van Dyck modelled his half-length of the armoured Charles on the *Otho* he was not alluding to that Emperor's infamous personality but invoking a generalised Caesarean image enhanced by the glamour of Titian's pictorial style. Here, in

The image of Charles I as a Roman emperor

1 Anthony Van Dyck, *Charles I and M. de St Antoine*.

the St James's picture which confronted an entire *galère* of Caesars good and bad, he makes King Charles outface them all with a kind of lofty composure, as if to decline or transcend characterisation, and follow the customary course of representing the ruler as an idealised figure, who projects a persona rather than a personality.

To consider the picture carefully, however, is to see that the withholding of expressiveness, which endows its protagonist with a preternatural eminence, is not just the usual device of the court artist but a quality ascribed to the sitter. To seek for moments of externalised narrative in Van Dyck's Caroline portraits is usually misleading: they make their impact in visual rather than dramatic terms. A lead in this case is given by the motif of the triumphal arch, shown not as a discrete structure which a viewer might virtually 'see round' (and therefore an item in a narrative) but as an enveloping visual field, rendering the notion of triumph indefinite, and perhaps generalised, not confined to a specific point in time. The casually draped curtains, which muffle parts of the architecture, assist this diffusion of the narrative into the visual; and their theatrical air recalls the court masques of the 1630s, which their producer and designer Inigo Jones insisted were the opposite of dramatic narratives, 'nothing else but pictures with light and motion.'[5] Van Dyck's emphasis on visuality is concentrated in the looks of the two figures in the composition, that is, in the way that their individual gazes see and are seen.[6] The subordinate figure of M. de St Antoine, Charles's riding master, looks up at the King with an expression of poignant respect, which plays across his features so as to indicate not just routine deference but a more charged state of mind; the King, paying him no attention, looks straight ahead with an indeterminate focus, as if regarding the viewer of the picture, while looking far beyond the viewer at the same time. The look of the subordinate points up that of the ruler: its restricted scope and overt emotion act as a foil for the far-reaching abstraction of the imperial gaze, while at the same time helping to unfold its meaning.

Both gazes are 'spread' alongside each other, distributed through adjacent vertical zones of the picture space. St Antoine's upraised gaze is compactly mimicked by the helmet which he holds in front of him, tilted towards the King with a kind of uncanny attentiveness, and is simultaneously extended behind him by the diagonally twisting curtain with its folds and highlights, suggesting the substance of his dutiful thoughts reaching towards the King's face with ectoplasmic animation. The same pattern recurs with the principal figure: the King's grave, ample regard is mimicked by his horse and condensed into the exquisitely narrow form of the animal's head; at the same time it fans out behind him into the variegated skyscape. The sequence by which each figure's gaze is condensed into a motif nearer the spectator (helmet, horse's head) and expatiated into a field farther off (curtain, sky) is the same in both cases, so that each gaze offers to be read not just at face value but in a larger context of visual phenomena. But whereas with St Antoine this sequence follows a restricted linear path, across a shallow space defined by the arch at his back, in the King's case it broadens out into the expanses of the sky. Both tripartite sequences combine in a larger relationship, parallel but asym-

The image of Charles I as a Roman emperor

2 Inigo Jones, Oberon in *Oberon, the Fairy Prince*, 1611.

3 Antonio Tempesta, Caius Caesar (Caligula) from *The Twelve Caesars*, 1596.

metrical, like a main plot and a sub-plot (or by-plot) in a play of visuality.[7] Within this signifying structure the King's countenance, seemingly impassive at first glance, reveals itself as first tinged and then charged with meaning. The complexion of the skyscape, which elaborates his gaze in abstract

The image of Charles I as a Roman emperor

paraphrase, becomes an index of depths and nuances within the mind, and the play of cloud and sunlight brings to attention a kind of facial weather which hints at the atmospherics of a various interior life.

In accord with the conventions of early modern ruler portraiture and the favoured Stuart doctrine of divine right, Van Dyck represents the King transcending the vagaries of merely human nature. At the same time, to show the peaceful Charles, who had no victories in war to celebrate, as an imperial *triumphator* is to suggest that this transcendence has been won not by military but by moral conquest. The painter's achievement is to reinvent the familiar neo-antique role in these terms, to psychologise the imperial persona without demoting it to the level of common humanity, by using an art both 'representational' and 'abstract', complementing the composure of the monarch's countenance with the soulful expressiveness of the pictorial field.

While Van Dyck's portrayal of Charles as an unusual kind of neo-Roman emperor, a hero of the inner life rather than a stern warlord, resorts to a certain level of abstraction, its suggestions are spelt out in more concrete detail by the King's masques of the 1630s. Their titles alone dwell repeatedly on the theme here taken up by the painter: *Love's Triumph through Callipolis, Albion's Triumph, Britannia Triumphans*; so that when the Inns of Court presented a masque at Whitehall in 1634 they not only fell into line but ingeniously summed up the trend by calling their production *The Triumph of Peace*. In his own masques the King would either lead a group of 'perfect lovers' or 'ancient heroes' or else have a named part – Albanactus or Britanocles – as a reincarnation of an antique emperor. These idealised identities tended to recapitulate and develop roles devised in the previous reign for his elder brother Prince Henry, in the brief phase of court entertainments between the Prince's coming of age and his sudden death. Although those festivals had medievalising, chivalric scenarios, they incorporated Roman imperial imagery into their overall design, and worked out a method of making it significant which was to be employed in the Caroline masques. Henry's two principal festivals were written by Ben Jonson and designed by Inigo Jones, who together devised a way of combining medieval and classical elements which owed something to the Italian romantic epic and its recent English offspring, *The Faerie Queene*; the second production, *Oberon, the Fairy Prince* (1611), is in part an *hommage* to Spenser. In this masque Jones designed a costume for Henry as Oberon (figure 2) based on the *Twelve Caesars* of Antonio Tempesta, a suite of engravings which reimagines the emperors in neo-chivalric terms, in the style of the equestrian pageants staged in Medicean Florence.[8] The design is eclectically derived from the images of Augustus, Caligula (figure 3) and Domitian, and is evidently meant to project an equally eclectic notion of antique chivalry, rather than to allude to those historical figures. In the previous production however, *Prince Henry's Barriers* (1610), Jones had enhanced the

55

John Peacock

4 Inigo Jones, St George's Portico in *Prince Henry's Barriers*, 1610.

Prince's role with more specific allusions to imperial Rome. The text represents Henry as the Christian knight Meliadus (originally a figure from Arthurian romance) whose mission is to restore the decayed House of Chivalry. This appears in the first scene as a prospect of Roman ruins; in the second scene they have regained much of their pristine integrity, and a new edifice has risen in their midst, St George's Portico (figure 4).[9] It is in this new site of chivalry, associated with Meliadus/Henry, that Jones evokes antique imperial exemplars for the idealised Prince.

In the restored Roman cityscape which forms the scene of a revived chivalry, the principal buildings are associated with the Emperor Trajan. The perspective vista shows a reconstruction of the Forum of Trajan, with his celebrated Column, surmounted by the Emperor's statue; adjacent is the Torre delle Milizie, believed to have been the barracks of Trajan's soldiers.[10] These architectural allusions link Prince Henry to the most virtuous and powerful of all Roman rulers; and the link is pointed up in the text, where Henry is addressed by the title voted to the emperor by the Senate, 'worthiest

The image of Charles I as a Roman emperor

5 Inigo Jones, Albanactus in *Albion's Triumph*, 1632.

John Peacock

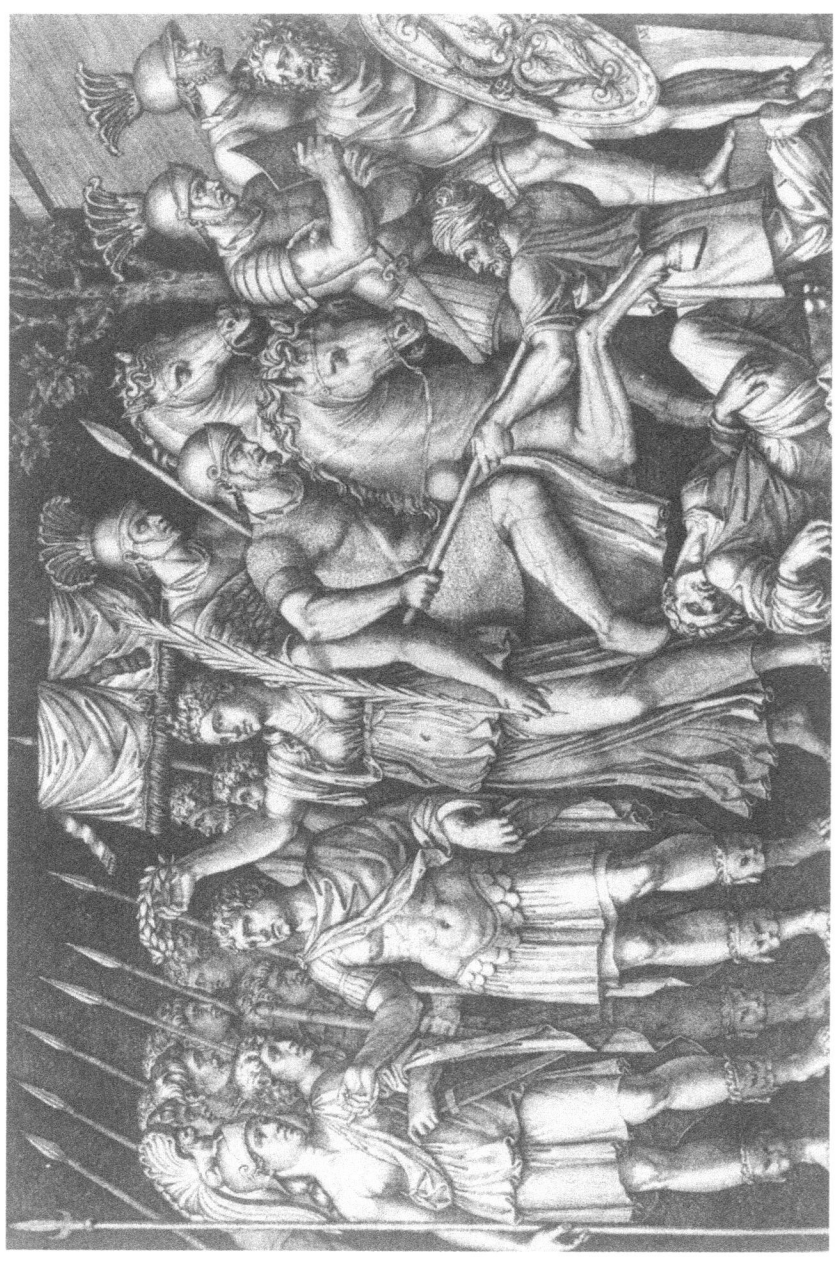

6 Marcantonio Raimondi, *Trajan crowned by Victory* from the Arch of Constantine.

prince' (*optimus princeps*).[11] Trajan's worthiness was augmented by the tradition dating from late antiquity that he could be regarded as an honorary Christian: Pope Gregory the Great was believed to have prayed for his soul and secured his admission to Heaven.[12] The figure of a Christianised Trajan fits neatly with the other emperor who is evoked by this scene. The new building which now appears at its centre, St George's Portico, is a hybrid structure which at first seems pure fantasy. But certain striking features, along with its blend of classical and gothic styles, recall St John Lateran, the first Christian basilica in Rome, founded by Constantine. As apologists for the English Reformation pointed out, Constantine, the first Christian Emperor, was born in Britain:[13] St George's Portico links imperial Roman *virtus* with pristine British Christianity. The historical symbolism of Jones's scenic architecture endows Henry with a composite imperial identity: he is both Trajan and Constantine, *optimus princeps* and godly British emperor.

The same composite role was revived for King Charles a generation later in the masque *Albion's Triumph* (1632), where he appears as the Romano-British Emperor Albanactus. Inigo Jones's design for his costume (figure 5) is derived from an antique Roman bas-relief (figure 6) which shows Trajan being crowned by Victory:[14] although originally designed for a Trajanic monument this was later set into the Arch of Constantine, where it appears with the new dedication '*Fundatori Quietis*' (to the establisher of peace); and the same words were to figure on one of the arches erected for Charles's coronation entry into Edinburgh the following year.[15] The panel on which Jones modelled the King's image was part of a whole collection of relief sculptures from earlier imperial monuments which Constantine incorporated into his triumphal arch. They record the deeds of three of the most virtuous rulers of the empire – Trajan, Hadrian and Marcus Aurelius – and by appropriating and reusing this imagery Constantine identified himself with his most eminent predecessors. Jones in turn identifies King Charles, as Albanactus Caesar, with the prestigious duo of Trajan and Constantine,[16] the imperial paragons of princely virtue and true religion.

Jones had done the same for Prince Henry a generation before. But this time there is a new constituent in the composite image of imperial majesty. It can be seen at the climax of the production, when the masquers make their appearance. The printed text gives this description: 'The Scene is changed into a pleasant Grove of straight Trees, which rising by degrees to a high place, openeth it selfe to discover the aspect of a stately Temple; all which, was sacred to JOVE. In this grove satt the Emperour ALBANACTUS, attended by fourteene Consuls ...'.[17] Only a rough sketch survives of Jones's design for this scene (figure 7),[18] but this shows the unusual architecture of the 'stately Temple' clearly enough to suggest its provenance. The portico of two storeys, the second consisting of small roundheaded arches between the entablature

7 Inigo Jones, Sketch for 'a stately temple' in *Albion's Triumph*, 1632.

The image of Charles I as a Roman emperor

8 Jacques Androuet du Cerceau, *Basilica of Alexander Severus*, 1584.

above the columns and the pediment, is not found in any recorded antique building (although the same arches occur as an undisplayed structural feature within the portico of the Pantheon). It is taken from an etching in the *Livre des édifices antiques Romains* by Jacques Androuet du Cerceau, which includes reconstructions of lost buildings. Du Cerceau's print shows the Basilica of Alexander Severus (figure 8),[19] an ambitious project which was never completed, and of which no trace remained; but the Emperor's fame procured it a kind of virtual existence. Early modern writers who narrated his life and praised his benign rule improved on their antique sources, declaring that this building 'full of beauty and magnificence' had been finished, and inventing details of its appearance.[20] Pirro Ligorio's topographical plan of ancient Rome (1561) included a reconstruction of it, elaborated from the minimal description which survived. His authority as an antiquarian ensured that this plan was reprinted and imitated; and certain items were excerpted, scaled up and reworked for Du Cerceau's series of '*édifices antiques Romains*', including the 'Basilica Alexandri Severi'.[21] As it has a façade very like a temple front, it can easily be paraphrased into 'the aspect of a stately Temple'. In this way a work of potent architectural fantasy, attributed to a paragon of imperial rule, becomes associated with King Charles in Jones's masque.

The surrounding 'grove' in which the masquers are discovered has a similar provenance. The greatest public work that Alexander Severus did carry through was his baths, described by Jones as 'the most Cellebrated' in Rome,[22] which were probably connected with the Basilica; and adjacent to them he

61

planted a grove of trees.²³ In Leon Battista Alberti's seminal treatise *De architectura*, owned and studied by Jones, Alexander's grove is cited as an example of how to enhance the effect of public buildings, and is paralleled to the grove next to the Academy in Athens, 'consecrated to the Gods'.²⁴ Again, such associations prompt Jones's design for the 'pleasant Grove ... sacred to JOVE' which forms a ceremonial setting for the Romano-British 'Emperour ALBANACTUS'.

An immediate link between the two emperors is geographical: according to a tradition current in the seventeenth century, Alexander had spent time in Britain and was buried at York.²⁵ But the implicit comparison being made here relies more substantively on his personal and political character.

Already in late antiquity Alexander Severus was being represented as an exemplary ruler, akin to the succession of 'good' emperors between Nerva and Marcus Aurelius. His reputation was handed down to the early modern period by the *Historia Augusta*, in a biography attributed to Aelius Lampridius. This was addressed to Constantine, and included numerous recollections of Trajan, points of reference which indicate its approving tone.²⁶ It was supplemented by the *History* of Herodian, which is by contrast partly critical;²⁷ but the eulogistic treatment by Lampridius prevailed. His account was rewritten in the sixteenth century by Antonio de Guevara for his *Década de Césares* (a sequence of lives from Trajan to Alexander), with supplementary material from other antique sources and additions of his own.²⁸ As a councillor of Charles V, Guevara offered his Caesars as *exempla* to be followed or in some cases avoided by a modern Roman emperor, so that he strives even more than Lampridius to show Alexander as an ideal ruler. The English courtier and diplomat Sir Thomas Elyot went even further, devoting an entire volume to 'the actes and sentences notable, of the most noble emperour Alexander Severus', entitled *The Image of Governaunce*, that is, the pattern of righteous and effective monarchy; he had Henry VIII in his sights. As Elyot's book was variously reprinted, and Guevara's was translated into other European languages,²⁹ the idealised figure of Alexander as an exemplary ruler became well established in early modern culture. When the French writer Marin Le Roy, Sieur de Gomberville chose to celebrate the government of the young Louis XIII he published a detailed comparison between him and Alexander Severus, with the Emperor's reign foreshadowing the King's.³⁰ This was in 1622, only ten years before a similar parallel was implicitly made in *Albion's Triumph* to glorify Charles I, who was by then Louis' brother-in-law.

This parallel can be discerned not only in the pivotal scene where Albanactus and his 'consuls' are revealed but in other parts of the masque. According to Guevara, Alexander built a sumptuous addition to the imperial palace, centring on a colonnaded courtyard where the most noted antique statues in Rome were gathered and displayed.³¹ This is matched in the opening scene of

The image of Charles I as a Roman emperor

9 Inigo Jones, A Roman atrium in *Albion's Triumph*, 1632.

Albion's Triumph, 'which represented a *Romane Atrium*, with high collombs of white Marble ... and betweene every retorne of these Collombs, stood Statues of gold on round pedestalls, and beyond these, were other peeces of Architecture of a Pallace royal'.[32] Jones's design for the scene (figure 9) shows that the traditional plan of a Roman atrium has been paraphrased on an imperial scale, to form the setting for an ideal collection of antique statues including, for example, the Farnese Hercules.[33] This evocation of Alexander's palace is appropriate to his modern reincarnation, the Emperor Albanactus, as Charles had recently completed his purchase of the Duke of Mantua's art collection, which included a wealth of classical sculpture.

His patronage of art and architecture was the first of several respects in which Charles could be likened to Alexander Severus. The Emperor had been a lover of painting, and a talented painter himself; so early modern writers concerned to raise the status of the visual arts repeatedly invoked his name.[34] As well as collecting sculpture to adorn his palace, he comissioned new work from sculptors; and he not only employed architects on his building programmes but awarded them salaries to be paid by the state.[35] In the end, while his cultural interests matched those of Charles I, the scope of his cultural patronage went far beyond what the King would be able to achieve; and part of the impact of *Albion's Triumph*, with its grandiose scenes recalling Alexander's Rome, is to express aspirations on a scale which could never be realised in practice, to create the fantasy of an ideal imperial culture.

The Emperor could also be compared to the King because of his impeccable moral character. When he succeeded his notorious cousin Heliogabalus, his first move was to purify the morals of the court. The spirit of these reforms is caught precisely in Lucy Hutchinson's famous characterisation of Charles I, which represents him in classical vein as a high-minded pagan ruler, like those whom she called the 'best emperors': 'The face of the court was much changed in the change of the king, for King Charles was temperate, and chaste, and serious; so that the fools and bawds, mimics and catamites of the former court, grew out of fashion ... Men of learning and ingenuity in all arts were in esteem, and received encouragement from the king, who was a most excellent judge and a great lover of paintings, carvings, gravings, and many other ingenuities ...'.[36] By associating strict morality with a love of the arts this recalls Alexander's character as described in the *Historia Augusta*; and it alludes to one specific passage, detailing how he expelled eunuchs, courtesans, and catamites from his court.[37] Like Charles, he regulated his household with the strictest propriety, as he did his own life: for the French translator of Guevara 'he was above all modest and chaste, and never known to break his marriage vows'.[38]

Alexander resembled the King further in his attitude to religion. Being *pontifex maximus*, he took his duties as head of the state religion very seriously, and, after the heretical deviations of Heliogabalus, initiated a programme of reform, restoring the images of the gods to their shrines and returning to traditional patterns of worship.[39] He made his observances every seven days in the temple of Jupiter Capitolinus[40] (which, the spectators were presumably meant to understand, is the 'stately Temple ... sacred to JOVE' on 'a high place' revealed in *Albion's Triumph*). He extended tolerance to Judaism, and to Christianity, which he respected as a religious faith in its own right, and even worshipped Christ among his household gods and tried to make this worship public: 'Unto CHRIST he would have made a temple in *Rome*, and placed him in the number of their Gods ... but the priestes of the temples dissuaded him, saying: that they had received aunswer of the oracle that if he should perfourme that acte, all other temples should perishe, and all persons would convert themselves and become *Christians*.'[41] As a Christian emperor *avant la lettre*, with his moral discipline enhanced by personal piety, respect for ritual, and deep sense of public religious duty, Alexander emerges as an even closer match for Albanactus.

The image of Charles I as a Roman emperor

The parallel is made complete by Alexander's style of government. He exercised power in consultation with small groups of advisers, or sometimes delegated it to such groups, especially in religious affairs. The average size of these groups is reflected in *Albion's Triumph*, when Albanactus appears 'attended by fourteene Consuls'. Alexander had appointed fourteen former consuls to hear legal cases within the city of Rome; and in his religious capacity he formed one of the *quindecimviri*, the fifteen keepers of the Sibylline Books.[42] He became accustomed to conciliar administration when he succeeded to the empire as a minor, and was appointed a group of tutelary advisers by his grandmother and mother, Moesa and Mamaea. In the words of Herodian, published in English translation in 1629, 'they selected out of the Senate 16 ancient, grave, and honorable Peeres, for Assistants and Counsellors to the Prince: without whose Suffrage and Consent, nothing was to passe as an Act of State. Which manner of Government was wondrous pleasing to the People, Souldiers, and Senators ...'.[43] With the addition of supreme executive power, which Alexander assumed when he came of age, exercising it with firmness and benevolence, this anticipates the image of personal rule displayed at the centre of *Albion's Triumph*, when Charles appears attended by his 'Consuls'. The Latin term had been glossed 'as it were counsailours' in Elyot's *Image of Governaunce*, which refers to Alexander's 'privy council' as if to present him as an obvious precursor of early modern personal monarchy.[44]

The comparison between Charles I and Alexander Severus, propounded visually in Inigo Jones's scene designs for *Albion's Triumph*, also informs the text by Aurelian Townshend. The central theme of the masque is that the triumph of Albanactus is a moral triumph: he does not engage in destructive military conquest, but is victorious over his own passions. His rule is not belligerent but peaceful; and in the concluding scene the figure of Peace appears in the heavens, 'alone triumphant'.[45] The same theme of a triumphal association between self-mastery and peaceful rule of his empire is seen in the life of Alexander. Lampridius in the *Historia Augusta* gives a lengthy account of the Senate trying to force Alexander to accept honorific titles such as 'the Great' (*Magnus*), which he steadfastly declined as disproportionate; this aroused such admiration that 'the Emperor returned home in the manner of one celebrating a triumph'.[46] And Guevara notes that he 'naturally ... was inclined unto peace': for many years under his regime of discipline and self-discipline 'the Empire enjoyed most perfect peace and tranquillitie ...'.[47]

When war was eventually threatened by Artaxerxes King of Persia he tried to avoid it by diplomacy. Guevara attributes to him a letter addressed to Artaxerxes, arguing that peace is not only a desirable but a rational alternative:

> we salute thee with peace, for that wee bee lovers thereof: and ... unto Princes that ... have not peace, it were lesse evil to be dead. It may chaunce, that the warre which a man hath against his own proper sensualitie sufficeth, but that he must invent

warre against some straunge countrie. A man that may not subdue his heart, which within his own body is imprisoned, thinketh he to conquere the whole world that is placed in so great libertie? ... The Prince that may not persuade him selfe to conforme his wil and mind to the judgement of one onely person, doth he think to constreine all persons to be appliant to his onely judgement?[48]

The philosophical style accords with Alexander's favourite reading as reported by Lampridius: Plato's *Republic*, and Cicero's *De re publica* and *De officiis*.[49] The topic of self-conquest, in the war against the ruler's own unruly instincts, and the pedagogic tone in which it is expounded, are transposed by Townshend into the antimasque of *Albion's Triumph*. He writes a mock-Platonic dialogue between a 'Plebeian' who has witnessed and enjoyed the spectacular triumphal procession of Albanactus, and an enlightened 'Patrician' who has shunned it, in the knowledge that the Emperor's aptest victory is in the moral realm: 'I have seene this brave ALBANACTUS CAESAR, seene him with the eyes of understanding, vew'd all his Actions, look't into his Mind, which I find armed with so many morall vertues that he dayly Conquers a world of Vices ... And in that fashion he Triumphes over all the Kings, and Queenes that went before him. All his passions, are his true Subjects.'[50]

The speaker of this tribute is named Platonicus; and his lesson is confirmed in the final scene by the figure of Peace, who explains that she has returned from heaven after having 'left the World displeas'd' because of

> Fond Men that strive more for a Province there,
> Then looking upward to possesse a Sphere ...[51]

Albanactus, like Alexander, instead of 'inventing warre against some straunge countrie', strives for a supremacy in virtue.

Townshend's text fills out the comparison with reference to the late imperial panegyrics of Claudian. As these were all written to celebrate the consulates of the Emperor or his lieutenants, they are apposite to the gathering of consuls in which Albanactus makes his appearance. Their adulatory tone suggests a language of poetic eulogy which can enhance the image of the righteous ruler drawn from the historical instance of Alexander Severus. When, for example, in the final scene Peace appears from the heavens, a group of other allegorical deities who have preceded her sing in unison 'Imperious Peace her selfe descends!'[52] The initial phrase, which perfectly sums up the scenario of the masque, is quoted directly from Claudian: 'imperiosa quies'. It comes from his panegyric *On the Consulate of Manlius Theodorus*, where the poet describes a similar descent by Astraea, the goddess of justice who had abandoned earth for heaven; Townshend's Peace similarly returns, as we have seen, after having 'fled to Heaven, and left the World displeas'd'. Astraea urges Manlius to put his philosophical studies into practice by assuming the office of consul; he accepts her challenge, and the poet agrees that only the man of reason, who is 'on a par with the gods' (*dis proximus*) and endowed with a 'divine temperance' (*divina modestia*) can rule the state effectively:

> peragit tranquilla potestas,
> quod violenta nequit, mandataque fortius urget
> imperiosa quies.[53]

As Ben Jonson, Townshend's predecessor in the writing of court masques, had paraphrased it in his text for James I's coronation entertainment (1604), 'a calme and facile power, [is] able to effect in a state that, which no violence can'.[54] Townshend's reuse of Claudian's phraseology is appropriate to the symbolic action of the masque: he takes a moral or psychological quality and externalises it as an allegorical figure with a general import. The 'calme ... power' with which the Emperor Albanactus pacifies the unruly tendencies of his own nature secures 'imperious Peace' over his entire realm.

Claudian's panegyric moves on to its concluding section, in which the muse Urania summons the gods to prepare games in the amphitheatre to inaugurate the consulate of Manlius: there are to be combats of wild beasts, together with theatrical entertainments. Both motifs find their way into *Albion's Triumph*. The various types of theatrical performers enumerated by Claudian figure in the balletic antimasques which follow the dialogue of the Plebeian and the Patrician: clowns, mimes, flautists, lyre players, acrobats.[55] And that dialogue itself takes up the imagery of wild animals (in Claudian's text, bears, lions and leopards) to praise the victorious self-control of Albanactus, who 'dayly Conquers a world of Vices, which are wild Beasts indeede. For example Ambition, is a Lyon; Cruelty, a Beare; Avarice, a Wolfe. Yet he subdues them all.'[56]

Here, to fit the representation of the protagonist, Townshend adapts Claudian in a manner the reverse of his use of the image *imperiosa quies*: whereas that had been magnified from metaphor into spectacle, the uncongenial imagery of animal combat is refined from a notional spectacle into a metaphor. The equation of vices to beasts had already been made by Claudian in an earlier panegyric *On the Fourth Consulate of Honorius*. The poet imagines the Emperor as a young prince receiving advice from his father Theodosius, who describes the make-up of the human soul according to Plato, and the necessity (to quote from another masque by Jones and Townshend) for 'the Irascible and concupiscible parts' to be 'obedient to the rationall and highest part'.[57] He warns against the soul's baser dispositions to anger and to lust, which is like an insatiable beast of prey; political supremacy is meaningless if one is a slave to the monsters of vice:

> tunc omnia iure tenebis
> cum poteris rex esse tibi.[58]

Self-command is the only true title to imperial power. The Platonising vein of the speech is aptly reproduced by Townshend's preceptor Platonicus; and this final aphorism matches the personal motto of Charles I, adopted when he was heir to his father's throne: '*Si vis omnia tibi subjici, subjice te rationi*' (if you wish all things subject to you, subject yourself to reason). These were words that greeted the King the following year, when the masque became a temporary reality, as he passed under the triumphal arches on his coronation entry into Edinburgh: they were significantly inscribed on an escutcheon displayed by Clio, the muse of history.[59]

The imperial role devised for Charles in *Albion's Triumph* is a complex one, but its different elements can be distinguished. In his costume design, which fashions an ideal image of the King as a Roman emperor reincarnate, Inigo Jones makes the appropriate references to Trajan and Constantine, first tried out for representations of Prince Henry over twenty years before. Then in the architecture of his set designs he reaches beyond these familiar models to evoke a new imperial exemplar, Alexander Severus, whose political and personal virtues are associated with the King by various touches in Aurelian Townshend's scenario and text. Some of these touches are conveyed with reference to Claudian's panegyric poetry, which is used to provide not further patterns for the ideal ruler (the historical Honorius, for example, was quite insufficient) but an appropriate language in which he can be celebrated: Townshend had never written a masque before, and needed to develop an idiom. He managed well; and the composite role of the Emperor Albanactus which evolved from these composite resources is subscribed with a deft signature at the end of his text. The full chorus sings a 'Valediction' to King Charles and Queen Henrietta Maria which concludes:

> Long live they so, and Brest to Brest,
> May Angels sing them to their Rest.[60]

The allusion is clear, to the King's beloved Shakespeare, and the valedictory words of Horatio:

> Goodnight sweet Prince,
> And flights of angels sing thee to thy rest.[61]

In a gesture of well-tempered cultural nostalgia, Townshend compliments Charles (the Dane, on his mother's side) as a Hamlet who has actually fulfilled his destiny 'to have proved most royal', a philosophical prince who has matured into a philospher-king.

To the courtiers who witnessed *Albion's Triumph*, not every feature of the idealised identity composed for the King would have been as legible as the final allusion to Shakespeare. Years before, Ben Jonson, using similar material from Claudian's panegyrics (and from other classical poets) in his contributions to the London 'arches of triumph' for the coronation entry of James I, had envisaged that only a minority among the crowds would appreciate his classicising allegories, 'so presented, as upon the view, they might ... declare themselves to the sharp and learned'.[62] In a masque audience at Whitehall, largely composed of the educated upper classes, 'the sharp and learned' would have been well represented, although there were probably many more versed in ancient history and Latin literature than were knowledgeable about Roman antiquities and classical architecture. Not all the references to antiquity which enabled Jones and Townshend to create the ideal figure and milieu of Albanactus Caesar might have registered on their audience as *imitatio* or allusion. Nonetheless the density of those references was bound to make a suggestive and telling effect, preparing the way for further 'imperial' representations of the King during the decade of the Personal Rule.[63]

NOTES

1 Jeremy Wood, 'Van Dyck's "Cabinet de Titien": the contents and dispersal of his collection', *Burlington Magazine*, 132 (1990), 680, figs 1–2.

2 Roy Strong, *Van Dyck, Charles I on Horseback* (London: Allen Lane, 1972), pp. 45–57.

3 Oliver Millar, *The Tudor, Stuart and Early Georgian Pictures in the Royal Collection* (2 vols, London: Phaidon, 1963), i, pp. 93–4, no. 143; Oliver Millar, *Van Dyck in England* (London: National Portrait Gallery, 1982), pp. 50–2, no. 11.

4 Harold Wethey, *The Paintings of Titian. III. The Mythological and Historical Paintings* (London: Phaidon, 1975), pp. 235–40, no. L-12, figs 32–50.

5 *Tempe Restored*, lines 49–50, in O&S, ii, p. 480; Cedric C. Brown, *The Poems and Masques of Aurelian Townshend* (Reading: Whiteknights Press, 1983), p. 94.

6 For a more developed account of Van Dyck's work in these terms see John Peacock, 'Looking at Van Dyck's *Scipio* in its contexts', *Art History*, 23 (2000), 262–89.

7 For Van Dyck's recognition of the theatricality of the Stuart court, *ibid.*, 280–6.

8 Bartsch XVII.146.598–609, reproduced in Sebastian Buffa, *The Illustrated Bartsch. 35. Antonio Tempesta* (New York: Abaris, 1984), pp. 325–7; John Peacock, *The Stage Designs of Inigo Jones: The European Context* (Cambridge: Cambridge University Press, 1995), pp. 281–2; A. M. Nagler, *Theatre Festivals of the Medici 1539–1637* (New Haven and London: Yale University Press, 1964), pp. 126–30.

9 O&S, i, pp. 158, 163–5, nos 36–7.

10 John Peacock, 'Jonson and Jones collaborate on *Prince Henry's Barriers*', *Word and Image*, 3 (1987), 180–3.

11 Ben Jonson, *The Speeches at Prince Henry's Barriers*, line 211, in C. H. Herford and Percy and Evelyn Simpson (eds), *Ben Jonson* (11 vols, Oxford: Clarendon Press, 1925–52), vii, p. 329.

12 Peacock, 'Jonson and Jones collaborate', 183–4.

13 Frances A. Yates, *Astraea: The Imperial Theme in the Sixteenth Century* (London and Boston: Routledge & Kegan Paul, 1975), pp. 42–3.

14 O&S, ii, pp. 452, 469, no. 204; Peacock, *Stage Designs of Inigo Jones*, pp. 128-9, 132-3.

15 *The Entertainment of the High and Mighty Monarch Charles King of Great Britaine, France, and Ireland, into his Auncient and Royall City of Edinburgh, the Fifteenth of June, 1633* (Edinburgh, 1633), p. 11: 'The face of the Arch had an *Abacke* or Square with this inscription, Carolo, Mag. Brit. Reg. Jacobi filio Princi: optimo, maximo, libert. vindici. Restauratori legum, fundatori quietis, Conservatori Ecclesiae, Regni ultra Oceanum in Americam Promotori. S.P.Q.E.P.'

16 Jones was aware that the Arch of Constantine was a pastiche of earlier monumental sculpture from previous reigns: see John Peacock and Christy Anderson, 'Inigo Jones, John Webb and Temple Bar', *Architectural History*, 44 (2001), 32-3.

17 Brown, *Townshend*, p. 83; O&S, ii, p. 456, lines 259-62.

18 *Ibid.*, p. 464, no. 193.

19 Jacques Androuet du Cerceau, *Livre des édifices antiques Romains, contenant les ordonnances et desseings des plus signalez et principaux bastiments qui se trouvaient à Rome du temps qu'elle estoit en sa plus grande fleur* (Orléans, 1584), plate 26.

20 For the earliest description of the unfinished basilica see Aelius Lampridius, *Severus Alexander* XXVI.7-8 in *Scriptores Historiae Augustae*, ed. and trans. David Magie (3 vols, London and Cambridge Mass.: Heinemann, 1953), ii, p. 229; enhanced early modern accounts in Sir Thomas Elyot, *The Image of Governaunce compiled of the Actes and Sentence Notable, of the most noble Emperour Alexander Severus* (London, 1549), fol. 66, and Antoine Allegre, *Decade, contenant la vie des empereurs, [de] Traianus ... [jusqu'à] Alexandre* (Paris, 1557), p. 527. For Elyot see Mary Lascelles, 'Sir Thomas Elyot and the legend of Alexander Severus', *Review of English Studies*, n.s. 2 (1951), 305-18; Allegre's book is an elaborated version of the imperial biographies of Antonio de Guevara – see below n. 28.

21 Amato Pietro Frutaz, *Le piante di Roma* (3 vols, Rome: Instituto di Studie Romani, 1962), i, pp. 61-2; ii, plates 25, 30.

22 Inigo Jones, *Roman Sketchbook* (facsimile, London, 1832), unpaginated.

23 Lampridius, *Alexander*, ii, pp. 225, XXV.3-5.

24 *L'Archittetura di Leon Battista Alberti, tradotta in lingua Fiorentina da Cosimo Bartoli* (Monreale, 1565), p. 245; for Jones's ownership of this text see John Harris, Stephen Orgel and Roy Strong, *The King's Arcadia: Inigo Jones and the Stuart Court* (London: Arts Council, 1973), p. 217.

25 George Abbott, *A Briefe Description of the whole World ... Newly Augmented and Enlarged ... The Sixt Edition* (London, 1624), sig. N2r: 'Divers of the Emperours were here in person, as *Alexander, Severus*, who is reputed to be buried at Yorke.' (In fact this is a mistake for Septimius Severus.) I am grateful to the editors for this point.

26 Lampridius, *Alexander*, ii, pp. 178-313 (Constantine addressed 306, LXV.1); Sir Ronald Syme, *Emperors and Biography: Studies in the Historia Augusta* (Oxford: Clarendon Press, 1971), pp. 95-8.

27 *Herodian*, ed. and trans. C. R. Whittaker (2 vols, London and Cambridge Mass.: Heinemann, 1969-70), book VI, ii, pp. 78-145; *Herodian of Alexandria His History Of Twenty Roman Caesars and Emperors* (London, 1629).

28 Antonio de Guevara, *Una década de Césares*, ed. Joseph R. Jones (University of North

Carolina Studies in the Romance Languages and Literatures, no. 64, Chapel Hill: University of North Carolina Press, 1966); first published in 1539.

29 The original edition of Elyot in 1544 was reprinted in 1549 and 1556; Guevara was translated into French by Antoine Allegre, and into English by Edward Hellowes as *A Chronicle, Contayning the Lives of Tenne Emperours of Rome ... Compiled by the most famous Syr Anthonie of Guevara* (London, 1577).

30 Marin Le Roy, Sieur de Gomberville, *Remarques sur la vie du Roy. Et sur celle d'Alexandre Severe. Contenant la comparaison de ces deux grands princes, & comme les propheties de l'heureux regne du Roy* (Paris, 1622).

31 Guevara, *Una década de Césares*, pp. 484–5, elaborated by Allegre, *Decade*, p. 525: '*Il feit en son palais un nouveau corps de maison ... tout le devant duquel estoit de porphyres, & divers marbres apportez de Grece, & taillez industrieusement. En la court du palais feit poser plusieur colomnes, & sur icelles mettre la plus part des statues antiques, qu'on peut trouver en Rome.*'

32 Brown, *Townshend*, p. 76; O&S, ii, p. 454, lines 41–6.

33 O&S, ii, p. 461, no. 191; John Peacock, 'Inigo Jones and the Arundel marbles', *Journal of Medieval and Renaissance Studies*, 16 (1986), 83. The idea of enlarging the 'atrium' of the ancient Roman house to a magnificent scale evidently came to Jones via Palladio's design for the Convento della Carità in Venice: see Andrea Palladio, *I quattro libri dell'archittetura* (Venice, 1570; facsimile Milan, 1969), II.vi.

34 *La Pittura di Leonbattista Alberti tradotta per M. Lodovico Domenichi*, in Alberti, *L'Archittetura*, p. 317; Romano Alberti, *Trattato della nobiltà della pittura* (Rome, 1585), in Paola Barocchi, *Trattati d'arte del Cinquecento* (3 vols, Bari: Giuseppe Laterza, 1960–2), iii, p. 203 (and for other references see iii, p. 614, index entry 'Alessandro Severo'). According to Lampridius, *Alexander*, pp. 230–1, XXVII.7, the emperor himself was a gifted painter; and Allegre, *Decade*, p. 527, has him making a collection of paintings, which he put on public display.

35 Lampridius, *Alexander*, pp. 226–7, XXV.8, XXVI.4; 232–5, XXVIII.6; 266–7, XLV.4; Vincenzo Scamozzi, *L'Idea della archittetura universale* (2 vols, Venice, 1615), i, p. 19.

36 Lucy Hutchinson, *Memoirs of the Life of Colonel Hutchinson*, ed. N. H. Keeble (London: Weidenfeld & Nicolson, 2000), p. 67.

37 Lampridius, *Alexander*, pp. 242–3, XXXIV.2–4.

38 Allegre, *Decade*, p. 536: '*Sur tout estoit pudique & chaste, & ne sçait on que jamais rompist la loy de mariage.*'

39 Whittaker (ed.), *Herodian*, VI.3; Hellowes, *Chronicle*, p. 436; Allegre, *Decade*, p. 530.

40 Lampridius, *Alexander*, pp. 264–7, XLIII.5.

41 Hellowes, *Chronicle*, p. 449, based on Lampridius, *Alexander*, pp. 266–7, XLIII.6–7, and see pp. 218–19, XXII.4 (on toleration); see also *The Imperiall Historie or the Lives of the Emperours, from Julius Caesar ... unto this present Yeere ... First Written in Spanish by Pedro Mexia ... Translated into English by W. T.: and now Corrected, Amplified and Continued to these times by Edward Grimestone* (London, 1623), p. 163. Elyot, *Image of Governaunce*, fol. 91v even makes him a secret Christian.

42 Lampridius, *Alexander*, pp. 240–1, XXXIII.1–2; pp. 218–19, XXII.5. It should be added that fifteen was the normal size for a group of masquers in the 1630s, so that the correspondence of numbers may be coincidence.

43 *Herodian His History*, pp. 2-3.
44 Elyot, *Image of Governaunce*, fols 22v, 45r.
45 Brown, *Townshend*, p. 87; O&S, ii, p. 457, line 385.
46 Lampridius, *Alexander*, pp. 198-9, XII.2; for the entire episode pp. 186-99, VI.1-XII.3.
47 Hellowes, *Chronicle*, pp. 452, 457.
48 *Ibid.*, p. 453.
49 Lampridius, *Alexander*, pp. 236-7, XXX.1-2.
50 Brown, *Townshend*, p. 81; O&S, ii, p. 455, lines 202-12. The motif of conquering vices echoes the Senate's acclamation of the Emperor in Lampridius, *Alexander*, pp. 194-5, IX. 5: 'vicisti vitia, vicisti crimina, vicisti dedecora.'
51 Brown, *Townshend*, p. 87; O&S, ii, p. 457, lines 391-3. The words of Peace seem to put a flattering construction on the King's unaggressive stance towards the recovery the Palatinate: see Peacock, 'Arundel marbles', 78. At the same time they make a slighting allusion to Louis XIII's recent military campaigns in northern Italy, especially his invasion of Monferrato, praised by Jean-Louis Guez de Balzac, the most famous French prose writer of the age, in *Le Prince* (Paris, 1631). This strident celebration of Henrietta Maria's brother as a mighty leader, very different in tone from Gomberville's earlier volume comparing him at a younger age to Alexander Severus, in effect presented him as the antitype of Charles I; it was published towards the end of 1631, just as *Albion's Triumph* was being planned.
52 Brown, *Townshend*, p. 88; O&S, ii, p. 457, line 419.
53 'A calmly exercised power accomplishes what a forcible one cannot, and a sovereign quietude more strongly presses its commands'. *Panegyricus dictus Manlio Theodoro consuli*, lines 239-41, in *Claudian*, ed. and trans. Maurice Platnauer (2 vols, London and New York: Heinemann, 1922), i, pp. 356-7.
54 Ben Jonson, *Part of the King's Entertainment in passing to his Coronation*, lines 467-71, in Herford and Simpson (eds), *Jonson*, vii, p. 98.
55 *Panegyricus dictus Manlio*, lines 309-24, in Platnauer (ed.), *Claudian*, i, pp. 360-3; O&S, ii, p. 456, lines 247-54; pp. 465-9, nos 194, 196, 198, 201-2.
56 Brown, *Townshend*, p. 81; O&S, ii, p. 455, lines 206-8.
57 *Tempe Restored*, 'The Allegory': Brown, *Townshend*, p. 104; O&S, ii, p. 483, lines 350-1.
58 'When you can be king over yourself then shall you hold rightful rule over the world.' *Panegyricus de quarto consolatu Honorii Augusti*, lines 261-2, in Platnauer (ed.), *Claudian*, i, pp. 304-5.
59 *The Entertainment of the High and Mighty Monarch Charles King of Great Britaine*, p. 14.
60 Brown, *Townshend*, p. 89; O&S, ii, p. 458, lines 457-8.
61 *Hamlet* V.11.351-2 in William Shakespeare, *The Complete Works*, ed. Peter Alexander (London, 1951).
62 *Part of the King's Entertainment*, in Herford and Simpson (eds), *Jonson*, vii, p. 91, lines 263-5.
63 See for example the Van Dyck portraits noted above; the sculptor Hubert Le Sueur's

neo-antique bust of the King (c. 1638, Stourhead), discussed in Charles Avery, 'Hubert Le Sueur, the "unworthy Praxiteles" of King Charles I', *The Forty-Eighth Volume of the Walpole Society 1980–1982* (Glasgow, 1982), pp. 158–9, 184–5, no. 33, plate 58 (a), and John Peacock, 'The visual image of Charles I' in Thomas N. Corns (ed.), *The Royal Image: Representations of Charles I* (Cambridge: Cambridge University Press, 1999), pp. 217–18; the King's masques later in the 1630s, such as *Coelum Britannicum* (1634), discussed in Peacock, *Stage Designs of Inigo Jones*, pp. 314–24; and the unrealised project to rebuild Temple Bar as a modern version of the Arch of Constantine (c. 1636), discussed in Peacock and Anderson, 'Inigo Jones, John Webb and Temple Bar', 29–38.

Chapter 4

'From his Matie to me with his awin hand':
the King's correspondence during the
period of personal rule

Sarah Poynting

From the time of Charles I's accession, documents reveal how closely he worked with his Secretaries of State and other trusted officers. Letters and speeches drafted by Lord Keeper Coventry bearing the King's amendments; aide-memoires of private meetings with him by Lord Carleton and the Earl of Totnes, followed by the letters or warrants emerging from those discussions; minutes of business to be presented to him for his decision or signature; letters between Secretaries of State Conway and Coke transmitting his instructions: all bear witness to Charles's close involvement in both the mundane bureaucracy of government and the formulation and presentation of policy.[1] The surviving manuscripts ebb and flow in a mostly predictable pattern, with surges of documents accompanying major events. Parliaments particularly engender floods of messages, answers and declarations. It is clear from those letters that might be regarded as in some way 'personal' (a peculiarly difficult thing to define) how far the business of being a king pervaded every aspect of Charles's existence. He had no relationship that was not primarily defined by his kingship. Only a few letters from Carisbrooke Castle in 1648 suggest a sense of odd relaxation from this pressure.

Documents written in the King's hand, as endorsements by a number of recipients referring to 'his Majesty's own hand' make clear, were regarded as especially significant. Such documents are, with the exception of 1638–39, rarer during the 1630s than at any other period during Charles's adulthood. However, it is not the number of records on any given subject that is significant, so much as the fact that he chose to write them at all. With bureaucratically competent Secretaries of State, councillors and clerks, there was no necessity for Charles to write his own letters – still less official letters or drafts of documents. The concomitant significance placed on them by their recipients was shared by their author: Charles wrote himself when he had a particular interest in the subject of the letter, when he wanted to keep it private, and when he wanted to express individual praise or displeasure. These documents provide information about the subjects that particularly exercised him, and his personal and working relationships, rather than a balanced cross-section of the key issues of the period.

A survey of holograph records can only ever be a partial account, dependent as it is on the haphazard nature of manuscript survival. Perhaps the most significant gap in the 1630s documents is constituted by the complete loss of correspondence between Charles and Henrietta Maria: when writing to Secretary of State Sir Francis Windebank while absent from London in 1639 he refers regularly to his letters to her, which would without doubt have been written by himself. This, though, is consistent with the pattern of survival of the King's correspondence with his wife.[2] However, there are reasons other than the chance destructiveness of time for the lack of large numbers of letters to figures that one might expect to be in receipt of them, such as William Laud or Windebank's fellow Secretary of State Sir John Coke, whose archives are otherwise substantial. Charles's non-parliamentary rule was 'personal' not only in his direct control of government but in the extent to which that government was conducted in private meetings in which the King gave verbal orders for action to be taken: it is this aspect of his rule that makes it so peculiarly difficult to establish degrees of responsibility for policy decisions. Coke usually joined Charles on his progresses, as well as travelling north with him in 1639, leaving Windebank in London, so the preponderance of letters to the latter is unsurprising. However, the very small quantity of correspondence surviving at all with both Laud and Coke may also indicate that those letters that were written were deliberately destroyed. The King's regular practice of apostiling (making marginal responses to) Windebank's letters and returning them to him for action extended to them both, but only a handful of such documents survive. Moreover, in 1637 Windebank complained with some bitterness to the Earl of Leicester concerning Coke's failure to pass on information or knowledge to him other 'than what he cannot keep from me'.[3] It is possible that Coke's tendency towards reserve resulted in his viewing correspondence with the King as too important and too private to risk its dissemination. If so, this would be particularly true of any communications written by Charles himself.

However, despite the loss of important documents, manuscripts can offer evidence that is not otherwise available, even when the content of the original is faithfully transmitted in print (as it too often has not been). Insertions and deletions in documents have frequently not been recorded when published, removing a layer of information about the writer's construction of an argument or second thoughts. The hand(s) in which a document is written may be suggestive of a network of working relationships; and while calendars and indexes can note these, they have, unfortunately, proved to be not always accurate.⁴ The distribution of paper, as identified by watermarks, may provide similar evidence, and even an apparently minor visual element such as a change in ink colour can provide clues as to the composition of a letter or its handling by its recipient.⁵

'YOUR LOUING FREND': THE EARLY 1630s

The recipients of letters in the King's hand in the early part of the decade were the Marquis of Hamilton and the Earl of Menteith (or Monteith/Monteithe/ Muntethe, as Charles variously spelt it). Menteith was the King's inside man on the Scottish Privy Council, appointed by him to the Lord Presidency in 1628. Both Charles's view of Menteith's function, and his intentions concerning the convention of estates called in 1630, are manifested in the first section of the instructions he wrote out carefully in June: 'You must command the Chancelor in my name, that no motion bee made in the Conuention but vnder the hand of the Clarke Register, & you must command the Clarke Register that he present none but eather those he shall receaue warranted vnder my hand, or by your aduyce.'⁶ The mainly financial articles he proposed privately were not identical to those he transmitted publicly through his Secretary of State for Scotland, Sir William Alexander (created Viscount Stirling later in the year), nor, indeed, as Maurice Lee has shown, to the issues on which he desired Menteith to gain the agreement of the convention.⁷ However, this opening clause establishes clearly the ground rules under which he considered it should operate. Following correspondence illustrates the King's nervousness that these rules might not be observed. In two letters written on 18 June, he ordered Menteith ('my pleasure is that') to 'incurage' 'all my seruants to show themselfes reallie to be soe' by furthering his service at the convention.⁸ This final phrase, demanding a public manifestation of support, is characteristic of Charles's style, as is his statement that 'those businesses, which shall at this tyme bee propound in the Conuention, bee so just, as I haue littell cause to suspect oposition'.⁹ The confidence expressed, though, is belied by the anxious repetitiveness of the sentiments in each letter, as well as by his feeling it necessary to write them at all. The first directs Menteith particularly to the 'encouragement' of Lord Chancellor Dupplin and the Earls of Mar and Haddington, and the second to that of the Archbishop of St Andrews, of whom the King twice makes the point that he is being singled out as special in being sent a letter all to himself, suggesting that Menteith may have been intended to show the letters to those concerned as a way of exerting pressure. Charles may have supposed that the effect would be reinforced by the 'in his Majesty's own hand' factor (although in the case of Archbishop Spottiswood this could have been undermined by the King's evident difficulty in finding the right complimentary words with which to describe him – two adjectives have been heavily deleted before he settled on 'one of my cheefe & able willing seruants'). When writing in his own hand, Charles was both more and less than simply the monarch. The formal 'we' used in scribal letters, signalling the full weight and authority of his majesty, is exchanged for 'I', suggestive of a private relationship and apparently a substitution of distance by intimacy, however temporary. Since his position, though, could never be forgotten, the effect of the first person singular was rather to enhance his formal power than to derogate from it, bringing the additional influence of the personal claim implied in it to bear on the recipient (although in one case, as we shall see, Charles himself seems to have been unsure which would be more persuasive).

Of the issues that were discussed at the convention, the one in which the holograph records show the King took a personal and continuing interest was reform of the Scottish fishing industry. As Lee has said, 'The plan for the fishery was the one economic proposal directly affecting Scotland which captured Charles's imagination.'[10] Clear accounts of this failed enterprise have already been published, and I do not intend to go over the same ground.[11] However, while both Sharpe and Macinnes refer to documents on which the King has made notes or added a postscript, the extent to which his interest is underlined by records in his own hand has not been specifically noted. In July 1631 he wrote a brief letter to Menteith to say that he expected an account of his progress on the subjects of the various instructions he had been given, adding that: 'ye must deale about the reseruations for the fishing business to keepe out those places from being reserued that I haue tould you of, becaus I foresee that otherwais that great business whereof I haue had so great a care of, will runn a hazard.'[12] In November he was still exercised by the problem of reserved fishing grounds and drew up a clause to present to the London committee on fishing in an attempt to solve it. According to Coke's minute of agreements made at the meeting, this was intended to protect poor fishermen dependent on those grounds for their livelihoods, who the King intended should be provided for 'by his royal power & grace'.[13] Perhaps unsurprisingly for a scheme emanating from Whitehall, this was not sufficient to reassure the Scots.

In the same year Charles was dealing, with an odd mixture of extreme secrecy and flamboyant publicity, with an affair emanating from Scotland whose ramifications have never been fully explored.[14] The case of the Earl of Ochiltree does not make an appearance in his letters until May 1632, although it had first erupted a year earlier when Ochiltree reported to the King a story passed on to him by Lord Reay that troops being levied by the Marquis of Hamilton for service in Europe would be used to depose him. Reay's chief informant – and one of the main conspirators – was named as David Ramsay, a favourite of Hamilton's. Charles's belief in the innocence of the Marquis was manifested immediately upon Hamilton's return to court from Scotland in May by having him sleep in his own bedchamber, but Reay and Ochiltree were committed to their lodgings. The Venetian ambassador reported that the arrests had given rise to much speculation, 'because the whole affair has been carried out with the most extreme and extraordinary secrecy'.[15] The next development, however, seems to have been designed for maximum publicity. Ramsay was brought over from Holland and confronted with Reay, at which point he not unnaturally denied everything and declared his desire to clear his name. It was decided that as neither man could produce sufficient witnesses, the case between them should be heard by the Court of Chivalry with a view to its being decided through a trial by combat, a course of action on which Charles seems to have been especially keen. After a number of postponements, though, in May 1632 he decreed, Richard II-style, that it should be called off, since Ramsay had not been proved guilty of treason despite Reay's efforts. By August both had been released. In the meantime, the Earl of Ochiltree had been transported to Edinburgh and held under close confinement in the Tolbooth. In December 1631 he was charged before the Court of Session with lease-making (making slanderous statements likely to prejudice the relations between king and subjects), to which he put forward such an effective defence that judgement was repeatedly deferred, since his Majesty so clearly required a guilty verdict.

It was not until the Reay/Ramsay affair was almost concluded that Charles committed himself to paper, writing to Hamilton that he had not wished to send 'halfe newes', but 'thought fitt to bee the first aduerticer of [the ende of] it to you'.[16] In part the King wanted to put across his own view of the aborted proceedings. However, his main reason for writing was 'that ye may so know D: Ramsay: that ye may not haue to doe with such a Pest as he is, suspecting he may seeke to insinuat him selfe to you, upon this occasion; wherfor I must desyer you as ye loue me, to haue nothing to doe with him'. Ramsay was not treasonable, but 'no wayes iñocent', with a 'virolent tonge' and 'foolish presumtius cariage'. In his next letter, written following Ramsay's release, he felt it necessary to reiterate this warning: 'I hope ye will remember, what I haue sayd concerning him alreddie.'[17] Kevin Sharpe has argued that although capable of eloquence, Charles saw the art of persuasion as unnecessary.[18] These letters to Hamilton give us a rare early glimpse of the King feeling unable to issue an order, however politely phrased. His figuring of Ramsay as a kind of serpent, and the hint of emotional blackmail in 'I must desyer you as ye loue me' certainly constitute attempts at persuasion, strategies which would become increasingly prevalent during the 1640s. In this case, his assumption of failure is suggested in the second letter: 'Dauid Ramsay, as I imagen, will meet with you befor ye cum hither.' A king who can 'imagen' an event that he would have preferred to forestall has ceded – and must know he has ceded – a measure of control. It is a remarkable reflection on the accepted balance of power between the two men.

Charles's letters to Menteith (at this time briefly Earl of Strathearn) on the subject of Ochiltree share none of this attempted blandishment: they are curt to the point of irritability. Strathearn had evidently informed the King of Ochiltree's likely acquittal, which Charles seemed to accept, ordering him ('we therfore I command you') not to allow the trial to go ahead, but to ensure that Ochiltree 'com not within 50: Myles of ~~our~~ my Court, upon paine of my hauiest displesure'.[19] The deletions are indicative of a curious blurring of the monarchical office in his conduct of the affair, which he tried to keep as private as he could, by contrast with the grand drama of the Court of Chivalry. Six weeks later Charles repeated his order, adding that he 'thought that I should not haue beene trubled' with it any more.[20] From this letter's repeated mention of warrants, it appears that Strathearn might have preferred to receive a more formal command from the King than a letter in which even he did not appear to be sure whether he was acting in his private or his public role. In the event, the Scottish justices and Privy Council seem to have been disinclined to incur either the King's or indeed Hamilton's displeasure by freeing the Earl. Charles ordered his removal to Blackness Castle in May 1633, with the apparent intention that he should stay there for life. It is a further confirmation of the strength of Hamilton's influence. Ironically, the King's final letter to Strathearn (reduced to Earl of Airth) in these years is one ordering him to retire to the country because of accusations against him that in claiming the earldom of Strathearn he aimed at the Scottish throne, the same accusation made against Hamilton.[21] Charles does not appear to have given any real credence to the case against Strathearn (who might otherwise very well have joined Ochiltree in Blackness), even though he declared him guilty of making treasonable speeches. But William Graham, successively Earl of Menteith, Strathearn and Airth, had few political friends but several powerful enemies, among them the Marquis of Hamilton.

The King's nine letters to Hamilton in 1631–32 while the latter was in Germany are naturally concerned largely with his activities there, but because Charles sent the earlier ones by Sir Henry Vane, he did not feel the need to enlarge on the 'publike & priuat' instructions Vane took with him.[22] Charles apologised twice for the shortness of these letters, blaming it on his own laziness, but three of the last four letters, not carried by Vane, are considerably longer. This is another manifestation of the personal conduct of government through private meetings, when trusted bearers of verbal information were given covering letters recommending them to the recipient. It was a mode of communication that the King would use even more frequently within the three kingdoms during the 1640s, when even ciphered documents could be dangerous in the wrong hands. In fact, in the shorter letters, without the pressure to discuss business, Charles was as relaxed and chatty (if briefly so) as he ever was in writing, except perhaps to Buckingham. He delivered a disrespectfully comic homily on the evils of drink, writing (in a passage omitted by Burnet when he printed the King's letters to Hamilton): 'I doe obserue (hoping you will doe so too) to what an estate drinking hes brought most of the Princes of Germanie; as you may easilie judge, by what you haue seene of my Vncle:'.[23] In a pattern often seen in Charles's letters, his final compliments were subtly varied to indicate the immediate feelings he wished to convey towards the recipient (the dropping of a customary 'constant' or 'loving' must often have been the cause of anxiety in interpreting the semiotics of the signature). The particular warmth he felt for Hamilton at this time is signalled both by the opening 'Iames', and in the courtesy of his drawing attention to their (extremely distant) kinship with 'Your louing frend & Cousin'.[24] In the first of his longer letters, in which he proffered some mild criticism of one of Hamilton's military decisions, this is mitigated not only by an assurance that he had shared this with no one else, and that no one else had voiced it, but by a boosting of the pre-signature line to 'constant louing frend & Cousin'.[25] His main concern was to extricate Hamilton from a problematic situation without loss of face, and in his final letter, of September 1632, which called Hamilton home, he expressed his affection in a simple epigram: 'ye shall be no sooner cum, then wellcum'.[26] Significantly, in 1638, despite the trust reposed in the Marquis by Charles, 'Iames' had become 'Hamilton' (and would always remain so), and the loving kinship downgraded to 'asseured constant frend', occasionally augmented by the addition of 'most'. Hamilton's return to at least partial favour in 1646 was met by an almost frantic accumulation of adjectives suggesting either guilt at Hamilton's imprisonment in 1644–46 or an effort to convey sincerity: 'most asseured reall constant faithfull frend'. Love and kinship are still, though, noticeably absent.

'FOR YOUR SELFE, APOSTYLED': THE MID-1630s

Charles's desire for order (as he saw it) in the church hardly needs repetition. However, it is worth looking briefly at one of its manifestations, in the attention he paid to certificates of archiepiscopal visitations to dioceses under his archbishops' care. These he apostiled with comments and orders for action, a mode of communication that, in its brevity, lends itself to a bluntness of tone that, particularly considering that the recipients were his two most senior churchmen, can verge on rudeness ('see that by the next Yeare ye giue me a good account thereof').[27] Most of his notes are concerned with control and punishment, and notably fail to indicate much interest in the independence of the judiciary. Laud's anxiety about the limits of his or the High Commission's authority was repeatedly swept aside: 'Informe mee of the Particulars, and I shall command the Judges [at common law] to make them Abjure'; 'What the High Commission cannot doe in this, I shall supplie, as I

The King's correspondence during personal rule

shall fynde Cause, in a more powerfooll way'; 'Demande there [the judges'] helpe and if they refuse, I shall make them assist you'; 'if faire meanes will not, power must redresse it'.[28] It may be indicative of differences in Charles's relationship with his two archbishops that these unembarrassed and unqualified assertions of monarchical authority appear only in the apostiles to Laud's certificates; or it may, again, simply reflect the nature of manuscript survival.

This brusque decisiveness, untinged by any hint of doubt, is also sometimes found in the King's apostiling of Windebank's letters that makes up the bulk of documents written in his hand from these middle years. However, here the tone is much more varied, reflecting not only the greater range of subject matter, but also Charles's occasional uncertainty as to the best way of achieving his aims, as well as the nature of his relationship with his Secretary of State. Windebank's every utterance comes veiled in wreaths of humility ('Neuertheles in my poore opinion wch in all humility I submit to yor M: wisedom, & craue pardon if I erre ...'[29]), but the wreaths are used to decorate expressions of his own thoughts that he feared the King might not agree with. What emerges from the apostiles, though, is the degree of trust placed in Windebank by Charles personally and politically (often, for the King, indistinguishable). In a short holograph letter to Windebank (signed simply 'Your frend'), Charles let him know that he had shown the Earl of Holland some of Sir Arthur Hopton's dispatches 'to keepe jelousies out of his head'.[30] Considering Charles's views on the maintenance of hierarchy, this reflection on one of his nobility to someone who was seen, when he was appointed, as 'brought out of the dark' suggests a degree of ease in the relationship.[31] The King's sarcasm in his apostiles is much more often directed against others and shared with Windebank than directed against him. Indeed, on occasion, Charles evidently and rather unexpectedly felt the need to soothe his anxious Secretary, even (perhaps especially) following the summer of 1636 when Windebank found himself in temporary disgrace and under house arrest after the King believed rumours that he had been bribed by the Spanish. Charles's tendency to absolve himself of blame (in the case of these accusations writing 'Mist[r]is Fame must beare all'[32]) manifests itself even in minor matters like the appointment of court places, when Windebank found himself in the awkward position of having to tell the King that he (Charles) had promised a position to one person and then given it to someone else. 'If I haue erred in this you must haue part of the blame, for it passed through your hands', Charles commented.[33] Perhaps, though, there is in this note an implication not so much of evasion of responsibility but of a rueful, almost playful, sharing of it. When Charles similarly promised one office to two people, he admitted his mistake frankly, putting his 'littell error' down to 'want of memory'; but he still left the problem to be dealt with by his Secretary. He also left the unfortunate Windebank to tell the Earl of Arundel 'in a discreet way' that the latter was angry 'without reason'.³⁴ It is possible that for Windebank, so aware of the vast distance between himself and his sovereign, those odd moments when Charles narrowed it – revealing his irritation with his nobles, implying sympathy for the Secretary's anxieties, or claiming him as joint author of a mistake – constituted a real reward for the difficulties he underwent for him. It is not especially surprising to find the King putting off his public aloofness in letters to Hamilton, a marquis of royal blood; much more that he should do so to any extent at all with the comparatively lowly Secretary. Charles's success in winning round some of the young parliamentarians appointed to wait on him during his imprisonment at Carisbrooke Castle in 1648, and the cordiality of the relationships that his letters imply he established with them indicate that he was capable of charm, but his choice of its beneficiaries is not predictable. However, insofar as one can judge from his correspondence, they tended to be either those he regarded as near-equals (Buckingham, Hamilton, Rupert) or people who, like Windebank, were properly aware of their inferiority. In each case, though, genuine liking appears to have been a necessary element. Perhaps to his detriment, politic charm does not seem to have been part of the King's armoury.

The ease in Charles's relationship with Windebank was evidently one experienced more by the King than the Secretary of State. Nevertheless, as Windebank's letters progressed a degree of relaxation entered into them in the way he addressed Charles. The humility manifested does not disappear, but it does diminish, and by the late 1630s it is combined with a willingness to make the occasional caustic comment, to join the King with himself in the expression of opinion. In 1639, in writing of the dangers of allying themselves with Spain, Windebank cited 'so many yeeres experience of their amusing Treaties' as proof of Spanish unreliability; and later disparagingly added 'yor M: hath had sufficient experience by the interposition of Princesse Phalsburg, & may perceaue by that Romanze in Sr Art: Hopton's lre, how capable women are of such greate affaires.'³⁵

Windebank's comment on Spanish treaties, and similar cynicism about the French, reflected the years he had spent attempting to make a treaty with both: it is the major subject of his letters to Charles throughout the mid-1630s. Treaty documents bearing amendments in the King's hand, as well as the apostiled correspondence, show how closely they worked together. Charles carefully weighed the Secretary's reports, analyses and proposals, agreeing, praising, arguing or dismissing as he felt it appropriate. One of Windebank's blunter communications concerning disagreements between Viscount Scudamore, ambassador to France, and the Earl of Leicester, ambassador extraordinary ('the businesse in my poore vnderstanding, being of very greate consequence & requiring haste'³⁶) pushed the King into writing immediately to Leicester.³⁷ In his letter one of the inherent difficulties arising from tête-à-tête policy-making becomes apparent: the potential for misinterpretation, or differently remembered interpretations. This, at least, is how Charles addressed the problem: 'I thought fitt at this tyme to explaine a discurce that past betwine you & mee.' If, however, Charles's verbal instructions concerning communications with Scudamore had been as contradictory as this letter, Leicester's confusion (whether wilful or not) as to what information he was obliged to pass on to Scudamore is understandable. The collection of clauses beginning 'yet' and 'but' left Leicester in a position where whatever he did could be argued to be acceptable; or conversely (should he find himself out of favour) wholly unacceptable. While the King evidently felt – or intended to convey – that he had dealt with the matter not merely promptly but decisively, his assurance to Scudamore, sent through Windebank, that he 'much wonder[ed] at this mistaking in the E: of Lester' and had 'cleered this mistaking with my owen hand' was found distinctly unsatisfactory by the Viscount.[38] Leicester also complained about Charles's opaque instructions, which Ian Atherton has suggested were deliberately ambiguous.[39]

Sir Thomas Wentworth, too, must have received assurances from the King with mixed feelings. In the mid-1630s Charles wrote to him in his own hand about every six months, supplementing his longer official communications with more private thoughts. The King generally praised Wentworth's good judgement ('my Letters would rather seem Panegyricks than Dispatches'[40]) and shared his opinions with him freely, especially on the subject of parliaments, warning him to take heed of 'that Hidra ... you know, that here I have found it as well cunning as malitious'; though with typical lack of prescience he also advised the Lord Deputy that 'young one's are ever most tractable'.[41] Wentworth was an 'asseured Frend', rather than simply a 'Frend' like Windebank and Leicester. The personal warmth expressed to Hamilton, however, is absent. When Wentworth persisted in suing for an earldom on the grounds that this sign of his Majesty's approbation would silence his enemies, Charles first assured him that he was not displeased, as 'noble Minds are always accompanied with lawful Ambitions'. Later, however, he issued a crushing, haughty rebuke: 'if [your Enemies] can once find that you apprehend the dark setting of a Storm, when I say no, they will make you leave to care for any thing in a short while but for your Fears. And believe it, the Marks of my Favours that stop malicious Tongues are neither Places nor Titles, but the little Welcome I give to Accusers, and the willing Ear I give to my Servants.'[42] Even the King's most favoured servants had to learn where the line was drawn that they might not cross, when they would cease to be given a willing ear.

Sarah Poynting

'WEE AR LYKE TO BEE ALL SHAMED & UNDONE':
THE LATE 1630s

The overwhelming majority of the King's holograph letters during the 1630s date from 1638 and 1639. His correspondents are still those from the earlier part of the decade: Windebank, Hamilton and Wentworth; even Menteith (as Earl of Airth) reappears briefly. However, the relationship between Charles and the first three of these underwent an alteration. From a situation in which the King communicated individually with each of them on different subjects, he created a network, of which Laud was also a member, in which the interconnections were crucial for the conduct of private business. This was, of course, a result of the increasing focus on Scotland almost to the exclusion of every other issue, but it is reflected not only in the content of the letters, but in their mode of composition and interchange.

Charles's rarer absences from London in late 1636 and 1637 led to a temporary lessening of apostiled letters between himself and Windebank (only three in 1637); there are then sporadic clusters of them during 1638. While the negotiation of a treaty with one of the European powers remained an issue, by the end of the decade finding an ally against the Scots had joined, if not altogether displaced, recovery of the Palatinate as Charles's main foreign concern. Letters to Wentworth become more frequent in 1638 and the first half of 1639, though they are mostly brief and concerned with the provision of Irish troops for the possible Scots war. However, the wording is telling for what it reveals about Charles and his expectations of his colleagues. In a particularly characteristic turn of phrase, he wrote that one of the Lord Deputy's long letters was not unpleasing 'for good Counsel and chearful obeying of my Commands cannot but be always acceptable to me'.[43] Charles's inability to listen to 'good Counsel' has been often rehearsed, but his frequent requirement for 'cheerfulness' – a not merely unquestioning but smiling readiness to follow – in his servants and supporters has not been noted. The unconsciously contradictory juxtaposition of 'good Counsel' with 'chearful obeying' in itself shows just why the King's counsellors found it so problematic to offer advice. Windebank's willing submissiveness was always 'acceptable', and it is a further sign of Charles's trust in and reliance on his Secretary that he told Wentworth that he should not 'think it odd, that I have and shall use Windebank's Pen, in Dispatches to you, sometimes of greatest Consequence and Secrecy'.[44]

All of this correspondence is outnumbered by Charles's letters to Hamilton, which have been more exhaustively analysed than any other of his communications. As Conrad Russell has written, this was 'a rare time when the main outlines of policy were being formed by letter'.[45] However, rather than adding to the extensive examination of that policy, what I wish to consider is again the evidence the letters provide of the King's working methods and relationships, as well as looking at what their language suggests about his outlook. In the periods when Hamilton was with Charles, the full extent of their collaboration is revealed in documents signed by the King but drafted in Hamilton's hand. His private instructions as commissioner of 16 May 1638 and a warrant of 18 May, superscribed by Charles but otherwise written by the Marquis, are in the latter's best hand and look like fair copies.[46] A letter from Charles to Hamilton in September endorsed 'my instructione for the Biss:' (bishops), signed and with the place (Oatlands) and date in the former's hand, resembles rough scribbled notes, and could have been done at Charles's dictation, or possibly copied in a hurry by Hamilton with a few changes being made, presumably at the King's direction, as he wrote.[47] Letters to the new commissioner, Traquair, and to the Archbishop of St Andrews in 1639 are more revealing. Though Hamilton invariably endorsed these as 'copies' they are clearly drafts, at times almost unreadable because of the number of deletions and insertions, in one by Charles himself as well as by Hamilton (at one point in the letter there are three layers of interlineations as well as the original deleted line), and in the letter to the Bishop, by Laud.[48] Donald has rightly said that it is not possible to be sure if Hamilton was functioning as more than an amanuensis.[49] Nevertheless, experience of the King's earlier collaborative documents suggests that Hamilton was more actively involved in the drafts, although undoubtedly under instruction from Charles.

The closeness of the triangular working group – Charles, Hamilton, Laud – is confirmed during Hamilton's absences in Scotland, when he wrote almost as regularly to the Archbishop as to the King, and Charles used Laud to write to Hamilton when he did not have the time to do so himself.[50] Windebank was on the edge of this group: new instructions sent to Hamilton in April 1639, authorising him 'to invade & enter oʳ said Kingdom of Scotlande by force of armes & in hostile manner' are in his hand.[51] In the same month Charles wrote in his own hand to his Secretary with a new proclamation 'to be Printed with all speede & secresie (my Lo: of Cant: onlie excepted & those who of necessitie must know it)', and ordering him to suppress the former version. It is interesting that the King felt obliged to explain himself: 'As for the alterations, I shall onlie desyer you to obserue, that albeit ~~that~~ I speake not of all, yet I promis no more then I did:'.[52] Wentworth was linked with the group both by Charles's use of Windebank to write to him, and more significantly by Laud's closeness to him.

Of course, Charles's personal relationship with Windebank differed fundamentally from that with his royal cousin and sharer of his bedchamber,[53] but the working relationships were at times more similar than might be supposed. The King supplied both of them with blanks bearing his signature so that they could carry on business in his absence. Windebank was punctilious in accounting for them,[54] and equally careful to ensure that he had written orders for action to be taken. For example, when given a direction for Balthasar Gerbier, he wrote to Charles, 'I most humbly beseeche yo' M: either to signify so much yo' selfe to M' Gerbier vnder yo' hande, or else to commande me to do it vnder my hande.'[55] To make his point the more clearly, 'vnder yo' hande' has been inserted. Charles's response was to underline the last clause and apostile it 'I command you to doe it.' Following some confusion with Sir Henry Vane, Hamilton, too, requested that if the King wanted something to be positively obeyed he should send word under his own hand. The possibility for misunderstanding has already been touched on in relation to the Earl of Leicester, and is made apparent in Charles's reply of 18 April 1639 to Hamilton, that 'I beliue nether of vs, expressed our selues, so cleerelie as wee might.'[56] Like the Earl of Menteith in 1632 pushing for a formal warrant to deal with the Earl of Ochiltree, neither Hamilton nor Windebank wished to find himself in a position of taking responsibility for having done the wrong thing. When Hamilton undertook to spy on Covenanters coming to Berwick, he took care to obtain a 'priuat uarrant' from the King indemnifying him against any prejudicial outcome of his covert actions.[57] More unexpectedly, Charles also wished to be able to show that he had support for his actions, writing in his letter of 18 April that he had asked for clarification of Hamilton's advice 'cheeflie to show Hen: Vane, that your judgement went along as well as your obedience'. In September 1638, in response to a request from Windebank for instructions on a business concerning the Earl of Leicester's negotiations, he wrote 'It is a business that requyres no great haste yet is very nyce therfor I will stay whille I may speake with you.'[58] While Windebank was always cautious in taking action, he was increasingly confident in giving advice on the course of the ever more complex treaty negotiations (by this time there was hardly a European power that was not involved in them). The King even entrusted him (not altogether enviably) with messages for Henrietta Maria, requiring Windebank 'to transcrybe so much of [Gerbier's] letter to mee as I haue marked in the syde & to show it to my Wyfe to make her see what bissi boddies her Mother hes about her'.[59] A few days later, when Windebank reported from a meeting with the Queen that she told him she had 'written so lately [to Charles] that now she wolde forbeare', Charles underlined 'she wolde forbeare' and responded plaintively, 'Yet, tell her that I cannot anie, from wryting to her.'[60]

If the King's occasional insecurities and dependence on his small group of servants (to use his own word) are revealed in his letters, the vocabulary that he employed about his opponents when writing to Hamilton can hardly have left the Marquis in any doubt as to the problems he faced in trying to bring the two together. Much of this is well known, particularly his reference to himself as having no more power than 'a Duke of Venice' as long as the Covenant was in force. But the terms Charles used, often repetitively, to describe his opponents are equally notable. He attacked the 'piuisheness' of the General Council, their 'follies', 'impertinencies' and 'madd actes'. In so belittling them, the King made it much more difficult for himself to recognise not only their point of view (an evident impossibility for him) but their power.[61] In a strikingly Shakespearean expression, Charles wrote of coming 'my selfe in Person accompanied lyke my selfe', of showing 'my selfe, lyke my selfe': in full monarchical authority.[62] The implication is that this display of sovereignty would in itself have a salutory effect on his recalcitrant subjects. This apparent confidence, though, is as often qualified. In a letter to Wentworth in June 1639, the King wrote that he would go himself to Edinburgh against the advice of 'many wise Men', because 'nothing but my Presence at this Time in that Country can save it from irreparable Confusion'; but he added 'Yet I will not be so vain as absolutely to say, that I can.'[63] His own irreparable confusion emerges most clearly in a letter to Hamilton the month before:

> It is trew, that (according to my Proclamation) I would rest quyet for the tyme, vpon ther yelding mee Siuill Obedience; but that must be vnderstude, by demanding Pardon, for there, by past, disobedience, & randring vp, what they vnjustlie possess, of myne, & others: less then this, I will not bee content of, no, not for the present; for all this, I doe not take my self, to bee in such a case as to Conquer them; yet I dout not, but (by the grace of God) to force them to Obedience, (in tyme) what by stopping of there Trade, & other Courses; the w^{ch}, rather then not doe, I shall first sell my self to my Shirt [64]

The splutter of commas and parentheses (excessive even for Charles, who tended to over-punctuate) produces the effect of breathless anger and incredulity, but this is a very neatly written letter, a fair copy rather than a draft. The effect is, at least in part, calculated: if this were a speech from a play, the urgent anapaestic metre and use of alliteration in the final clause would be assumed to be deliberate.

From this point financial problems and the concomitant inadequacy of his forces began to outweigh all other issues in the King's letters. 'I shall desyer you to take heede, how ye engadge me in Monie expence', he wrote to Hamilton in May 1639. A few weeks later he ordered him: 'I set you loose, to doe what mischeefe ye can doe upon the Rebelles for my seruice, with those men ye haue, for ye cannot haue one man from hence.'[65] In an apostile to a letter from Windebank concerning supplies, he told him that without them 'wee ar lyke to bee all shamed & undone, & so tell the Comittie for Monie from me'.[66] Ten days later he signed the Treaty of Berwick.

The calling of the General Assembly in Edinburgh following the Pacification saw the re-emergence of one of Charles's former correspondents: he reappointed the non-covenanting Earl of Airth (Menteith) to the Privy Council and ordered him in his own hand to attend the Assembly. When, in

September 1639, Airth wrote requesting directions as to how to carry himself towards the King's commissioner, Traquair, Charles told him to withhold advice unless asked for it, 'for I suspect the issew will not be so faire, but that he will be glad to lay the burden on other Mens shoulders to ease his owen'. This comment on Traquair implies a continuing personal trust in Airth as well as a desire – perhaps guilt-induced – to protect him from further trouble. However, one of the last surviving letters written in the King's hand in the last days of the Personal Rule indicates that protection was no longer even offered to his Scottish supporters: 'Douglas / according to my promis, I thinke it is nou tyme to send you word to looke to your selfe, for I will not warrant you from the insolencie of the Couenanting Rebelles longer then the 13: of the next Moneth:'[67] On 'the 13: of the next Moneth' the Short Parliament opened; preparations for war had already begun.

With the end of personal rule, the King's small group of correspondents from the 1630s rapidly fragmented. Of them all, only the marginalised and ruined Menteith survived until the Restoration, dying in 1661, when it was calculated that the Crown owed him £50,000 (it was never recovered). Hamilton's varying fortunes during the civil wars came to an end when he followed Charles to the scaffold, being put on trial a week after the King's execution on 30 January 1649, and beheaded in March. The three Englishmen, Windebank, Wentworth (now Earl of Strafford) and Laud, more immediately fell victim to their close association with royal policy. After the House of Commons drew up charges against him, Windebank fled to Paris in December 1640 where he died in 1646. In April 1641 Charles assured Strafford, shortly after the latter had been found guilty of treason by the House of Commons, that 'upon the Word of a King' although he could no longer employ him, he would 'not suffer in Lyfe, Honnor or Fortune'. The King finally signed himself as more than an 'asseured Frend': for the first and last time he was the Earl's 'constant faithfull Frend'.[68] Less than three weeks later Charles signed the Bill of Attainder that sent Strafford to his death. In March 1641 Laud was committed to the Tower, also accused of treason, though not put on trial until 1644. His execution in January 1645 caused Charles to reflect that 'nothing can be more euident then that Strafords innocent bloode hath beene one of the great Causes of Gods Iust Iudgements upon this whole Nation, by a furius Ciuill War, bothe syds being hitherto almost equally punished as being in a maner equally guilty; but now, this last Crying Bloode being totally theirs, I beliue it is no presumption to hope that heerafter his hand of Iustice will be hauier upon them, & lighter upon us.'[69]

It hardly needs to be pointed out that whether or not it is presumptuous, it is always a mistake to anticipate the future on the basis of knowledge of divine justice.

NOTES

1. See, for example, House of Lords Record Office, Main Papers, 12 May and 6 June 1628 (letters to the House of Lords drafted by Coventry with amendments by the King); PRO, SP 78/79, fol. 120 ('Memorial ... by word of mouth from his Ma^{ty}', by Dudley Carleton, 12 July 1626); PRO, SP 16/22, fol. 70 (memorial of meeting with the Earl of Totnes, 8 March 1626).

2. The only surviving letters from Charles to his wife (remarkably few in relation to the number he must have written) are mostly drafts that remained in his own possession, as well as a few that were intercepted.

3. *Calendar of State Papers, Domestic Series, 1625–49*, p. 550. It may also be the case that Coke felt some resentment at Windebank's having been entrusted with treaty negotiations with the French of which he himself knew nothing, despite being the Secretary of State with supposed responsibility for relations with France. Windebank was still having problems with Coke in 1639, when he was driven to complain to the King about him (Bodl., MS Clarendon 16, fol. 94, 24 April 1639).

4. O. Ogle *et al*. (eds), *Calendar of the Clarendon State Papers Preserved in the Bodleian Library* (5 vols, Oxford, 1869–1970), for example, repeatedly misidentifies Windebank's hand and even occasionally the King's (Bodl., MS Clarendon 25, fol. 147, letter to Prince Rupert of 14 September 1645, is not holograph).

5. Not all of these elements in manuscript production are relevant to this article, but for an example of watermark evidence, see letter from Charles to Henry Firebrace of 26 July 1648, which is on the same paper as a letter to Firebrace from Jane Whorwood of 27 July: given the closeness of the King's imprisonment, this seems particularly significant (BL, Egerton MS 1788, fols 36 and 38).

6. NAS, GD 229/4/35, 2 June 1630.

7. Charles Rogers (ed.), *The Earl of Stirling's Register of Royal Letters* (2 vols, Edinburgh, 1885), ii, p. 462; Maurice Lee Jr, *The Road to Revolution: Scotland under Charles I, 1625–37* (Urbana and Chicago: University of Illinois Press, 1985), pp. 99–104.

8. NAS, GD 220/4/36, 18 June 1630.

9. *Ibid.*, no. 37; a very similar statement is made in no. 36, with slight differences in wording.

10. Lee, *Road to Revolution*, p. 102.

11. *Ibid.*, pp. 102–5, 170–1; Kevin Sharpe, *The Personal Rule of Charles I* (New Haven and London: Yale University Press, 1992), pp. 250–2; Allan I. Macinnes, *Charles I and the Making of the Covenanting Movement, 1625–41* (Edinburgh: John Donald, 1991), pp. 108–13.

12. NAS, GD 220/4/43, 31 July 1631.

13. PRO, SP 16/203, fol. 84 (draft by Charles) and fol. 83 (minute by Coke), 19 November 1631.

14. I gave a preliminary paper on the case at the conference 'The 1630s: Interdisciplinary Approaches' (Keele University, 2002) which is being expanded into an article.

15. *Calendar of State Papers, Venetian Series 1629–32*, p. 523, 4 July 1631.

16. NAS, GD 406/1/159, 8 May 1632.

17. *Ibid.*, no. 160, 1 August 1632.

18 Sharpe, *Personal Rule of Charles I*, p. 180.
19 NAS, GD 220/4/49, 17 July 1632.
20 *Ibid.*, no. 52, 30 August 1632.
21 NAS, GD 220/5/65, 7 May 1633. The letter is signed and dated by Charles, but is otherwise scribal. For a clear account of this tangled plot, see Lee, *Road to Revolution*, pp. 119–25.
22 NAS, GD 406/1/154, 21 September 1631.
23 *Ibid.*, no. 153, 8 September 1631; Gilbert Burnet, *The Memoires of the Lives and Actions of James and William Dukes of Hamilton and Castleherald, &c* (London, 1677), sig. C4.
24 Conrad Russell has tentatively suggested that Charles may have used Christian names in letters only to recipients of royal blood (*The Fall of the British Monarchies 1637–1642* (Oxford: Clarendon Press, 1991), p. 55, n. 91); in fact he addressed both Henry Jermyn ('Harry') and Will Murray thus. Russell gives the incorrect impression that the King was still using Hamilton's Christian name at the end of the decade.
25 NAS, GD 406/1/158, 30 April 1632.
26 *Ibid.*, no. 161, 24 September 1632.
27 Archbishop Neile's certificate for dioceses in the charge of York in the year 1633 is in the state papers (PRO, SP 16/259, fols 167–72); Laud's for the years 1633–38 are printed in W. Scott and J. Bliss (eds), *The Works of the Most Reverend Father in God, William Laud* (7 vols, Oxford, 1847–60), v, part 2, pp. 317–70, from Lambeth MS 943; quotation taken from Neile's certificate, fol. 169.
28 Laud, *Works*, v, part 2, pp. 337–8, 355, 366.
29 Bodl., MS Clarendon 7, fol. 107v, 27 August 1635.
30 *Ibid.*, fol. 35, 6 August 1635.
31 Quoted in the *DNB* entry on Windebank as having been said by Sir Thomas Roe.
32 Bodl., MS Clarendon 10, fol. 64, 2 September 1636, apostiled 3 September.
33 Bodl., MS Clarendon 7, fol. 177, 21 October 1635.
34 Bodl., MS Clarendon 9, fol. 70, 18 May 1636; MS Clarendon 10, fol. 30v, 14 August.
35 Bodl., MS Clarendon 16, fol. 140v, 31 May 1639; MS Clarendon 17, fol. 35v, 9 July.
36 Bodl., MS Clarendon 9, fol. 96, 1 June 1636.
37 BL, Additional MS 24023, fol. 12, 2 June 1636. A second letter (fols 13–14, 18 October 1636) is concerned with details in clauses of the treaty under negotiation.
38 Bodl., MS Clarendon 9, fol. 97, 2 June 1636 (apostile on Windebank's letter of 1 June).
39 For details of the disagreement between Leicester and Scudamore, see Ian Atherton, *Ambition and Failure in Stuart England: The Career of John, First Viscount Scudamore* (Manchester: Manchester University Press, 1999), ch. 6, esp. pp. 187–92.
40 William Knowler (ed.), *The Earl of Strafforde's Letters and Dispatches* (2 vols, London, 1739), i, p. 365, 22 January 1635.
41 *Ibid.*, p. 233, 17 April 1634; and as note 36.
42 Knowler (ed.), *Strafforde's Letters*, i, p. 332, 23 October 1634; ii, p. 32, 3 September 1636.
43 *Ibid.*, ii, p. 244, 21 November 1638.

44 *Ibid.*, ii, p. 262, 28 December 1638.
45 Russell, *Fall of the British Monarchies*, p. 43.
46 NAS, GD 406/1/10480 and 10482.
47 *Ibid.*, no. 398, 9 September 1638.
48 *Ibid.*, no. 1030 (to the Archbishop of St Andrews, 6 August 1639); to Traquair: 1032 (20 August); 585 (with corrections by Charles, 4 September); 1031 (1 October).
49 Peter Donald, *An Uncounselled King: Charles I and the Scottish Troubles, 1637–1641* (Cambridge: Cambridge University Press, 1990), p. 203.
50 See, for example, NAS, GD 406/1/162, 8 November 1638, holograph letter of Charles to Hamilton, when he added in the margin 'the rest ye will fynd answered by my Lo: of Cant:'.
51 NAS, GD 406/1/10538, 7 April 1639.
52 Bodl., MS Clarendon 16, fol. 88, 20 April 1639.
53 In October 1639 Hamilton wrote to Windebank that the shortness of his letter would be excused by his 'lying in his Majesty's chamber' (*Calendar of State Papers, Domestic Series, 1639–40*, p. 22).
54 PRO, SP 16/427, fol. 97, 14 August 1639.
55 Bodl., MS Clarendon 14, fol. 167v, 22 September 1638.
56 NAS, GD 406/1/10541 and 10543: Hamilton to Charles, 15 April, Charles to Hamilton, 18 April 1639.
57 NAS, GD 406/1/809, 17 July 1639. The text is in Hamilton's hand, signed, dated and endorsed as being to the Marquis by Charles.
58 Bodl., MS Clarendon 14, fol. 156, 17 September 1638.
59 Bodl., MS Clarendon 17, fol. 31: Windebank to Charles, 6 July 1639, apostiled Berwick, 10 July.
60 *Ibid.*, fol. 38v: Windebank to Charles, 11 July 1639, apostiled 14 July.
61 NAS, GD 406/1/10508, 9 October 1638; 10514, 29 October; 10527, 7 December.
62 *Ibid.*, no. 10492, 25 June 1638; 10527, 7 December. As Shakespeare's usage in *Timon of Athens* shows (Act 1, scene 2, opening stage direction: 'Then comes ... Apemantus, discontented, like himself'), the phrase does not necessarily have martial connotations, but they may be implied in Charles's letters both from context and by allusion to the Prologue of *Henry V*.
63 Knowler (ed.), *Strafforde's Letters*, ii, p. 362, 30 June 1639.
64 NAS, GD 406/1/10550, 10 May 1639.
65 *Ibid.*, no. 10558, 13 May 1639; 10563, 2 June.
66 Bodl., MS Clarendon 16, fol. 174v, 8 June 1639.
67 NAS, GD 406/1/10565, 27 March 1640, to the Marquis of Douglas. A similar letter was sent to the Earl of Nithsdale.
68 Knowler (ed.), *Strafforde's Letters*, ii, p. 416, 23 April 1641.
69 Charles to Henrietta Maria, 14 January 1645 (House of Lords Record Office, Naseby Papers, no. 13).

Chapter 5

Henrietta Maria in the 1630s: perspectives on the role of consort queens in *Ancien Régime* courts

Caroline Hibbard

Henrietta Maria arrived in England as a girl of fifteen, intensively educated in her natal court of France for the role she took up as consort to Charles I. She joined the long succession of English consorts, whose lives and activities have attracted less attention than they deserve.[1] These women often deployed greater material resources, and enjoyed more visibility at court, than any other figure save the king. While the reign of Elizabeth I has been a magnet for students and the general reading public, our view of how courts functioned, and the role of women at them, has been seriously skewed by this anomalous and lengthy reign. In particular, the nature of Elizabeth's political role as the final arbiter of policy has meant that the political influence of consorts is usually, and usually unfairly, derided. We are only beginning to construct analytical tools for court history; and until that task is further advanced, we are apt to retreat instinctively into anachronistic views of what constituted the 'political' – focusing on what was debated in parliament or in the press, and neglecting underlying issues of patronage, appointments, and the control of money.

The historiography of Henrietta Maria reflects our failure to construct useful models for discussing consorts. The last biography of Henrietta Maria to incorporate substantial new research is from the 1970s; interesting work in several disciplines remains unrecognised in a recent popular biography.[2] A new paradigm is beginning to address the public import of apparently 'private' royal activities such as entertainments and artistic patronage, and will need to build a broader context for the issues of place, or appointment, at court, where the queen had well-recognised influence.[3] Earlier models for women's history, with their emphasis on struggle and on commoners, have been unhelpful for the study of elite women, and court women in particular. Although elite women's records have been underexplored, and in that sense they may be 'forgotten figures', the records are abundant. And despite the patriarchal structures within which they had to operate, elite women (and queens most of all) were guaranteed a place at court, indeed they were essential to court life; they scarcely had to elbow their way in. But, as always, our recognition of female agency needs to be accompanied by elaborations of how, in any particular historical situation, it operated.[4]

The chronological and cultural distances separating the Stuart consorts from their predecessors have inhibited comparative study. While work on medieval queens has progressed rapidly,[5] we have not always recognised the continuities in court life between the reign of Edward I and the late seventeenth century. And in the shorter range, over fifty years separated the last Tudor consort, Katherine Parr, from the arrival of the first Stuart consort, Anna of Denmark. In the meantime, the Reformation profoundly upset all the international relations of Europe, including dynastic constructions. It made of religion a divisive rather than an international unifying element.

Most relevant for Henrietta Maria, foreign-born queens consort scarcely form a class at all in early modern England. Anna of Denmark provides one previous post-Reformation model, but although close in time she was not in other ways entirely comparable.[6] When Charles himself, in an early marital spat, referred to his mother's establishment as a precedent for some economy he wished to impose on his wife, she indignantly replied that there was no comparison – Denmark was not France.[7] That Henrietta Maria was a daughter of France never for a day left her mind, although how it played out was fairly complex.

In fact, we have to go back over a hundred years to find a comparable figure to Henrietta, in Catherine of Aragon. She was another Catholic whose religion became a major issue; but because she was *less* politically effective – she did not help raise a civil war – and because she had a generous and learned biographer, she has had a very different historical afterlife.[8] Catherine's role in policy, her patronage of learning and the arts, her pride and independence, should all be remembered when we evaluate her successor, come to England from another superpower. In 1501 Catherine too had been a girl of fifteen. In 1509 Henry VIII, newly married, evinced at least as much ardour and attachment as Charles would display in 1628. For the first decade of his reign, the King discussed with her matters of statecraft and high policy; he trusted her advice in foreign affairs and received ambassadors in her chambers. But after 1525 she was in the political shadows.

By contrast, Henrietta's role increased after the first decade, and it is this that makes it so challenging to build a consort model from her career; for this royal marriage was as politically disastrous as it was personally successful. She was and is seen as an alien who fatally divided the King from his people, and contributed to the onset of the civil war. The Queen had a terrible press from the onset of the Long Parliament, straight through the civil war, and afterwards.[9] She has never really recovered from this early, politically motivated demonisation, which made her the quintessential evil counsellor – a foreign intruder, meddlesome, and wielding dangerous sexual power. The parliamentary attacks on the Queen found resonance on the other side, in the royalist and post-Restoration need for a scapegoat. This more traditionally political part of her story, which picks up in the late 1630s, is already familiar;[10] it has made it difficult to look at the earlier period. Even by her sympathisers, the Queen is viewed as a threat to her husband, a drain on his material resources and on his claim to the loyalty of his subjects – in short, a negative, a diminution of the King, and an ultimately fatal one.

By contrast, I will here concentrate on elements of commonalty, qualities and activities she shared with other consort queens whose ultimate impact was less dramatic, but who also mattered politically in the broader sense of influence over patronage, appointments and resources. In so doing, I will suggest that her very success at fulfilling her traditional roles was twisted against her in the accusations of her enemies, such was the fragility of consort reputations. Royal consorts could evoke responses rooted in misogyny and xenophobia, but they were also celebrated and welcomed as assets to the marital courts, providing numerous forms of amplification. Reigning queens might find themselves running a sort of men's club, where all the characteristic strengths – bold, incontrovertible, even brutally wilful leadership – were by definition male, but this particular paradox did not affect queens consort. Like the Queen of Heaven, who was ceaselessly invoked as their model, they were intercessors, conveyors of charity and mercy, and these traditional virtues outlasted the Marian imagery through which they were formerly elaborated. Their mediatory role was available because they were wives, and even more crucially mothers, of kings.[11]

In all these respects – fecundity, mediation and generosity – Henrietta Maria conformed to a positive model for queens consort, in opening up and strengthening the court of Charles I. The promise of fecundity was foreshadowed in the richness of material goods that she brought with her, as was the political and cultural connection with France. Cultural mediation would be played out in her extensive patronage of the arts and fine crafts – sometimes independent, sometimes joint with the King – while, finally, the existence of her court and later those of the royal children offered scope for queenly generosity, and amplified the opportunities for royal service, particularly for women. Only later would fecundity, mediation and generosity be caricatured as wantonness, foreign betrayal and arrogation of power.[12]

This amplification is symbolised by the new Queen's arrival – the baggage she brought with her. The wedding party (a flimsy word for what it was) was the transference of an auxiliary court across the Channel. Such bridal trips were deliberately lengthy (three to six weeks was common) and magnificent, with elaborate welcomings in cities along the way; the new queens arrived heavily laden, displaying on their person and in their train the splendour of the court from which they had come. In 1445 Margaret of Anjou, coming to marry Henry VI, had a train of 1,500 at the start of her journey and was accompanied by the French King; in passing through Paris she had been given relics from the treasury of Nôtre Dame. Catherine of Aragon had also come to the Channel edge in 1501, after a more than four-month journey, with a train composed of those who would see her on board, those who would cross and stay for the wedding, and those who would form a 'permanent household of some sixty persons', ranging from ladies to seamstresses, pages and cooks. Later, Anne of Cleves had a slow and expensive trip in a horse-drawn chariot similar to that used by Henrietta, with over 250 persons and almost as many horses; one-third of her attendants were to leave her at the shore, another forty or so would return from England after the wedding, and almost ninety remained in her household.[13]

And so with Henrietta Maria. French inventories show much of what went across with the French princess in the spring of 1625. She took boatloads of furnishings in an era when soft furnishings were literally the 'stuff of courts'.[14] There were chapel ornaments for the use of her Oratorians,[15] and household furniture for the twelve priests and their four servants. There were jewels entrusted to the Queen's *dame d'atour* (chamberwoman), stable supplies, and the many items of both furniture and textiles given by the King her brother: four 'chapelles' in velvet, and bedroom suites (as we would call them) for the Queen and half a dozen of her ladies, including bedsteads. There were toilet items, boxes for curling irons, bed and chapel linen, silver and gold plate for the chapel and the table (and a chamber pot), outfits for her pages, and of course rich clothing for the Queen.

The Queen, then, added to the materiality of the court, both with what she brought, and by her continued establishment there. If she added wealth to the court, a new queen was also expensive; but that was part of the point of acquiring her, like any work of art or piece of conspicuous consumption. She was a capital investment, and would provide generous yields. This was certainly, and importantly, the King's own view – Charles I's view. The court was enlarged by the presence of this human treasure, a princess of France, by the progenitive hopes she brought with her, and by the literal treasure she carried. A segment of the French court was transplanted to England, and this increased the political, social and cultural resources available to the English court. The project of the marriage would bring into being subsidiary projects shared by the royal couple.

Needless to say, the conversion of England was not one of these shared projects, although it was one that the young Queen cherished. Her husband quickly became impatient with the French priests surrounding her, and was glad enough to be able to expel them in 1626; but, unlike many of his subjects, the King did not object to his wife's religion as though it were a blemish on her. On the contrary, he facilitated her practice, and regarded this as a point of honour. He acceded, too often for political expediency, to her mediating efforts on behalf of co-religionists, but he blocked her attempts to convert his own children, and later famously told his eldest son to obey his mother in all saving religion. In general he treated her religion as her birthright, no more to be disparaged than her French and Italian parentage. The King's studied conversations with the papal agent George Con in the late 1630s suggest a man who thought it ungentlemanly to dispute in religion. Adherence to established religion was inseparable from the defence of established order, and religious conformity could not be separated from the rest of governance. Yet he felt a commitment to unity and tolerance, and would prefer that differences of religious opinion not affect his political or personal relationships.[16]

Most importantly, the King did not feel defiled by sexual intimacy with a daughter of Rome – the view that some of his subjects would come to take. In the eyes of the King and those who thought like him, Catholicism was not like pitch that dirtied and stuck.[17] At the centre of the court was a deeply charged sexual relationship between the King and a Catholic woman. In the eleven years from January 1630 to the end of 1640, the Queen was pregnant fully half the time – she again got pregnant soon after rejoining the King in 1643.[18] None of this suggests a sexually tepid marriage, despite one biographer's allegations to that effect.[19] The fervour began, unusually, not at the time of the marriage, but after Buckingham's death, when reports of court observers suggest sexual infatuation. After 1632 there were two healthy sons, and by 1635, as the Venetian ambassador reports on the latest birth, there is a hint in his tone that there is almost a superfluous fecundity in the royal family.[20]

This cross-confessional union was celebrated in entertainments that seem to point to larger political and religious opportunities. As the court was teased throughout the early and mid-1630s with discussions of possible reunion between England and Rome, so Erica Veevers has described how the court entertainments of that time evoked 'the common heritage of spiritual beauty which Anglicans and Catholics shared', celebrating in a quasi-religious manner the union between the King and the Queen.[21] Thus, in this interpretation, the entertainments were designed to suggest the possibility of harmonious relations between the faiths. Melinda Gough's recent re-examination of *Tempe Restored* has again emphasised its connection to an earlier tradition of eirenic or *politique* court ballets sponsored by Catherine de Medici in the 1580s.[22] A deliberate cosmopolitanism, with an eirenic overlay, also characterised a wider range of the Queen's artistic patronage than we have previously recognised.

In addition to the French version of the Counter-Reformation, Henrietta Maria imported a general programme for court life, based on her French experience and partly derived from the Italian models familiar to her mother. This is visible – barely, because of difficult sources – from her very arrival at court.[23] The thread was picked up after the Restoration: she returned to England then with an elaborate scheme for redoing the gardens at Greenwich based on Le Nôtre's work for the French King. John Peacock's studies of her early dealings with Inigo Jones have given us the clearest picture of the way in which Henrietta's taste, formed at the French court, immediately influenced the settings of court entertainments and the decoration of palaces. She appears as someone with firm ideas, if not yet a fully developed taste.[24]

Given her upbringing, this is not surprising. Marie de Medici, her mother, was one of the great patrons and rebuilders of Western Europe, and Henrietta had lived at her mother's court during the height of this activity.[25] The Luxembourg palace was partly complete by 1623, a banquet being held there in February 1624, and Rubens's Marie de Medici cycle was installed in the gallery in time for the celebrations honouring Henrietta's marriage in May 1625. The Luxembourg project involved not only architecture, but sculptural decoration inside and out, wall and ceiling paintings, elaborate interior painted decoration, hung paintings and tapestries.[26] Another image in Henrietta's mind as she left for England would have been that of her childhood residence St Germain: the palace and its gardens engraved themselves on her heart as models of rural pleasure that she would try to replicate in England. She came to England, then, with ideas about what courts, palaces and gardens should be like, and a determination to shape her new environment. All this casts doubt on a recent verdict that there is 'no reason to think that Henrietta Maria, who was then only fifteen years old, was at all informed about art'.[27] In regular contact with Jones and with other artistic intermediaries such as Nicholas Lanier and Endymion Porter, and with Van Dyck himself (for whom she sat, it is estimated, no fewer than twenty-five times in the eight years from 1632 to 1640), she would have had every opportunity to learn.

And however we evaluate her taste, there is little denying her energy. This is visible in a number of areas. She was the chief patron of architecture at the Caroline court. Of the dozen or so royal properties still used by the court at this time, a total of six palaces were in her jointure by 1630, while Wimbledon would be added in 1639. Only three palaces were clearly used by the King, and he pursued almost no building at these sites despite elaborate plans for one of them, Whitehall.[28] In contrast, the Queen set about remodelling and redecorating her palaces from an early date. Somerset House received immediate attention; work at Greenwich began soon after it was added to her jointure in 1629. Outside, she redesigned the palace gardens and stocked them with fruit trees and plants sent for from France. 'Claude de Molette', appointed 'new chief gardener' in December 1627 at a wage of £120 a year, would design a garden for the Queen at Wimbledon in the years just before the war.[29] Like so many of her other French employees, he seems to have migrated to the court after her arrival.

Her cultural activities before Buckingham's death should not be underestimated; her early entertainments and intervention in the Mantua art negotiations suggest she was invigorated by competition with Buckingham for the King's attention.[30] But there is no doubt of the watershed represented by the month of August 1628. This month saw both Buckingham's assassination and the arrival of much of the Mantuan collection – a coincidence not usually noticed. This is the month when the royal love affair began, and also an extraordinary period of artistic activity and planning at the court in much of which the Queen is likely to have been involved.[31] It is difficult to document her participation, but Orazio Gentileschi seems to provide an example. He had been at her mother's court in 1625, came to England in 1626, and after Buckingham's death, it would seem that his main patron was the Queen. Ultimately, he would do the ceiling painting for her great hall at Greenwich, as well as several pictures there.[32]

One aspect of the new-found intimacy between King and Queen, then, was their shared love of the arts, and desire to be honoured as patrons. In addition to her redoubtable mother, the Queen would have at court by 1628 another mature model (and perhaps advisor) for such activity; for after Buckingham's death the Earl and Countess of Arundel returned to England. Alathea Talbot Howard, Countess of Arundel, now recognised as a connoisseur and substantial patron of painting in her own right,[33] would later ally with the Queen in the project of the papal agency; but they may already have found a common interest in the fine arts.

The Queen's patronage of painting has been but partly explored, and it is difficult to extricate her commissions from those of the King.[34] But certainly her reputation as a patron would be greater had her husband not been such an extraordinary connoisseur. He chose to house a number of his acquisitions in her palace at Somerset House where he spent much time in her company, so there is a certain artificiality in separating their patronage. In particular, most of the sculpture and painting from Mantua was lodged at St James's, Somerset House, and later at Greenwich, as well as Whitehall. This, I would suggest, was a shared activity like the commissioning of masques and performing in them. In the 1630s, the exchange of agents with the papal court would be sweetened for the King by the access it provided to artists under Barberini patronage, all of this negotiated through the Queen and thus heightening her role.[35]

Even in the realm of visual arts, her patronage was not exclusively Catholic, but included associates of the Huguenot court physician Theodore de Mayerne, whom she steadfastly preferred (to the horror of the French court, who had tried to impose their Catholic doctor on her), such as the miniature-painters Jean Petitot and Jacques Bordier. In sculpture her activities as an individual patron and joint patron with the King are even clearer. The sculptor François Dieussart, originally brought to England by the Earl of Arundel, did substantial work at her renovated Somerset House chapel. Hubert Le Sueur was employed by both King and Queen by 1630; and in the mid-1630s was working extensively at Somerset House.[36]

A richly documented area of patronage is that of luxury goods, including clothes and furnishings. Already by March of 1628, the Queen's debts to 'tradesmen' amounted to £30,000;[37] these included jewellers, perfumers, and artists of various kinds, and provisioners of luxury foodstuffs and fine textiles. These craftspeople were predominantly French, but they had not come with the Queen; rather they belonged to the sizeable community of French artisans already established in London who found the Queen's favour without being formally attached to her household.[38] Her bills for dress and textiles – especially important when she was giving masques or giving birth – were very large through the 1630s; Gentile the embroiderer and Ralph Grynder the upholsterer appear regularly on her pension and payment records. Her tradesmen's bills reveal a steady commissioning of furniture, and the acquisitions of both King and Queen ended up mainly in her palaces.[39] Obviously, the furnishings were as shared as the palaces were. The King paid for many of them, and enjoyed them as he enjoyed the paintings from Mantua that he hung in those buildings; but this joint project of furnishing would have been deeply influenced by the Queen's tastes – and the money spent out of her own budget on such purchases suggest that this was a major interest for her.

But easily the most constant area of joint royal patronage was music. Unlike most of the artists and craftspeople, the musicians were in more or less continual service or attendance, members of the official royal households and receiving pensions and wages.[40] The composer, singer, and lutenist Nicholas Lanier was unusually versatile, in that he also became a trusted connoisseur and purchaser of paintings for the King. He was Master of the Musick to the King and directed some of the music in the Queen's masques. But he was archetypal of the Queen's musicians, and of the whole court milieu, in that he reflected both French and Italian cultural influences, negotiated between the French and English courts, served both King and Queen, was a naturalised foreigner, and held chamber appointments in addition to that of musician. Most of the musicians had a wide range of accomplishments, being singers, composers, and/or choreographers as well as instrumentalists.

Musicians had accompanied the Queen from France, to serve and honour her during her journey, but they were not intended to stay. For her new establishment, which never numbered more than fifteen, Henrietta could draw from a large stable of established royal servants, a number of whom, like Lanier and the organist and composer Richard Mico, were from families of French descent long living in London. She also added and recruited a few men of other nationalities, such as the Irish harpist Daniel Cahill – not all of them Catholic, for there was the noted German violist and composer Dietrich Stoeffken. The Master of the Queen's Music from 1625 to 1642 was Lewis Richard, who had also served Queen Anna in that post. Richard chose and trained the 'little singing boys', for the Queen's chapel. These, and the instrumentalists that he supervised in the chapel, also performed in masques, at dinner, and in small concerts.

During this reign the already significant number of French musicians in royal employ was accentuated, and Catholic musicians such as Mico and the organist and composer Richard Dering were attracted to the court, while the Queen's chapel provided a showcase for the latest in Catholic sacred compositions. In addition to the musicians, and of great importance in the masques, were the dancing masters/choreographers (usually also players and composers), of whom Henrietta had three, all French.[41] One of these – Jacques Boucan alias Cordier – had been moving between the English and French courts for years, while he and Simon de la Pierre had served the court in the previous reign. Both now served the King as well as the Queen; and La Pierre, who had been dancing master to King Charles when Prince of Wales, became dancing master to this next generation of royal children.[42] The place and use of dance at court suggests most strikingly the futility of trying to isolate the King's and the Queen's patronage, and encourages us to see, as typical also in the visual arts and fine crafts, a model of joint activity if not formal patronage.

From the moment of her arrival, the Queen was a new and potent player in the luxury market, patronising foreign craftsmen and popularising foreign fashions. Her expenditures sustained many in the capital city; when it seemed the Queen would be leaving London in 1642, a number of tradeswomen petitioned that she might stay, for without her custom, they claimed they and their families would be ruined.[43] Yet by then she was already becoming a symbol of wanton extravagance, almost a thief, whose trip to Holland in 1642 to pawn items of royal jewellery would be pilloried in the parliamentary press as the sale of the 'crown jewels.'[44]

This pervasive French cultural influence at the court did not, however, translate into any predictable or sustained pro-French foreign policy.[45] The English court was rather preoccupied with, than allied with, the French through much of this period. Our understanding of the Queen's position vis-à-vis foreign policy has been bedevilled by anachronisms and credulous readings of French reports. French ambassadors had privileged access to court because of the Queen; they could attend her informally, as emissaries from her brother, and this provided opportunities for discussion with the King. But this did not have the consequences hoped for by the French government; and there are successive ambassadorial reports excusing how little their access yielded for French policy. They variously attributed this to Henrietta's immaturity and frivolity, or to her failure to understand what was at stake. These comments have formed the basis for far too many generalisations about her indifference to 'politics', and create a misleading chronology for her life and outlook, according to which she only begins to focus on the real business of politics as the Scottish crisis develops, and then becomes in the 1640s, as is clear in the correspondence of that decade, an indefatigable politician.

In fact, the Queen was always energetically loyal to France, by which she would have understood, primarily, the French royal family and its associates. She had been manifestly unhappy during the Anglo-French war of the 1620s, and showed no pleasure at the English peace with Spain in 1630. But the key to her activities and attitudes is the Day of Dupes of 10 November 1630, which turned her mother into an exile from France, usually entertained at courts hostile to the French government, while her brother Louis XIII continued to rule under the dominance of Richelieu. The French ambassadors sent to England thereafter were agents of Richelieu, and Henrietta Maria did not view his aims as necessarily corresponding to the best interests of France. Ambassadors always need explanations for their failures; and it is hardly surprising that those from France put her antipathy to Richelieu's interests down to ignorance or immaturity.

But as Malcolm Smuts detailed in 1978, she had shown herself a determined intriguer as early as 1629 – first against the Anglo-Spanish peace, then in various movements of opposition to Richelieu.[46] Her allies were a varied group including some English courtiers, and Richelieu's enemies at the French court or in exile; until the late 1630s they never included Spanish agents or pro-Spanish courtiers. Until 1635 the chief figure at court associated with a policy of friendship with Spain was the Earl of Portland, whom she detested; and she voiced hostility to other courtiers such as Windebank precisely because they were 'Spanish'. The 'puritan party' which Smuts delineated, the great courtiers clustered around her in the early 1630s, favoured a sea war against Spain and its concomitant, the calling of parliament.

Moreover, she was not isolated from French persons and influences even during the Anglo-French war of the 1620s. Historians have, in this matter, adopted the perspective of contemporary Englishmen about the French in her household: that in the beginning there were far too many, then they were expelled, after which there were almost none. The only lay persons usually mentioned in print are the Queen's chamberwoman Mme de Vantelet, and her old nurse Françoise Garnier; but there were many more. In fact, after the summer 'expulsion' of 1626 – itself an only more raucous version of a queen's traditional farewell to those of the natal court – there remained twenty or so French in chamber positions, who enjoyed a more than proportional share of the Queen's pension allowance. In the household 'below stairs' there were also the Queen's French cooks, and in some antechamber her dressmakers, all of them brought with her and retained for decades.

After 1626 the French lay element in the household was primarily a family constellation of the Vantelets and the Garniers, built around the Queen's French women. Because it was that, it reflected the influence of Marie de Medici, who had installed these families in the households of her children decades before. Unlike most of the ecclesiastics in her household, therefore, who were close to Richelieu's government right up to 1642, Henrietta's lay servants (like the Queen herself) had divided loyalties after the falling out between the Queen Mother and Richelieu. Throughout the 1630s, French government agents would attempt to exert leverage through the Vantelet family and others in the Queen's circle who were vulnerable to pressure because of their relatives in the French court. The French derived little more than information about the court; but their efforts helped sustain a constant and sometimes intense cross-Channel traffic. Some of the Queen's French servants are known mainly through the passes for travel issued to them, as they tended to their business in Paris and did the Queen's errands.

This Anglo-French exchange did not end with the outbreak of war in 1642; Henrietta's exile and court in Paris were a focus for royalists. And this constant cultural connection had a lasting impact on the Stuarts and on portions of English society. As the Queen's religious practice influenced her sons, making their conversion a real and ultimately winning option, so the Queen's cultural orientation, which made the English court in the 1630s a place drenched in French influences and full of French persons, laid a foundation for her sons' experiences of the Interregnum and for some of the choices they would later make.

The consort amplified the court not only by her magnificence, consumption and exercise of cultural patronage, not only by the intensification of international contacts that she enabled, but also by the sheer addition of places, and especially places for women. The presence of a consort pointed up the court's important function as a marriage market, and provided unusual scope for female entrepreneurship. Subsidiary courts always opened up new worlds of place, attractive to aristocrats for the honour, the chance for profit, and the opportunity to help friends and family.[47] Only a minority were interested in what we would recognise as 'policy' issues. The enlargement of numbers through a subsidiary court helped to sop up the incessant aristocratic demand for place that always exceeded supply in the seventeenth century. As John Plumb pointed out, the seventeenth-century court 'could not satisfy the aspirations, social or pecuniary, of a political nation that was constantly growing in size and authority'; but until the Glorious Revolution it still remained the sole institution that could provide that 'sense of possession' that underlay political stability.[48]

That this queen too would provide a wealth of new opportunity was never doubted. The departure of the French was long anticipated. Entries in the Lord Steward's books in early 1626 show that servants of James and Anna were hanging around waiting for places, and a number of 'supernumeraries' were appointed until slots fell vacant.[49] If there was unwillingness to serve the new Queen on grounds of religion, the records are silent on this, although some non-courtiers may have been deflected from seeking out her court for this reason.

Courts were always sites for elite female activity, but the space available to them varied. The consort court provided more positions for women, special perquisites for them, and a constant ritual display of the court's function as a marriage market in the appearance and activities of the maids of honour. Moreover, most of the 1630s were a time of peace; and times of peace highlighted the activities in which court women always played a major role – entertainments, marriage negotiations, and the daily ritual of the palace. Every royal ceremony was an occasion for the distribution of gifts and leftovers,[50] and each royal lying-in brought substantial rewards in kind to the closer attendants. In such a milieu the domestic and the public were thoroughly intertwined, and where this is the case the status of women is typically higher.

The full official household of the Queen numbered over 200; and men filled almost all the most important offices.[51] Men also filled all of the lesser courtly, and most of the menial, jobs. After 1626, the men and women of the household were chiefly English and Scottish, in three main groupings: English families that went back to the Tudor household in royal service; Scottish families that had come in with James I and Anna of Denmark, and who descended on the new Queen immediately the French were gone; and, finally, the Villiers connection.

Despite the dominant role of males in the formal governance of the household and the supervision of its revenue, only a handful of men had as much daily access to the Queen as did the ten or so women who at any one time were in official attendance on her.[52] These were Susan Feilding, Countess of Denbigh, her Mistress of the Robes, Lady Thomasina Carew, Keeper of the Sweet Coffers, and (at any one time) three to six 'chamberers' (married ladies of the bedchamber) and three to six maids of honour. These were the women whose access to the Queen, and through her to the King, gave them access also to numerous perquisites. In some cases they literally lived off the King and Queen.[53] They were frequently the recipients of handsome monetary gifts, as well as pensions of £300 or more per annum. When the maids of honour married, in alliances often arranged or at least facilitated by the King and Queen, they could expect large wedding gifts or expensive jewellery from the royal couple.[54] Yet none of these court women, apart from the Countess of Feilding and one or two of her daughters, is ever mentioned by name in the biographies of the Queen, and they seldom appear in literary primary sources. But they provided the constant milieu in which the Queen and her family moved, and their destinies clearly mattered to a solicitous King who arranged marriages, offered princely gifts, and stood godfather to several children. They were part of the common enterprise of the royal couple.

The household women included numerous French chamberers over the years, three of them married to Englishmen,[55] but few Scots apart from the Countess of Roxburgh. The other women at the Queen's court were English, most of them the sisters or daughters not of the great nobility, but of the courtier families with whom Charles I had grown up. Here were a few chamberers, and many maids of honour, such as Anne and Elizabeth Killigrew, from a family that had provided three generations of courtiers. Two of the English maids of honour married Scots in the king's chamber during the 1630s, both remaining as chamberers for the Queen after their marriage.[56] The royal couple's patronage and generosity brought place and profit to these women and their families, and also served the end of initiating or sustaining strands in the crisscrossing dynastic alliances at the court. They exemplify two patterns, both encouraged by King and Queen: members of their respective households marrying each other, and the French marrying into English gentry.

A final and crucial element among the women was added by the Villiers connection, whose court position was kept alive in the 1630s by Susan Feilding, Countess of Denbigh. She was the late Buckingham's sister and worked in consort with her son-in-law James, Marquis of Hamilton. The King bore a constant affection to Susan Feilding, and the prominence she enjoyed from the beginning of the reign – she was one of those who went to meet the new Queen at Dover – was not substantially diminished after Buckingham's death. Her access to the King seems to have been independent first of her brother, then of the Queen. In 1639 the Venetian ambassador commented on the King's attitude to the Countess and the Marquis of Hamilton, 'for both of whom the king has a singular affection'.[57]

The Countess was politically astute, a real court entrepreneur. Her position in the Queen's household and the favour she enjoyed enabled her to control large sums of money and to have a say in the composition of the female side of the court. The latter role is especially evident in the appointment of maids of honour, many of whom are part of the family or its clientele. Elizabeth Beaumont, 'mother of the maids' until the mid-1630s, was one such. Eleanor Villiers was maid of honour from 1630 to 1634, when – having fallen from honour with at least one (and allegedly half a dozen) men of the court – she was sent packing. Among the maids of honour were also two of the Countess's nieces, Elizabeth and Goodeth Arden, and two young daughters of Lucy, Viscountess Falkland, who had been taken under her wing.

The Countess enjoyed a central role in the Queen's household by virtue of her office as Mistress of the Robes, a position she held from 1627 to the outbreak of civil war. Of the Queen's estimated £20,000 per year budget, £4,000 was allotted to the Robes, an additional £500 to linen, and £4,000 to the privy purse. A large part of all these funds passed through the Countess's hands, as we can see from the Signet Office docquet books.[58] An annual £2,500 allocated to New Year's gifts distributed by the Queen also fell partly under her control; she signed the lists of arrears and of additions. One way or the other she had access to up to two-thirds of the Queen's declared income; the remaining amount, over £7,000 for wages and pensions, not infrequently fell in arrears, and special pleading might be necessary to extract the money from the Exchequer – pleading of the sort for which she was well placed.

There were additional sources of potential revenue for her, in the provision of furniture and jewellery to the royal couple – 'a rich bedstead and furniture' in November 1629 at £1,500, repaid by the Queen's special request, £250 for a diamond in March 1631, £2,000 for furnishing the Queen's bedchamber and nursery in 1633.[59] The Queen's 'lying-ins' were occasions for large additional sums of expenditure for linens and physicians – £2,000 in 1630 for the birth of Charles, Prince of Wales, lesser sums for the children who followed. The Countess's husband, the Earl of Denbigh, was Master of the Wardrobe for the King, a position analogous to her own; but when she used an intermediary with the King, she turned not to her husband, but to Hamilton, or occasionally one of the men of the king's bedchamber. The pivotal and powerful role of the departments of the Wardrobe and the Robes is exemplified also in a later reign, when Sarah, Duchess of Marlborough was Mistress of the Robes to Queen Anne, as well as Groom of the Stole (head of the queen's bedchamber) and keeper of her Privy Purse.[60]

It is in family papers and the financial records of the court – not the printed literary records on which so many royal and court biographies have been based – that we discover that the Countess of Denbigh was a figure at least as important as her husband in the court world, as well as the clearly dominant figure in the household of Henrietta Maria. Mistress of the Queen's purse strings, advancing her son in the larger court and her female relatives and dependents within the Queen's household and in the marriage market – she emerges as a powerful figure in her own right.

The world of the court ladies was one where private lives were led in public and were part of the stuff of public life – where dynastic arrangements and patronage networks, as well as a role in the theatre of the court, were available to and manipulated by women. It was a greatly intermarried world in which both males and females made decisions in terms of family interests as much as individual preferences. It was a world of conspicuous consumption in which women were important spenders and controllers of purse strings, until 1638 when it began to be a world gearing up for war. There was, of course, no sharp break or rapid redirection of resources; Charles I famously continued to pay off debts to painters when he needed to furnish his armies for his own literal survival. Nevertheless, the pattern of patronage shifted dramatically when the King began to mobilise – those who could raise men, arms and supplies for the King began to edge out the diamond-sellers and linen-suppliers among the King's creditors. A court on a war footing was a milieu offering very different opportunities often to a different range of entrepreneurs.

The peacetime Caroline court before 1638 was full of ambition, and its dynamics can only partially be understood in terms of faction defined around policy. It was at least as much about place and its perquisites, and about the direct and indirect control of money.[61] Some of the structures of the court that have been sketched in above deserve more attention: the court as marriage market, advancing dynasties and creating alliances; the court as a cosmopolitan site of consumption and display, where large resources are deployed and controlled; the court as the fount of honour, where there is constant jostling for the appointment, the 'place', that carries both tangible and intangible rewards. In this perspective on the court, the consort's court would loom a good deal larger than it traditionally has.

NOTES

1 But see Margaret Howell, *Eleanor of Provence* (Oxford: Blackwell, 1998), John Carmi Parsons, *Eleanor of Castile* (New York: St Martin's, 1995), and especially Eric Ives, *Anne Boleyn* (Oxford: Blackwell, 1996). There is also a growing body of work on Scottish consorts, mainly medieval, e.g. Lois L. Huneycutt, *Matilda of Scotland* (Woodbridge: Boydell Press, 2003). This paper will not attempt to deal with Scottish consorts apart from Henrietta.

2 Alison Plowden, *Henrietta Maria: Charles I's Indomitable Queen* (Stroud: Sutton, 2001); cf. Quentin Bone, *Henrietta Maria: Queen of the Cavaliers* (Urbana: University of Illinois Press, 1972). See, for example, Sophie Tomlinson, '"She that plays the king": Henrietta Maria and the threat of the actress in Caroline culture', in Gordon McMullan and Jonathan Hope (eds), *The Politics of Tragicomedy: Shakespeare and After* (London: Routledge, 1992), pp. 189–207; H. Maddicott, 'The provenance of the "Castle Howard" version of Orazio Gentileschi's *Finding of Moses*', *The Burlington Magazine*, 140 (1998), 120–2; and Jonathan P. Wainwright, *Musical Patronage in Seventeenth-Century England* (Aldershot: Scolar Press, 1997).

3 For the former, see Erica Veevers, *Images of Love and Religion: Queen Henrietta Maria and Court Entertainments* (Cambridge: Cambridge University Press, 1989), and Clare McManus (ed.), *Women and Culture at the Courts of the Stuart Queens* (Basingstoke: Palgrave, 2003).

4   See Barbara J. Harris, *English Aristocratic Women 1450–1550* (Oxford: Oxford University Press, 2002), ch. 1.

5   Clarissa Campbell Orr, review of conference 'Medieval queenship' in *Court Historian*, 3:3 (December, 1998), 31–4. The essay volumes edited by John Carmi Parsons, *Medieval Queenship* (Stroud: Sutton, 1994) and Anne J. Duggan, *Queens and Queenship in Medieval Europe* (Woodbridge: Boydell & Brewer, 1997), with their associated bibliographies, are crucial resources.

6   Leeds Barroll's recent work on the Queen (*Anna of Denmark, Queen of England: A Cultural Biography*, Philadelphia: University of Pennsylvania Press, 2001) does something to elucidate the continuity of her cultural concerns and political ambitions across her successive careers in Scotland and England. Unfortunately it attempts to reconstruct her 'court' with no reference to the records of her household, relying instead on literary sources of greatly varying reliability. The best account of Anna's household is still the short section in Linda Levy Peck, *Court Patronage and Corruption in Early Stuart England* (Boston: Unwin Hyman, 1990), pp. 68–74.

7   C[alendar of] S[tate] P[apers] Ven[etian] 1626, p. 497.

8   Garrett Mattingly, *Catherine of Aragon* (Boston: Little, Brown, 1941), pp. 19–22, 119–40, for the following.

9   Caroline Hibbard, 'Henrietta Maria', *Oxford Dictionary of National Biography* (Oxford: Oxford University Press, 2004).

10 Caroline Hibbard, *Charles I and the Popish Plot* (Chapel Hill: University of North Carolina Press, 1983).

11 Gordon Kipling, *Enter the King* (Oxford: Clarendon Press, 1998), ch. 6.

12 Michelle White, 'Meddlesome Henrietta Maria' (PhD dissertation, York University, Canada, 2001), provides the best account of the propaganda of the 1640s. Dr White is preparing her work for publication.

13 Philippe Erlanger (trans. E. Hyams), *Margaret of Anjou, Queen of England* (Coral Gables: University of Miami Press, 1970), pp. 66–74; Mattingly, *Catherine of Aragon*, pp. 21–2; Retha Warnick, *The Marrying of Anne of Cleves* (Cambridge: Cambridge University Press, 2000), p. 116.

14 BL, Royal MS 136, fols 412–61 for transcripts of the inventories. See Kristin Neuschel, 'Noble households in the sixteenth century', *French Historical Studies*, 15 (1988), 595–622.

15 The Oratorians were a post-Reformation congregation of secular priests, founded in Italy and especially active in seventeenth-century France, where Richelieu's first 'grey eminence', Cardinal Pierre de Berulle (d. 1629), was their head.

16 The Queen's Chamberlain Dorset provides a similar model; see D. L. Smith 'Catholic, Anglican or puritan? Edward Sackville, fourth Earl of Dorset, and the ambiguities of religion in early Stuart England', in D. Hamilton and R. Strier (eds), *Religion, Literature and Politics in Post-Reformation England* (Cambridge: Cambridge University Press, 1996), p. 126.

17 A helpful analogy offered by Dr Pauline Croft during a question period at the conference 'Fornicating with the nine muses: the cultural patronage of William Cavendish', Oxford University, May 2002. See R. P. Cust and P. G. Lake, 'Sir Richard Grosvenor and the rhetoric of magistracy', *Bulletin of the Institute of Historical Research*, 40 (1981), 42–8, on popery as toxic.

18 Catherine of Aragon was also pregnant almost continually for the first nine years of her marriage; see Mattingly, *Catherine of Aragon*, p. 139.
19 Charles Carlton, *Charles I, the Personal Monarch* (2nd edition, London: Routledge, 1995), p. 107.
20 *CSP Ven 1633–36*, p. 501.
21 Veevers, *Images of Love and Religion*, pp. 174, 175–8, and ch. 6. For the reunion discussions, Hibbard, *Charles I and the Popish Plot*, pp. 38–51.
22 Melinda Gough, '"Not as myself": the Queen's voice in *Tempe Restored*', *Modern Philology*, 101 (2003), 48–67.
23 Caroline Hibbard, 'Translating royalty: Henrietta Maria and the transition from princess to queen', in *Court Historian*, 5:1 (May, 2000), 15–28.
24 John Peacock, 'The French element in Inigo Jones's masque designs', in David Lindley (ed.), *The Court Masque* (Manchester: Manchester University Press, 1984), esp. pp. 154–9. See also John Peacock, *The Stage Designs of Inigo Jones: The European Context* (Cambridge: Cambridge University Press, 1995).
25 In addition to this artistic patronage, Marie de Medici provided a model for her daughter as patron and participant in masques; Karen Britland traces the lineage of queenly iconography from Italy through France to England, and dissects its ambiguities, in 'An under-stated mother-in-law: Marie de Médicis and the last Caroline court masque', in McManus (ed.), *Women and Culture at the Courts of the Stuart Queens*.
26 On the Luxembourg, see Deborah Marrow, *Art Patronage of Marie de Medici* (Ann Arbor: UMI Research Press, Studies in Baroque Art History, no. 4, 1982), pp. 20–1, 39.
27 Jeremy Wood, 'Orazio Gentileschi and some Netherlandish artists in London', *Simiolus*, 28:3 (2000–01), 120.
28 On the palaces, see Arthur MacGregor (ed.), *The Late King's Goods: Collections, Possessions and Patronage of Charles I in the Light of the Commonwealth Sale Inventories* (Oxford: Oxford University Press and London: Alistair McAlpine, 1989), ch. 1.
29 A son of the man who had designed royal gardens at the French palaces of her youth. Roy Strong, *The Renaissance Garden in England* (London: Thames and Hudson, 1979), pp. 161, 186–97.
30 Michael I. Wilson, *Nicholas Lanier: Master of the King's Musick* (Aldershot: Scolar Press, 1994), p. 113. Marie de Medici had been angling to get part of the Mantuan collection.
31 The cataloguing of the King's paintings and other art objects was undertaken at this time, under the direction of Inigo Jones and Nicholas Lanier. See also Hibbard, 'Translating royalty', *passim*.
32 Most of his English production was in her lodgings by the end of the 1630s. Among the Gentileschi works is a *Finding of Moses* that seems to signify her own sense of mission about bringing true religion to England; she later took it to France, to the house in which she died. Gabriele Finaldi (ed.), *Orazio Gentileschi at the Court of Charles I* (London: National Gallery, 1999), pp. 24–32.
33 David Howarth, 'The patronage and collecting of Aletheia, Countess of Arundel, 1616–54', *Journal of the History of Collections*, 10:2 (1998), 125–37. Henrietta is known to have frequented Arundel House by December 1628.

34 Van Dyck's appointment in 1632 was as 'Principal Painter in Ordinary to their Majesties': Oliver Millar, *Van Dyck in England* (London: National Portrait Gallery, 1982), pp. 17–22, 34–5. By 1641 there was a keeper of the pictures for 'the queen's side', Daniel Soreau; see O. Millar, *A. van der Doort's Catalogue of the Collections of Charles I* (London: Walpole Society, 37, 1958–60), p. xvi.

35 The shipment arrived while Henrietta was lying in at St James's after the birth of Elizabeth, and the King had the pictures unpacked in her room. The absence of any 'pious subjects' apparently disappointed her, and was cited by Wood, 'Orazio Gentileschi', as evidence of her superficial tastes – I think unjustly, and based on dismissive comments by the eighteenth-century editor of Panzani's memoirs. Against this, we should note Panzani's report that the Leonardo was 'especially pleasing to her'.

36 Le Sueur had been serving the French Crown for at least a decade. For the suggestion that either Buckingham or the Queen enticed him to England, see A. MacGregor, 'King Charles I: a Renaissance collector?', *The Seventeenth Century*, 11:2 (1996), p. 157, n. 33.

37 PRO, LR 5/57, fol. 10v.

38 The household lists are the annual 'establishment books' that give names, positions and compensation. Of craftspeople, only William Petit the clockmaker is on any such list. Many more were listed as pensioners, such as 'the Queen's silkman', and others.

39 MacGregor (ed.), *Late King's Goods*; the title should include queen and prince, but it would have been unwieldy; the act authorising this survey specified: 'Act for sale of the goods and personal estate of the late King, Queen and Prince'. In most of this work, all the palaces are described as 'the King's palaces'. Of the thirty-six most valuable cabinets, thirty-one were at Somerset House alone; all the listed marble tables were at her palaces.

40 I am preparing an article on the Queen's music and musicians, expanding on the material in these paragraphs.

41 These figures are not on the official establishment lists, but are identified in multiple other reliable sources.

42 B. De Montagut, *Louange de la Danse*, ed. B. Ravelhofer (Renaissance Texts from Manuscript, no. 3, 2000) for information on court choreographers.

43 *The Humble Petition of many Thousands of Courtiers, Citizens, Gentlemens and Tradesmens Wives ... 10 of February 1641* (London, 1641[2]; Wing T1628).

44 Every English ruler pawned or sold some jewellery and commissioned more. The 'crown jewels' in the sense of the regalia were untouched until a parliamentary committee desecrated them several years later. See R. Lightbown, 'The King's regalia, insignia and jewellery', in MacGregor (ed.), *Late King's Goods*, pp. 267–8.

45 See my article 'A cosmopolitan court in a confessional age', in R. Corthell, F. Dolan, C. Highley and A. Marotti (eds), *Catholic Culture in Early Modern England* (forthcoming, Notre Dame Press).

46 R. Malcolm Smuts, 'The puritan followers of Henrietta Maria in the 1630s', *English Historical Review*, 93 (1978), 26–45.

47 R. Malcolm Smuts, 'Art and the material culture of majesty', in R. Malcolm Smuts, (ed.), *The Stuart Court and Europe: Essays in Politics and Political Culture* (Cambridge: Cambridge University Press, 1996), pp. 88–90; Robert O. Bucholz, *The Augustan Court* (Stanford: Stanford University Press, 1993), pp. 136, 149; Harris, *English Aristocratic Women*, pp. 3–15.

48 J. H. Plumb, *Growth of Political Stability in England 1675–1725* (London: Macmillan, 1967), p. 112.
49 PRO, LS 13/168, fols 272–95.
50 Jennifer Loach, 'The function of ceremonial in the reign of Henry VIII', *Past and Present*, 142 (February 1994), 45–55.
51 Chamberlain, secretary, treasurer, and members of the council that managed her financial affairs.
52 I distinguish the paid members of her household, who appear on the establishment lists, from the female aristocrats, mainly countesses, styled 'ladies of the bedchamber', a position unknown to the establishment books. These ladies were sworn in, and might even have rooms provided at court, but were unpaid. They could also find themselves thrust out suddenly, as happened with the Countess of Carlisle.
53 The Earl and Countess of Monmouth had served Queen Anna; he lamented that Anna's death cost them £1,000 a year because they now had to keep house for themselves and dependents, whereas formerly they had 'lived at no great charge': Robert Carey, *Memoirs of Robert Carey, Earl of Monmouth*, ed. F. H. Mares (Oxford: Clarendon Press, 1972), p. 76.
54 PRO, SO 3/8–12 (Signet Office docquet books 1624–42).
55 Marie Smith, 'underchamberer'; Chrestienne Vantelet married into the recusant Shelley family; Katherine Garnier married Thomas Arpe, Provider of the Robes.
56 Elizabeth Ashburnham married Patrick Maule, and Anne Killigrew married George Kirke.
57 *CSP Ven 1640–42*, p. 4.
58 PRO, SO 3/8–12.
59 PRO, SO 3/9 (November 1629); SO 3/10 (March 1631, October 1633).
60 Bucholz, *Augustan Court*, pp. 44, 50, 72–5. Sarah was Mistress of the Robes 1702–11.
61 Menna Prestwich, *Cranfield: Politics and Profits under the Early Stuarts* (Oxford: Clarendon Press, 1966) explored the profit to be made of office, setting a standard few biographers of other officeholders have been able to match.

Chapter 6

'The faction of the flesh': orientalism and the Caroline masque

James Knowles

The various forms of early modern orientalism and the masque have a long, interconnected history. From the earliest days of the Tudor masked entry, through the Elizabethan mask, the adopted disguises often included Turkish costumes or Persian robes. Indeed, the first masque of the Jacobean period was a masque of Indian Princes and a Chinese magician fabulously attired in 'loose robes of crimson satin embroidered with gold and bordered with broad silver laces, doublets and bases of cloth of silver, buskins, swords, and hats alike, and in their hats each of them an Indian bird for a feather, with some jewels'.[1] The geographical range encompassed by this orientalism, collapsing Near and Far East, apparently demonstrates how western imaginings of the orient confirm Edward Said's argument that Islamophobic western ideology created a monolithic and homogenised 'Orient'. Yet, in the 1630s, the trading, diplomatic and cultural connections in the east with a variety of regimes, including the Turkish and Persian sultanates, the Mogul princes of India and the principalities of the East Indies and even the imperial Chinese system, created a far subtler range of images and ideas about the east. These images combined direct observation from travel with long-accepted tropes from classical, Biblical and later sources, drawing upon the emerging ability to read indigenous descriptions and opinions as skills in Arabic and other Near Eastern languages developed.[2]

The high point of Caroline court orientalism, Davenant's *The Temple of Love* (1635), known to its contemporaries as 'the Queen's Masque of Indianes', illuminates the complexity of early modern responses to the orient, simultaneously deploying recognisably orientalist tropes alongside a more nuanced understanding of the east.[3] Most commentary on this masque emphasises its significance for the codification of courtly Platonism,[4] quarrels over the masquing personnel (notably the non-involvement of Lady Carlisle),[5] the gender politics of its presentation,[6] or the possible allegorical significance of the arriving Persian youths,[7] but little has been said about its eastern setting. In the only treatment of this aspect of *The Temple of Love* Stephen Orgel, who calls the masque a 'Persian entertainment', argues that the text allies 'Caroline reforms with the world of regenerative mysteries and epiphanies' without using contemporary knowledge of Persia to shape either the conception or design of the masque.[8] Certainly the term 'Indian' could cover a wide range of locations in the early modern period and Davenant's masque mixes Persians, Indian figures, and more general eastern imagery. Without denying the orientalist possibilities of this term, or that Davenant and Jones drew upon standard European iconographical sources for their 'eastern' imagery, this chapter shows how the Persian element in particular has a precise significance for Caroline interpretations of the orient. Within an orientalist text, this specificity complicates other images of the east, particularly the Turkish east, offering a reformed orientalism with particular resonances for the Caroline court.

The Persian specificity of *The Temple of Love* and the series of intertexts and commercial and cultural relations it suggests also highlight the complexity of early modern responses to the orient. Since its publication in 1978 most critical studies of western engagements with the east – and particularly the Near East – have been dominated by Said's 'Orientalism'; however, in the last few years scholars, especially those working in the early modern period, have begun to question the applicability of Said's characterisation of western approaches to the east.[9] Recent discussions of early modern orientalist writings question, particularly, the ahistoricism of Saidian orientalism, and Jerry Brotton, surveying the complex interactions of Europe with the Ottomans, has argued that 'To place the Ottoman beyond the remit of the development of early modern Europe is to emplot a much later geopolitical shift.'[10] Earlier J. H. Elliott commented that early modern 'insensitivity to the otherness of the Other', often seen as central tenet of orientalism, marks the 'different set of goals from our own', in which observers 'were struggling to discover resemblances not differences ... It was brothers not others, whom they wished to find.'[11] Indeed, Anthony Parr has argued that Persia, in particular, was 'not so much Europe's Other as its opposite or foil' and 'while the fascination with the glamorous east was later to become a disabling orientalism ... it was during the early modern period a positive alternative to views of Asia as either the home of barbarian hordes or the hellish doctrine of Islam.'[12] Several early modern scholars have suggested alternative terms for these complex engagements with oriental cultures, such as 'Arabism', or 'Ottomanism', used recently to describe the 'imperial envy' felt by English travellers who regarded the Ottoman empire as a potential model for nascent British imperialism.[13]

Although some of these discriminations about Asia were motivated by a desire to divide and rule, separating Sunni (Turkish) and Shi'ite (Persian) Muslims, the awareness of localised difference also belongs to the process of 'mutual adaptations' and 'interactive emergence' that characterised the developing trading and political systems both in the Persian Gulf and in the Indian Ocean and Far East.[14] One recent discussion of Edward Terry's accounts of his time at the Mughal court has commented that early travellers were not simply 'agents of an incipient colonial ideology', but rather 'they frequently appear as complex historical subjects struggling to interpret a different culture that challenges the stable categories and assumptions of English cultural and religious identity.'[15]

Caroline orientalist thought, then, differs from Saidian orientalism whilst also containing a proto-orientalism. Images of the exotic, luxurious, glamorous east, co-existed with more precise and specified recognitions of the differences in the east. In the case of Persia, in particular, a discourse around the typical oriental body, luxurious, sexualised, effeminate, and dangerous, jostled with images of austerity and virtue, a mixture found in the responses to Persia inscribed in Thomas Herbert's *A Description of the Persian Monarchy now beinge the Oriental Indyes, Iles and other Parts of the Greater Asia and Africk* (1634).[16] Most famously, however, one of the main early modern figures associated with the Near East, Sir Anthony Sherley, described Persia as 'differing so much from that which we call barbarousnesse ... it may iustly serue as great an *Idea* for a Principality, as Platoes Commonwealth did for a Government.'[17]

The Temple of Love exploits the doubleness of Caroline interpretations of Persia, presenting both the proto-orientalist reading of the Persian body alongside the austere and mystical Persian body. The fascination with the body in *The Temple of Love*, in contrast to its apparent Platonic rejection of the bodily, reveals political concerns around the status of both male and female bodies in Caroline culture. Significantly, this exploration of the more immediate body politics of Caroline culture looks outward, representing not only a courtly Platonic body politics but also examining the political body of the nation.

'ANTIQUITIES WE PRINCIPALLY DESIRE': CAROLINE COURT ORIENTALISM

Caroline travels to the east were spurred by a number of motives, diplomatic, mercantile, intellectual. By the 1630s the network of East India Company trading posts ('factories') and agents was established across the Near East, the Indian coast and the Far Eastern archipelagos, and trading and diplomatic ties had been cemented between many of the local rulers including the Persian shah and the Mogul emperor, visited by Sir Thomas Roe in 1616. This successful mission provided not only a model for future diplomatic contacts but also prompted Roe's discussion paper for the East India Company analysing the operation of a trading empire:

> All warr and traffique are incompatible. By my consent you shall no way engage your selves but at sea, wher you are as like to gayne as often as to loose. It is the beggering of the Portugall, notwithstanding his many rich residences and territoryes, that hee keepes souldiers that spendes it; yet his garrisons are meane. He never Profited by the Indyes, since hee defended them. Observe this well. It hath also beene the error of the Dutch, who seeke Plantation here by the Sword. They turne a wonderfull stocke, they poule in all Places, they Posses some of the best; yet ther dead Payes consume all the gayne. Let this bee received as a rule that if you will Profitt, seeke it at Sea, and in quiett trade.[18]

Roe's targets were not simply the Dutch East India Company but the ideologically motivated westwards colonialists who argued for 'plantation' rather than trade. The plantation model, based on encounters with less technologically sophisticated native peoples and the brutal imposition of western settlement and 'civilisation', has often obscured the more complex, mutual and negotiated exchanges found in the Indian Ocean and beyond. Eastern travellers often encountered higher forms of technological achievement, such as Chinese porcelain, Persian silk-weaving, or Indian dyeing industries, and many of the interactions operated in favour of Asian imports into Europe, to such an extent that it was a perennial problem for traders and visitors to obtain goods of high enough quality and status to impress their Asian hosts.[19] The importance of these technological interactions, and the challenge they presented to the west, can be seen in Shah Sufi of Persia's request to Charles I for access to an enameller, clockmaker, diamond cutter, 'aexquisite gouldsmith', 'curious Limner or Painter', gunner and maker of fireworks in return for the support offered to William Gibson, the East India Company's agent in Persia.[20]

Three particularly significant voyages in the late 1620s and early 1630s, closely connected to the court, capitalised on the renewed interest in eastern affairs created by the arrival of Sir Robert Sherley and the competing Persian representative, Naqd Ali Beg (1624–27), each mixing commercial and cultural concerns.[21] Dodmore Cotton's official embassy to Shah Abbas of Persia (1627–29) aimed to smooth over the ruffled diplomatic situation after Sherley's bid to act as an intermediary between London merchants and the Persian Shah and the subsequent dispute between Sherley and Ali Beg, although it also aimed at increased importation of silk, making London the centre of the European silk trade.[22] Although Cotton died en route, his secretary Thomas Herbert produced his *Description of the Persian Monarchy*.[23] The cultural impact of Herbert's book can be seen in Nicholas Wilford's 1637 mission. Wilford, a skilled draughtsman, was hired at Arundel's suggestion to undertake observations of the silk industry and its use of colour, and also to collect portable antiquities, such as bas reliefs, statues, coins, carved gemstones and Persian, Arabic or Greek books for the royal collection, as well as providing pictures of Persian monuments. Wilford was to 'exactly designe all auntient Buildings and Edifices such as are either famous for Antiquity or Architecture and particularly to note their forme and eligancy', copying inscriptions and carefully noting their size.[24] Such royal interest in Persian culture and, especially, commerce was not entirely welcome to the East India Company, as Charles I frequently attempted to circumvent the monopoly privileges of the Company. Thus, for example, in December 1635 shortly before the performance of *The Temple of Love*, Sir William Courteen and his associates received a royal licence to trade in all areas not exploited by the Company.[25]

Perhaps the voyage undertaken by William Feilding, 1st Earl of Denbigh between January 1631 and August 1633 reveals most about Caroline court orientalism. The mission generated one spectacular material outcome, not treasures or trade, but instead one of the earliest western representations of the Englishman abroad. Van Dyck's portrait depicts Denbigh as alert hunter, seasoned traveller, and explorer, accompanied by an Indian servant boy, Jack, who points towards a parrot. This portrait, painted c. 1633–34 to mark the Earl's return, probably for his daughter Mary, Marchioness of Hamilton (figure 10), illuminates the multifaceted nature of Caroline court orientalism. Most recently, it has been suggested that the Earl's striking clothing – he wears Indian silk pyjamas, but also a European shirt and shoes, while carrying a flintlock fowling-piece – places the Earl between east and west, while still maintaining his European identity.[26] This 'hybridity' characterises many aspects of the painting, so his servant boy wears a Persian-style turban as he gestures towards the parrot, tilting the image towards the kinds of exotic luxury goods (black servants and feathers) associated with later orientalism. In the sequence of inventories which list the painting, the boy becomes a 'blackamoor' by 1641–49.[27]

Given the repertoire of orientalist images the picture deploys, including a dubious background of palm trees and a visibly South American parrot, it is tempting to dismiss the picture as orientalist fantasy.[28] Yet the position and function of the Indian boy provide an important counterbalance to white power, contrasting with the role of black figures in other power portraits of the period such as Van Dyck's *Henriette of Lorraine* (now at Kenwood House), where the black servant's bare-headed crouching position marks his obedience, his blackness accentuating her whiteness.[29] Stallybrass and Jones comment on the 'informality' of the Denbigh image which punctures orientalist hierarchies. Indeed, one reading of the portrait (the family legend that it shows the lost Earl guided to safety by the boy) implies an even more radical dependence of the western traveller on local knowledge. Feilding's gesture of 'mild surprise' seems to recreate those unstable moments of encounter,

10 Anthony Van Dyck, *William Feilding, 1st Earl of Denbigh*

which as Jyotsna Singh has argued 'create an imaginary space upon [sic] which the reader can participate in the playful dynamic of cross-cultural meetings that elude the narrator's classifying grasp'.[30]

Feilding's trip differed from other missions. Although it acquired a semi-official status, as the Earl carried royal letters of introduction and travelled with royal support (and probably contributed to the necessary personal diplomacy to ensure the continuance of trading networks),[31] Denbigh also claimed primarily to have undertaken the voyage 'to better my vnderstanding and not impeach my estate'.[32] Certainly, the library at Newnham Paddox (the Feilding house in Warwickshire) evidences familial interest in travels and included copies of Knolles, Purchas and Sandys.[33] Feilding commissioned several charts for the voyage, including a magnificent map of the Indian coast, and he retained copies of the journals of the voyage in his library.[34] Despite this professed educative desire, as noted above, Feilding was supported by Charles I, who urged the reluctant East India Company to transport him even when the Earl also insisted on travelling in the primary ship of the voyage (as befitting his rank). Crucially, Charles also supplied Denbigh with a series of introductory letters to Shahjahan, the Mogul emperor, highlighting the 'fame and glory' of his rule, and to Shah Sufi of Persia stressing how Persian military prowess had 'inflamed the hearts of manie of our subjects' and praising the 'glorie' of the Persian royal court.[35]

William's trip, however, seems to have been considerably less successful than the painting and than implied in some contemporary reports that reproduced the orientalist trope of fantastic eastern wealth and heralded his return laden with jewels.[36] Having outfaced the Company, who were concerned no expense should devolve upon them and that the trip should not interfere with their trade, in Surat Feilding became entangled in the difficult relations between the governor and the Company. Feilding's departure for the Mughul court was marred by the confiscation of his horses and the East India Company factor reported that Denbigh was 'ill-accomodated for such a Iorney', a situation exacerbated by 'the base vsage, and disrespect of this Gouernor, who would not suffer him, to haue not one horse to Ride', so that Feilding 'was Inforced ... to Travell in Coaches such as the Country affordes.'[37] Nothing is known of the success of this visit, although the Dutch newsletters claim the earl received 6,000 rupees and numerous jewels and gifts. Notwithstanding, on his return to Surat, also according to the Dutch, Feilding was 'so badly received by the governor that he has been obliged to return on board the fleet in disguise leaving his goods in the hands of the custom house officers'.[38] Feilding then departed for Persia on the *Mary* and returned home from there on the *James* without reaching the Shah.

Both the Van Dyck portrait and the 1631 engraved portrait by Voerst which entitled him 'Ambassador to the high and mighty King of Persia' may have been attempts to project a successful image before, during and after the trip.[39] Correspondence from his wife sent out to Feilding whilst abroad details the power struggles that ensued in his absence as attempts were made to supplant his chosen deputy at the Wardrobe, so that the pictures may also serve to reassert Feilding's status at home, increased by the kudos of having travelled to exotic places as a personal, rather than formal, royal representative. For both Feilding and his wife the trip may have had more direct purposes since as Master of the Wardrobe and Mistress of the Queen's Robes the Feildings were involved in the commissioning and supply of clothing, and especially luxury items such as silks, for the monarchy and its entertainments. The Persian setting found in *The Temple of Love*, with its notably magnificent costumes, partly organised by the Denbighs, and the central position afforded to cloth in the proscenium arch (the central cartouche is 'crimson drapery', pleated and knotted in luxurious profusion) recall the importance of the eastern cloth trade in the Caroline world.

If the enhancement of personal status may have formed one motivation for the voyage, several writers noted there were other kinds of 'profit' from the trip.[40] For example, we know Denbigh carried with him Thomas Barlow, a mathematician, as his secretary, which resulted in Barlow's calculation of the height of Table Mountain.[41] The other material results of the trip were more varied, including the seventeen pieces of 'Mesopotamia cloth' (possibly muslin or printed cottons),[42] 'an old pagan coat', three kittisols (Oriental sunshades), a quilt, large numbers of tortoiseshell items, 'a bird of paradise', coral, crystal and gold bead necklaces, a gold Indian cup, and an 'Indian coat of satten wrought with silk and gold'.[43] Interestingly, at Denbigh's death in 1643 the inventory of his Whitehall apartments included 'one large Cabonet with seuerall Indian Toies and other things in it', 'an Indian cotte two quilts a Boulster and a Counterpoint', and 'fower Indian Chaires', along with silverware, fifty-six unidentified pictures, and oriental porcelain.[44] Perhaps the most intriguing gift acquired by Feilding is the 'east Indian Idoll of blacke brasse wch was by my lord Denbigh taken out of there Churches from there alter' and given to Charles I for the royal collection.[45] The idol joined Arabic books, other oriental antiquities, and Van Dyck's portrait, painted in Rome, of Sherley and his Circassian wife, Lady Teresa, a version of which Charles had also acquired.[46]

These voyages and their cultural products, ranging from western paintings to eastern temple idols, illustrate the range of information and images available about Persia at the Caroline court by the mid-1630s.[47] There is no evidence that Jones drew on this material for the design of *The Temple of Love*, and most of the visual sources can be traced to Vecellio (the design of the costume for the Persian youth),[48] the *balet de cour* (for the antimasque designs),[49] and Medici entertainments (for some of the scenery).[50] Thus the overall impression created by the masque conforms to a general eastern and orientalist exoticism, promiscuously mixing Persian, Turkish and African images.[51] John Peacock, however, has argued that the proscenium shows a 'hybrid' Doric order with an 'exotic inflection' to create a new '"Indian" order', embodying precisely the amalgamation of images, the discovery not of difference but similarity, that underpinned early eastern travels.[52] Within the generic expectations of the masque, *The Temple of Love* blends eastern and western ideas as, for instance, in the journey of the Persian youths westward in search of their ideal and enlightenment. As Stephen Orgel has noted the action of the masque replays the journey of the magi, but rather than interpreting the journey as an acceptance of western superiority as Orgel does, it is also possible to treat the echoes of the nativity as gestures towards ecumenism or the unification of east and west.[53]

Further evidence of the Caroline court's familiarity with the differences between Turks and Persians and awareness of the different trading and technological relations involved in the Indian and East Indian trades can also be seen throughout the design. The opening stage direction that describes the proscenium differentiates the Indian and Asian monarchies and distinguishes the Asian figure riding on the camel as wearing a 'turban and coat differing from that of the Turks'.[54] While Orgel argues that this shows an orientalist mindset incapable of conceiving the east apart from through the Turks, the distinction was widely acknowledged, and both societies are placed as equivalent monarchies. Here, the masque is framed, literally, by the very distinction which becomes so fundamental to the interpretation of the masque. Similarly, the headdresses shown are clearly Persian (the cross-folded Persian turban and the mitre, O&S, no. 299), while the cloth used would have appeared more obviously Persian to early modern eyes. Persian fabrics were widely known, as can be seen in the Greenbury and Van Dyck paintings of Ali Beg and the Sherleys, and the design for Indamora's costume (O&S, no. 315) shows floral sprigs while the headdress design (O&S, no. 316) is annotated with the question 'what sprigs'. Floral sprigs, especially the smaller versions found on the lighter silks imported during the seventeenth century, were one of the distinctive Persian designs and were often adopted by European designers.[55] These cloth patterns illustrate how recent attempts to read the oriental images of *The Temple of Love* have been clouded by post-orientalist preconceptions of what constitutes the 'Oriental'.

Davenant's fiction for *The Temple of Love* is framed by two well-known texts about Persia, one contemporary and one classical. First, Herbert's contemporary narrative, published in 1634, provided a ready source for ideas about Persia, bringing together etymology, geography, mythology and ethnographic observation. The *Travels* amalgamate a proto-orientalist preoccupation with Persian luxury and Asiatic tyranny with an appreciation of the ascetic and philosophical elements of Persian culture. Herbert not only describes the wonders of Persepolis, including a temple of Diana and the extraordinary remains of the magnificent palaces, he also emphasises the Persian obedience to their monarchs and their love of poetry. These rather general parallels are strengthened by the long description of the Indian brahmin priests which may have furnished Davenant's *The Temple of Love*. Herbert first associates the priests with classical philosophers commenting, 'Their priests are called *Bramyni* or *Bracahmani*, such as in old times from their quality, were named *Gymno-sophi*; as *Porphirius* the great Platonist ... dictates concerning them', and praising their philosophical method:

> *Tertullian* calls them *gloriae animalia*, *Apollonius* says, they were and were not earthly; their thoughts so transcendent, as if they were ravisht by the sweetnesse of that harmony the rolling of the Orbs in an exact diapazan send forth in their forced Motion. Their imagination flew beyond nature, beleiving that this Fabrick of the inferiour world was created of nothing, and made sphericall, yet subject to dissolution; that it had an efficient cause, it being unable to form itself, and that that cause is the commander of nature.[56]

Herbert's description of their 'ravishment' by celestial harmony is, perhaps, echoed in the Brachmani's songs with Orpheus (notably lines 398 and 438–43), while their dislike of polygamy parallels the chastity espoused in the masque.[57] Moreover, their commandments include the control of the senses, directly echoing the theme of *The Temple of Love*.[58]

The Temple of Love is equally informed by the most important text of the classical tradition about Persia: Xenophon's *Cyropaedia*. Xenophon's description of Cyrus was one of the central exemplars of humanist education, providing a key illustration of the combination of manly prowess and prudence required of the governing classes inculcated, crucially, through persuasion (the *Cyropaedia* is filled with examples of the king's speeches) and what Sidney called 'honest dissimulation', the stratagems required for rule.[59] Described by Philip Sidney as 'the portraiture of a just empire', and by Edmund Spenser as an image 'a gouernment such as might best be', both writers prefer Xenophon's imperial images to Plato's commonwealth as providing the most plausible model for men to emulate. Both writers regarded Xenophon's work as most likely to provide an effective image of government in contrast to Plato's feigned polity.[60]

Widely cited by Cicero and later Machiavelli, the *Cyropaedia* provides an image of what one critic calls the 'economy of empire', extending ideas from the *Oeconomicus*, and bringing together the management of the household and empire as a paradigm of good personal and political governance.[61] The English Xenophon becomes a figure of the prudent use of foresight and persuasion in the management of empire but also political events, bringing together military prowess and the ability to secure cultural transformation through personal persuasiveness, the combination of public display and austerity, and what has been described as 'imperial erotics'.[62] In the context of the masque this emphasis upon persuasive speaking has particular resonance and, as Lorna Hutson has argued, Xenophon shows 'Cyrus's incessant labour in the art of cultural production – the labour of ensuring the loyalty of a colonised people through the strategic innovation and reordering of customs and codes of living'.[63]

Many of the ideals expressed in Xenophon chime with Charles's own national reform project. Caroline household reforms are paralleled in Xenophon by the creation of a court where 'honourable' gentlemen wait on Cyrus. Moreover Xenophon's description of the religiosity of the Persian court (especially the continuous chanting of hymns) and his emphasis on the King's personal example ('By showing also his owne moderation and temperance, he provoked all others the rather to use the same') echo Charles's own continence.[64] The *Cyropaedia* also argues that 'it be evident that to obey a prince and a soveraigne availeth most the atteining of wealth and honour', presenting a highly ambiguous image of the honest dissimulations involved in power. Although Xenophon stresses persuasion as the main princely tool, the potential inherent in such manipulations could be used to support a strongly absolutist line. Xenophon comments how monarchies might be 'brought to nought by conspiracies of the commons'.[65] This last phrase, taken from the 1632 translation of the *Cyropaedia* by Philemon Holland, illustrates the political potential in Persian history. Significantly, Holland's translation was dedicated to Charles I, and some copies were issued with a further dedication to Lord Holland (who was a close confidant of Henrietta Maria).[66]

Holland's translation presented Persia as the ideal image of absolute imperial sovereignty and refined political and religious culture, providing a persuasive model for Charles's reformed, imperial Britain, a point encapsulated in the engraved title page.[67] Here Cyrus's spear and shield are juxtaposed with Charles's sceptre and shield, perhaps suggesting both the King's current pacificist methods, but also how he might become a military leader should need arise. This martial aspect frames the translation, and according to the title page the main features of the book will consist in 'treating of noble education, of princely exercises, military discipline, warlike stratagems, preparations and expeditions'. Much of the book, indeed, is given over to issues of military training, campaign planning and narratives of battles and encounters, often providing exhaustive detail about military equipment.[68] Such military issues had important resonances in the Caroline period in the light of disputes over the billeting of troops, coat and conduct money (which as the name implies concerned furnishment of troops and which was much resented as a royal and extra-parliamentary power), and Charles's attempts to fashion an exact militia. Although Xenophon's Cyrus seeks a standing army, Henry Holland, the translator's son, in his dedication to Charles in 1632, makes the links to militia policy explicit:

> Demaundeth your Majesty now, what he is, that dareth to approach so neere your Presence, as to speake of Warre in time of Peace? Give your poore vassal leave to answer in the submissive voice of a loyall subject: He is no Schollar professed, nor Martial man, yet a lover of learning; and being one of the Trained Band, to guard *Camera Regis*, always prest without your Imprest money ... (sig. II8r).

Holland's emphasis upon voluntary military service contrasts with the resistance that Caroline policy encountered, and the debate over the militia, particularly the extension of central government authority it represented through the enhanced roles of the lords lieutenant, meant that attempts to develop the militia were often regarded as 'unjustifiable interference verging on tyranny'.[69]

Caroline orientalism, then, need not simply reflect a vague mysticism. Some Caroline oriental connections were rooted in the hard material worlds of trade and technological exchange; oriental fantasy existed alongside more scholarly and informed attempts to understand the east, or find points of commonality. Within this complex, overlapping and sometimes contradictory range of possibilities, oriental images, even if lacking in specificity of architectural and visual detail, had precise resonances in Caroline culture. One such association lay in the *realpolitik* of state and military power as shown in the title page's dual image of Cyrus and Charles from the *Cyropaedia*, and in the interpretation of Persia as the ideal Platonic commonwealth. *The Temple of Love*, presented from within the Queen's household, offers Charles an image of the proper mode for conducting imperial sovereignty.

'THE FACTION OF THE FLESH' AND 'MODERN DEVILS': POLITICAL BODIES AND THE BODY POLITIC

The title page of *The Temple of Love* stresses Davenant's position as 'her majesty's servant' and the text, largely, represents the Queen's ideas, placed in dialogue with her husband's masques and, in this instance, echoing a text that one of her closest advisors had already gifted to the King. Mindful of the importance of *The Temple of Love*'s origins in the Queen's household, recent critical writing has emphasised how the significant gender politics of the masque articulate a tactful but forceful intervention in politics on behalf of the Queen. Martin Butler has suggested that the repeated performances 'reflect' *The Temple of Love*'s importance for the Queen as she re-emerged as a political force after her eclipse during the anti-Weston plot (1634), while the unusual combination of male and female masquers is deployed to advance female dominance (literally as normal masquing practice is reversed when they lead the men out to dance), and celebrate the superiority of refined female Will over male Understanding.[70] Although it has been suggested that the masque rejects bodily desire, the emphasis upon 'generation', and the final image of the united monarchs, point towards a subtler interpretation of Platonism, not as the repudiation of the body but, rather, *The Temple of Love* proposes its proper management, led, naturally, by the Queen's refined Will.[71]

The ideal Platonic commonwealth of *The Temple of Love* depends on the contrast between the disorderly bodies of the 'fantastic faith' (line 197) worshipped in the false temple and the new corporeality represented by the Temple of Chaste Love. The contrasting bodies of the text draw upon the dual idea of the oriental body, on the one hand sensual, luxurious and sexual (an orientalist body), and the reformed view supplied in part by Herbert and Xenophon. The act of re-reading the oriental body in these texts, itself a reformation of a common trope, becomes an analogy for the process of the reforming of the body of the state; but, also, its insistence on the textual body and its interpretation becomes a rejection of the readings of courtly bodies offered in contemporary political commentaries.

The antimasques of *The Temple of Love* are presented by three false magicians who have 'seduced the more voluptuous race / Of men to give false worship' (lines 173–4) in their temple rather than the true Temple of Love. The designs for these figures show their oriental qualities, but also their hybridity: one magician sports 'dogges eares' (O&S, no. 297); the watery spirits that present the antimasques are half-human, half-fish (lines 287–8); another is described as the 'fatt mage' 'like a Sir John Falstaff' (O&S, no. 299). Their incipient animality and the grotesque outsized magus emphasise the bodily qualities of the false Temple of Love, described in terms of humours, heat and luxury. Indeed, when the magicians hear of the new temple they fear that they will have to dispose of their 'bodily implements', that is 'Persian quilts, embroidered couches, / And our standing beds' (lines 206–8). Their plot to thwart the new 'humour' of 'Platonical' love (lines 204 and 240) is to use the spirits of air, water, fire and earth 'if not t'uphold the faction of / The flesh, yet to infect the queasy age / With blacker sins' (lines 266–8).

These are the typical bodies of orientalist thought. The exotic, sensuous, seductive body, especially associated with the Turk, runs throughout western writings on the Levant and clearly dominated thinking about Turkey. Harems, divans, eunuchs, barbaric luxury and unbridled desire, especially sodomy, symbolised the east for western observers. Robert Stodart, one of the members of Cotton's mission, deploys familiar orientalist tropes when he described how

> we cam into a garden very pleasant, full of poumecittorns and oranges, and many pleasant tanckes, and in the middle of this garden was a room built with timber ouer a tancke, wher ye kinge did vse to sitt himself. On the side of the garden was his haram, the roumes being wonderfull curiouse, ther floores being layd with

> Turkey carpets being wrought curiously with gould, with men and wemens pictures according to the maner of the cuntrye curiously paynted with gould and other fine colours. In some roomes ther was beds whervpon might tumble half a dosen of his conqupines att a time; in others ther was looking glasses besett round about for him to see in the maner of his bodie waging when he dallied with his conqupines; other roomes bestett ful of curious chenie wher he does vse to drinck coho, wyne and feast himself amongst his women ...
>
> I was curteously entertayned and brauely feasted after the maner of the cuntrey, with wyne and women and bugring boyes for the davnce before vs beside divers other lascivious sportes ...

Stodart's description with its alertness to Turkish artistic and cultural ability is mixed with images of the exotic ('coho', 'curious chenie') and the sexual ('conqupines', 'bugring boyes') and, in this instance, includes the additional 'bodily implement' of the mirror.[72] Here *The Temple of Love* confirms the orientalist expectations of many contemporary accounts of the east.

The antimasques of *The Temple of Love* develop from those of Aurelian Townshend's *Tempe Restored* (1632), deploying the parallel images of false worship, bodily transformation, and grotesque hybrids of human and animal, often connected to the orient. Thus in *Tempe Restored* Circe's false masque of animals, Indians and barbarians centres on the strange hybrid figure of the 'Pagoda', an 'Idoll' formed from a human body, with black wings, pointed gold shoes, elongated fingernails and a quasi-oriental headdress above an animal face.[73] This monstrous figure literally embodies the false worship promoted by Circean sovereignty and the debasement of the human into the bestial that her rule creates contrasted with the proper worship promoted by Henrietta Maria as Divine Beauty. Circe's improper physicality is echoed in her want of 'physic' to cure her distempered heart as she like her subjects is 'confined' by her bodily desires. In contrast, Henrietta Maria's descent and the power of the stellar Influences liberate from the body, offering, instead, 'music to all eyes'.[74] These images of improper bodily worship mirror Protestant readings of Catholicism, lending the imagery of false religions and idols much wider resonance in the context of the continuing criticisms of Henrietta Maria, her Catholicism and her theatrical performances, especially in Prynne's *Histriomastix* (1633).[75] The main thrust of this attack is on the lack of spirituality and the worldly fleshiness of Catholicism that can be traced in the 'voluptuous' celebration of Christmas and the excessive use of gestures that draw attention to the priestly body, confirming Prynne's hypothesis that Catholicism presents a false, theatrical form of worship, part pagan and part oriental in its origins.[76] The Persians and their cult of chaste love are the antithesis of bodily desire and, instead, in a neat reversal, the critics of chaste love are cast as false magicians conjuring bodily visions to entice and entrap their victims. The repeated use of 'sect' by the false mages to describe the cult of chaste love, actually renders them more sectarian, while their belief that the new regime is a transitory humour reveals their own dependence on humoural ideas.[77] Like Townshend's *Tempe Restored*, Davenant's *The Temple of Love* responds to Prynne through the very medium he criticised, using the idealised female body to reject his vision of bodily politics.

The Temple of Love replaces these orientalist bodies with an ascetic and mystical eastern body founded in the soul and what the Persian page calls 'a maidenhead belonging to the mind' (line 334). Like Carew's *Coelum Britanicum* (1634), Davenant's masque presents a morally reformed universe in which the disorderly body is banished, but in *The Temple of Love* the disordered body derives from the false imaginings of a false temple. The Shrovetide performance date acquires added significance here as it associates the masque with the rejection of the fleshly world while also stressing the masque's placement in a properly ordered cycle of festivity and restraint.[78] The Persian setting allows for the exotic and the mystical, but it is a vision that is carefully regulated and stresses the refined continence available in the religion of chaste love, where even love poets (those who allow 'false love in numbers [to] flow', line 97) are civilised by the religious ('purified', line 99) and Orphic poetry.

The Persians, easily assumed to be symbols of the luxurious east, read through the *Cyropaedia* and through Herbert's Brahmins, embody refinement, contemplation and, above all, moderation and continence, and the quest for perfect beauty. They combine both male and female qualities, symbolised in the mixed-sex train of attendants who accompany Indamora, and each gesture of the masque, from the sea-borne triumph of Indians which reshapes the birth of Venus, to the final tableau of the descent of Amianteros, rejects either the image of active females as mannish viragos, or as dangerously enticing bodies. In this way Davenant's masque provides an example of the 'imperial erotics' traced by Xenophon in operation, persuading the country to obedience through poetry and spectacle, and offering an image not of 'loose verse' (line 112), but of the truly civilising poetry of the reformed Orpheus.

This insistence on the disciplined female body raises an interesting question about how the court interacted with criticism from opponents, especially those beyond the court, as *The Temple of Love* rejects not only Prynne's view of women, but also other voices outside the court that were even more critical and vociferous. Contrary to the general view of the Caroline court that stresses its attachment to the ideals of married and Platonic love and which accepts the Stuart propaganda of a court reformed after Jacobean debauchery, the Caroline court suffered from continuous sexual scandals. In 1633 Rossingham reported Dr Dee's sermon extolling women, saying 'he spake so very much in commendation of virginity' but that 'Sure this doctor made no good choice of the court to commend virginity in.'[79] Rossingham's quip may seem misplaced and even to echo the slightly over-emphatic view of Prynne and his followers that Henrietta and her women were nothing but 'notorious whores', yet the Caroline court and especially Henrietta's household were riven with sexual tensions and affairs. Liaisons attributed to Lady Carlisle and Strafford were followed by the rerun of the Essex divorce when the unfortunate 3rd Earl divorced Elizabeth Paulet almost immediately after their marriage, and Lady Desmond accused her husband, George Feilding (second son of William) of impotence.[80] Information about the most famous scandal, the Castlehaven trial, circulated widely in manuscript and was the subject of much ribald verse and, indeed, even Feilding in India carried with him a copy of the proceedings against Castlehaven and 'divers other letters and bookes of newes' in his Indian trunk.[81]

More strikingly still, in 1636 a libel circulated against the ladies at court, in which three of the performers who danced in *The Temple of Love* appear (see appendix).[82] Although this poem only survives in a single copy amongst the papers of Gervase Holles, combined with other texts such as 'The Progress' (another attack on court morality) and the numerous satires on the Castlehaven scandal, such libels created a wider awareness of the sexual mores of the court, contradicting the monarch's insistence on married chastity and the image of a virtuous court promoted in Caroline propaganda.[83] Modern historians have suggested that libels contributed to the disillusion with the Caroline regime,[84] and significantly, the antimasques presented by the spirits for the magicians in *The Temple of Love*, include a 'sect of modern devils, / Fine precise fiends' sent to 'vex the world'. This description, which attributes criticism of the court to the over-punctilious puritans, culminates in the seventh entry which consists of 'A modern devil, a sworn enemy of poesy, music, and all ingenious arts, but a great friend to murmuring, libelling, and all seeds of discord, attended by his factious followers; all of which was expressed by their habits and dance' (lines 300–3).

Furthermore, the Second and Third Magicians' cries of 'News! News!' (line 234) and 'More of thy news' (line 242) suggest that the masque echoes Caroline concerns with the novel ('modern') phenomenon of news culture.[85] Alongside the libels the growth of newsbooks, especially those detailing foreign affairs such as the defeats of the Protestant cause during the Thirty Years' War, provided a significant pressure on the Caroline state and its non-interventionist policies. Concern about such newsbooks, libels and other unofficial methods of political communication was widespread and the Caroline authorities struggled to regulate the developing news market. Here, the inclusion of 'murmuring and libelling', precisely the kind of political libelling and gossips that undermined the image of the virtuous court, reduces these criticisms to unjustified disturbances (they are 'factious'), but also makes them the false creation of a body-obsessed set of deceiving magicians.

Nonetheless, this passage evidences a striking consciousness of a world beyond the court, and the mages describe the 'queasy' (unsettled, troubled) age, an image that stands against Caroline invocations of harmonious plenty in the Stuarts' 'halcyon days'.

In the world of *The Temple of Love* the libellers and murmurers are simply the phantasms created by the disordered imagination of voluptuaries, and they are easily banished by the arrival of the masque as 'at an instant' (line 360) the clouds and mists that have obscured the temple dissolve. Yet the oriental imagery of the masque also carries more sinister implications, for while the masque moves away from the image of eastern tyranny, even the Persians were noted for their absolutism and for a total intolerance of criticism.[86] Stodart's journal describes one instance where two men were sentenced 'for the delivering of a petition unto [the Shah] that he did not like the maner of writeing of it'. One man was 'drubbd soe that within a while after he died; the other, wch writt it [had] his hand cutt in the middle, the two fingers and them vp to the wriste', explaining that 'the king wheresoeuer he is doth execute his lawes and nobies els'. So, one implication of this masque and its use of orientalism is far from decorative and amusing, rather it subliminally suggests ideal kingship is absolute. Even though the Queen's reformation of the 'dull Northern isle they call Britain' (line 210) is couched in the language of purification and healing (notably lines 93–4), and in terms of reformed ('lawful', line 454) desire, the song that accompanied her entry praises Henrietta as 'both strict and kind' (line 455). Charles is celebrated as 'the mightiest' who rules 'b'example as by power' (lines 511, 513).

These reminders of the combination of persuasion and power are ultimately developed from the ideal image of Persian kingship supplied in the *Cyropaedia*. This is the other side of the Persian dress of this masque, not the Persia of mysticism, but of an imperial sovereignty enforced by strict laws and, ultimately, violence. It is an image rooted in *realpolitik* even if expressed in the terms of imperial erotics designed to both cloak and further power politics. This combination in *The Temple of Love* reminds us that the decorative surfaces of the Caroline masque can be highly charged, presenting a political argument for a harsh response to criticism, and also insists that real power depends upon the maintenance of a standing army – one of the main innovations of Cyrus. Here, the Queen's selection of an oriental image of monarchical rule mirrors the ancient British world so often imagined in the King's masques, but where both masque languages appeal to mysticism, the Queen's oriental imagery deliberately echoes Xenophon's more disturbing image of persuasion backed by power.

MASQUES AND THE 'QUEASY AGE'

Although contemporary observers noted the centrality of courtly Platonism to *The Temple of Love*, the oriental imagery does not simply reinforce an apolitical mysticism. In Caroline politics the mystical origins of power itself argues for absolutism rather than contractual theory, and as much as the language and action of this masque are encased in an image of civilising poetry and music, the Persian setting raises the possibility that mysticism also requires might. These kinds of nuanced political manoeuvrings, institutionalised in the dialogue established between the King and Queen's masques at the Caroline court, are difficult to describe since they depend upon inference and context more than direct statement. Indeed, the surface of the masque is precisely designed to both aestheticise and abstract rather than deal in direct political statement. Although the antimasques with their images of deformed bodies and minds are easily banished, their very presence, joined with the satire on sectarians, libellers and news culture of the 'queasy age', suggests that *The Temple of Love* marks more than the development of an intellectual fashion, responding to a critique already voiced against the women of the court. Indeed, even Lucy Percy's refusal to participate, traced by Julie Sanders not simply to personal clashes but to intellectual difference, may mark the political and factional contests that simmered in the Caroline court. Moreover, much as the language and ideas of the masque may seem remote from contingent political issues, the very presence of outside and disruptive voices argues greater consciousness of the wider political nation and its views.

There is a final parallel between the politics of the Caroline masque and orientalism. Recent post-colonial criticism has sought to dislodge the 'closed system' of Said's orientalism, which restricts how eastern encounters can be viewed, but which, as Said admitted before his death, depends upon an untenable homogenisation of the west as much as orientalism undoubtedly homogenised the east. For Caroline masque criticism, a similar flattening has occurred whereby, even as historians have begun to recognise the polycentricity of the Caroline court, literary critics have continued to restrict their interpretations of the masque to monolithic conceptions of power and its institutionalisation in the court. Although Davenant's oriental settings cannot simply be treated as genuine encounters with the east, nor are they merely oriental fantasies; they represent instead a complex engagement with a range of images and ideas about the east. Ultimately, of course, the masque practises an orientalist manoeuvre in its projection of English political concerns onto an eastern stage, but the range of possibilities that Caroline orientalism encompasses, the different kinds of encounter and exchange that early travel in the east allowed, stand as a reminder of the parallel range of possibilities that exist in the discovery of the different voices, cultures and ideas that made up the wider Caroline political culture. The challenge, then, for masque criticism is to shed its neo-orientalist readings of power politics and address itself to the full range of political voices and discourses available in Caroline culture.

APPENDIX

A lybell called ye health to diuers Lord and Ladies 1636[87]

A health to my Lady Dutchess   of Buckingham
that loues redd hayr so well
and to my Lord her husband
that made her belly swell

A health to my Lady Marques   of Hamilton
that hath so good a grace
and to my Lord her husband
with his ill fauored face

A health to my Lady Arundell
whose traualing days ar past
and to my Lord her husband
I hope twill be his last.

A health to my Lady of Kent
with her fat bouncinge
and to my Lord her husband
that fucks my Lady Hunt

A health to my Lady Pembroke
that lookes so like a witche
and to my Lord her husband
that so well indures ye switche

A health to my Lady Essex
who had once lost her fame
and to my Lord her husband
that is so ill at the game

A health to my Lady Dorsett
that of grauity hath store
anwhored to my Lord her husband
yt giues his soule for a whore

A health to my Lady of Warwick
beeing made a Countess glories
and to my Lord her husband
that loues to tell strange stories.

James Knowles

A health to my Lady Lindsey
that's quickly moou'd to rage
and to my Lord her husband
that brought his child on the stage

A health to my Lady Holland
of wemen shee's the best
and to my Lord her husband
that goes so neately dresst

A health to my Lady Dover
that was first wife to a citt
and to my Lord her husband
that hath more wrath than witt

A health to my Lady Denbigh
that groome o' the stoole to her grace
and to my Lord her husband
whose nose hath fyrd his face.

A health to my Lady Carnaruon
that's a pearl in eache mans ey
and to my Lord her husband
that will both sweare and ly.

A health to my Lady Newport
that loues to play and dance
and to my Lord her husband
that rann away in France

A health to my Lady Desmond
with her frend she loues to play
and my Lord her husband
that's oft sent out of ye way.

A health to my Lady Portland
yt was whipt to her marriage bedd
And to my Lord Her husband
with his great loggerhead

A health to my Lady Wimbledon,
but eighteene yeares of age
and to my Lord her husband
that's iealous of his age.

A health to my Lady Goring
in deuotion shee's not cooling
and to my Lord her husband
that hath got all by fooling.

NOTES

1 PRO, SP 14/6/21, Dudley Carleton to John Chamberlain, 15 January 1604.

2 G. J. Toomer, *Eastern Wisedome and Learning: The Study of Arabic in Seventeenth-Century England* (Oxford: Oxford University Press, 1996), and H. Daiber, 'The reception of Islamic philosophy at Oxford', in C. E. Butterworth and B. A. Kessell (eds), *The Introduction of Arabic Philosophy into Europe* (Leiden: Brill, 1994), pp. 65–82.

3 O&S, ii, p. 604 (inscription on no. 292, proscenium arch design). See also O&S, no. 295 (an Indian shore) where the masque is the 'Queens masque of Indamora'. All references to the designs are to this edition.

4 James Howell, *Epistolae Ho-Elianae*, cited in G. E. Bentley, *The Jacobean and Caroline Stage* (7 vols, Oxford: Clarendon Press, 1941–68), iii, pp. 216–17. The French *Recueil des Gazettes Nouvelles 1638*, ed. Theophraste Renaudot (Paris, 1639), 28 February 1635, noted the subject as 'l'Amour platonique', and the date of performance as 'le 20. de ce mois (jour du Mardi gras)'. I am grateful to Karen Britland for this reference.

5 Julie Sanders, 'Caroline salon culture and female agency: the Countess of Carlisle, Henrietta Maria, and public theatre', *Theatre Journal*, 52 (2000), 449–64, has argued that the personal rifts mark an intellectual difference over the nature of Platonism, showing how the inflections *within* Neo-Platonism allow us to envisage a much less monolithic Caroline culture.

6 M. Butler, *Theatre and Crisis 1632–1642* (Cambridge: Cambridge University Press, 1984), pp. 29–30; K. Sharpe, *Criticism and Compliment: The Politics of Literature in the England of Charles I* (Cambridge: Cambridge University Press, 1987), pp. 244–7.

7 E. Veevers, *Images of Love and Religion: Queen Henrietta Maria and Court Entertainments* (Cambridge: Cambridge University Press, 1989), pp. 134–43, argues that *The Temple of Love* contains an allegory of the arrival of the Roman envoy Panzani in England and that the Persian youths should be seen as Jesuits arriving to celebrate the emerging reform of the English (Indian) nation.

8 S. Orgel, 'Inigo Jones' Persian entertainment', *AARP: Art and Archaeology Research Papers*, 2 (1972), 60–2, and 'Plato, the magi, and Caroline politics: a reading of *The Temple of Love*', *Word and Image*, 4 (1988), 663–77, esp. 665 and 671.

9 To be fair, many of the simplifications of Said's orientalism have been generated by other post-colonial critics, and Said himself, shortly before his death, redefined orientalism in the aftermath of the Iraq War: 'The terrible reductive conflicts that herd people under falsely unifying rubrics like "America", "The West", or "Islam", and invent collective identities for large numbers of individuals who are actually quite diverse ... must be opposed': Edward W. Said, *Orientalism* (Harmondsworth: Penguin, 2003), Preface (2003), p. xxii.

10 J. Brotton, *Trading Territories* (London: Reaktion Books, 1997), p. 90. See also: L. Valensi, 'The making of a political paradigm: the Ottoman state and oriental despotism', in A. Grafton and A. Blair (eds), *The Transmission of Culture in Early Modern Europe* (Princeton: Princeton University Press, 1990), pp. 173–203, and K. Parker (ed.), *Early Modern Tales of the Orient: A Critical Anthology* (London: Routledge, 1999), pp. 1–35, esp. pp. 2–3.

11 Cited in A. Parr (ed.), *Three Renaissance Travel Plays* (Manchester: Manchester University Press, 1995), pp. 17–18.

12 A. Parr, 'Foreign relations in Jacobean England: the Sherley brothers and the "voyage to Persia"', in J.-P. Maquerlot and M. Willems (eds), *Travel and Drama in Shakespeare's Time* (Cambridge: Cambridge University Press, 1995), p. 20. Another impetus towards connections with the Near East was Archbishop Laud's continued ecumenical interest in the Greek church in Constantinople and Alexandria, partly fuelled by the desire to rescue classical wisdom from the hands of the Turks and the Catholics, but also by an awareness of the example offered for Anglicanism by the Greek church with its independent theological tradition: see H. Trevor-Roper, *From Counter-Reformation to Glorious Revolution* (London: Secker & Warburg, 1992), ch. 5.

13 For 'Arabism', see 'Introduction' in Parker (ed.), *Early Modern Tales of the Orient*, p. 4; for 'Ottomanism', see G. MacLean, 'Ottomanism before Orientalism? Bishop King praises Henry Blount, passenger in the Levant', in I. Kamps and J. Singh (eds), *Travel Knowledge: European 'Discoveries' in the Early Modern Period* (Basingstoke: Palgrave, 2001), p. 87.

14 J. E. Wills, 'Review article: maritime Asia, 1500–1800: the interactive emergence of European domination', *American Historical Review*, 98 (1993), 83–105.

15 J. G. Singh, 'History or colonial ethnography? The ideological formation of Edward Terry's *A Voyage to East-India* (1655 and 1665) and *The Merchants and Mariners Preservation and Thanksgiving* (1649)', in Kamps and Singh (eds), *Travel Knowledge*, p. 204.

16 T. Herbert, *A Description of the Persian Monarchy now beinge the Oriental Indyes, Iles and other parts of the Greater Asia and Africk* (London, 1634). The book bore the additional title page *A Relation of some yeares Trauaile begunne anno 1626. Into Afrique and the Greater Asia, especially the Territories of the Persian Monarchie*.

17 A. Sherley, *Sir Anthony Sherley his relation of his travels into Persia* (London, 1613), sig. E3r.

18 Sir Thomas Roe to the East India Company, 24 November 1616, repr. from BL, Additional MS 6115, fol. 140 in W. Foster (ed.), *The Embassy of Sir Thomas Roe to India, 1615–19* (Oxford: Oxford University Press, 1926), p. 303.

19 R. W. Ferrier, 'The terms and conditions under which English trade was transacted with Safavid Persia', *Bulletin of the School of Oriental and African Studies*, 49 (1986), 49, and I. Woodfield, *English Musicians in the Age of Exploration* (Stuyvesant: Pendragon Press, 1995), pp. 209–10.

20 PRO, EXT 6/2, fols 53–4, undated letter Shah Sufi to Charles I. This is presumably related to the Shah's request for paints (1636) and some artists may actually have gone to Persia: see R. W. Ferrier, 'Charles I and the antiquities of Persia: the mission of Nicholas Wilford', *Iran: Journal of the British Institute of Persian Studies*, 8 (1970), 53, and Ferrier, 'Terms and conditions', 64.

21 B. Penrose, *The Sherleian Odyssey: Being A Record of the Travels and Adventures of Three Famous Brothers During the Reigns of Elizabeth I, James I and Charles I* (Taunton: Barnicotts, 1938), pp. 211–41, and L. Lockhart, 'European contacts with Persia, 1350–1736', in P. Jackson (ed.), *The Cambridge History of Iran, Volume 6: The Timurid and Safavid Periods* (Cambridge: Cambridge University Press, 1986), pp. 386–96. The East India Company seems to have been involved in the appointment of Ali Beg (*Sherleian Odyssey*, p. 214) and supported him in London, although R. W. Ferrier's detailed study of the embassy ('The European diplomacy of Shah Abbas I and the first Persian embassy to England', *Iran*, 11 (1973), 75–92) argues that the East India Company found

itself in a divided position about the embassy, unwilling to offend either sovereign (p. 85). Ali Beg's portrait was painted by Richard Greenbury, later portrait painter to Henrietta Maria (1631): see M. Archer, *The India Office Collection of Paintings and Sculpture* (London: India Office, 1986), pp. 28–9 and plate III.

22 R. W. Ferrier, 'Trade from the mid-14th century to the end of the Safavid period', in Jackson (ed.), *Cambridge History of Iran, Volume 6*, pp. 412–90, esp. pp. 451–2 and 459–60.

23 Herbert (1606–82) later attended Charles I in prison (1647) and became a Groom of the Bedchamber. After the death of his patron the Earl of Pembroke in 1630 he travelled in Europe and his court connections in the 1630s are unknown. Herbert's *Travels*, however, went through four editions by 1677.

24 On his death Wilford's possessions included a copy of Herbert's book, 'a booke of perspectives', 'a booke of Architecture' and '12 sibilles in Black and Wte', a 'cover of a booke with draughts' and a copy of Quintus Curtius: see Ferrier, 'Charles I and the antiquities of Persia', 55–6.

25 For Caroline assaults on the East India Company monopoly, see R. Brenner, *Merchants and Revolution: Commercial Change, Political Conflict, and London's Overseas Traders, 1550–1653* (Cambridge: Cambridge University Press, 1993), pp. 169–81, and P. J. Marshall, 'The English in Asia to 1700', in N. Canny (ed.), *The Oxford History of the British Empire, Volume I: The Origins of Empire* (Oxford: Oxford University Press, 1998), pp. 264–85, esp. pp. 276–7.

26 P. Stallybrass and A. R. Jones, *Renaissance Clothing and the Materials of Memory* (Cambridge: Cambridge University Press, 2000), p. 53. They note the symbolic placing of the Earl between east and west as he originally carried a fur castor, an emblem of westwards enterprise, not a gun in the left hand. In fact, Feilding travelled with a 'Beaver hatt with a golde and siluer Band' (Warwickshire Record Office [hereafter WRO], Feilding MSS, CR2017/C2/188, 'A note of such things as are in my lord of denbighs Truncke').

27 The painting was given to the Marquess of Hamilton who had married to Denbigh's daughter (and who danced in *Temple of Love*). The various labels in the Hamilton inventories are discussed in G. Martin, *The Flemish School, c. 1600–1900* (London: National Gallery, 1970), pp. 54–5: see Stallybrass and Jones, *Renaissance Clothing*, p. 53.

28 The parrot has been identified as a Scarlet Macaw. Its distribution covers northern South America up into Mexico, not Panama, Columbia, east of the Andes to the Guianas and Trinidad, and south as far as eastern Peru, Bolivia and northern Mato Grosso, Brazil. 'They would have been one of the first substantial parrots encountered as a traveller ventured South from the now USA so presumably would have been one of the first to have its nest robbed of chicks which were then tamed sufficiently to travel with the early ships.' I am grateful to Owen Joiner and his colleagues at Jersey Zoo for this information.

29 C. Brown and H. Vlieghe (eds), *Van Dyck, 1599–1641* (London: Royal Academy, 1999), no. 74, notes the pose as 'respectful' (p. 264).

30 Oliver Millar, *Van Dyck in England* (London: National Portrait Gallery, 1982), p. 56; Singh, 'History or colonial Ethnography?', p. 204. Singh's important essay modifies the assumption that early narratives can simply be subsumed into a colonialist gaze of classification and domination.

31 D. Starkey, 'Representation through intimacy: a study in the symbolism of monarchy and court office in early modern England', in I. Lewis (ed.), *Symbols and Sentiments* (London: Academic Press, 1977), pp. 187–224, esp. pp. 199–201 on the role of the king's intimate servants as ambassadors/substitutes. Although Feilding was neither a privy councillor nor a member of the bedchamber he enjoyed 'fairly easy access to the king' as Master of the Wardrobe: see G. E. Aylmer, *The King's Servants: The Civil Service of Charles I, 1625–1642* (London: Routledge & Kegan Paul, 1974), p. 350. In a letter to Basil Feilding, July 1631, Mary Buckingham implies that the trip was an 'embassy' (WRO, CR2017/C17).

32 WRO, CR2017/C1/2.

33 WRO, CR2017/F13/1 (Library List, 1703), unpaginated, lists 'Knowles's Hist: of ye Turkes', Purchas, *Hakluytus Posthumus* (1625–6), and Sandys, *Travels* (1627). Later books included Herbert's *Travels* (1638) and Cartwright's *Plays* (1651). Amongst the MSS Ottaviano Bon's 'Il seraglio di Gran Turca', listed E. Bernard, *Catologi Librorum Manuscriptorum Angliae et Hiberniae* (1697), vol. 2, pt 1, pp. 35–9 as a quarto (now BL, Additional MS 18661) probably belonged to William's son Basil, ambassador in Venice (c. 1608–74), who collected Italian materials.

34 The charts, now BL, Additional MS 18664 A&B, represent a fragment of the collection of five maps by John Daniell, and eight other maps including 'an old Book, in large 4to' (probably now BL, Additional MS 18665) which 'contains four Maps, all very ancient' listed in the *Catologi*. The sea journals, BL, Additional MS 18649, include two copies of the journal of the *Mary* outward bound (England to India, February–October 1631) and one of the *Mary*'s trips between Surat, Masulipatan, Gombroom and Surat (May–September 1632). These MSS appear as two items (1498 and 1499) in the list of Feilding manuscripts in the *Catologi*, but are listed as three separate 'sea iornall' in the 1703 library list.

35 *Calendar of State Papers Domestic, 1629–31*, p. 329; ambassadorial credentials, Charles I to Shahjhan and Shah Sufi, private collection. See also BL, Stowe MS 177, fol. 209r (copy of Charles I to Shah Sufi).

36 *Calendar of State Papers Domestic, 1633–34*, p. 195 (Howell to Windebank).

37 BL, India Office Records, B14, pp. 37, 42, 49, 123 (Court Minutes, July 1630–July 1631), and E3/13/1418. A letter from Hopkinson at Surat (WRO, CR2017/C14) suggests a different order of action with the horses taken after Feilding's departure.

38 BL, India Office Records, I/3/18, Daniel Collier and Jacques Pars (Surat) to the Governor General at Batavia, 8 Aug. 1632 ('Hague Transcripts').

39 M. Corbett and M. Norton (eds), *Engraving in England, Part III, The Reign of Charles I* (Cambridge: Cambridge University Press, 1964), p. 204 and plate 101c. Voerst was engraver to Charles I (see p. 202).

40 Rumours of his new-found wealth may have spurred the accusations of private trading raised on Denbigh's return and there was some suggestion he might become ambassador at Constantinople.

41 R. C. Temple (ed.), *The Travels of Peter Mundy in Europe and Asia, 1608–1667* (5 vols in 6, Hakluyt Society, 2nd series, 17, 35, 45–6, 55, 78, 1907–36), ii, p. 323.

42 For printed cottons, see D. Jenkins (ed.), *The Cambridge History of Western Textiles* (2 vols, Cambridge: Cambridge University Press, 2003), i, pp. 494–5. I am grateful to Dr Lynn Hulse for the suggestion that these may be muslins.

43 PRO, SP 16/267/4.IV, 'Goods from the Seahorse', 18 September 1634. It is hard to be sure that all the listed goods are Feilding's although some, such as the 'roll sealed up' directed to Hamilton clearly are, and some may belong to Captain Quail in whose trunk they were stored: see Millar, *Van Dyck in England*, p. 56, and *Calendar of State Papers Domestic, 1634–35*, p. 2. Interestingly, Denbigh's goods were transported home on a royal ship rather than an East India vessel (the *Seahorse* was under Charles I's direct commission, see W. Foster (ed.), *The English Factories in India, 1630–1633*, ed. W. Foster (Oxford: Clarendon Press, 1910), p. xvi).

44 WRO, CR2017/F1, Inventory ('In his Lops bedchamber in the orchard at Whitehall'), 20 April 1643.

45 O. Millar (ed.), *Abraham Van der Doort's Catalogue of the Collections of Charles I* (Walpole Society, 37, 1960), p. 94 (see also p. 112), cited in A. MacGregor (ed.), *The Late King's Goods: Collections, Possessions and Patronage of Charles I in the Light of the Commonwealth Sale Inventories* (Oxford: Oxford University Press and London: Alistair McAlpine, 1989), p. 417.

46 Brown and Vlieghe (eds), *Van Dyck*, p. 160, n. 2.

47 Feilding's correspondence during his eastern sojourn included numerous letters, particularly from the women of the wider Feilding-Villiers, circle, three of whom danced in *Temple*, and from other figures associated with the Queen's household, such as the Countess of Buckingham (WRO, CR2017/C1/36), Thomasina Carew (CR2017/C2/151), Ursula Beaumont (CR2017/C2/195), Elizabeth Cornwallis (CR2017/C2/190), and Barbara Villiers (CR2017/C2/191).

48 O&S, nos 311 and 312, and compare O&S, ii, p. 623, figs 100 and 101, which show how the design combines Vecellio's Turkish and Persian costumes.

49 O&S, nos 303, 304, 307 are drawn from Rabel's designs for two ballets (*Ballet du château de Bicêtre* (1632) and *Ballet de la douairière de Billebahaut* (1626) and an engraving of Trajan's column): see John Peacock, *The Stage Designs of Inigo Jones: The European Context* (Cambridge: Cambridge University Press, 1995), pp. 144–9.

50 The design for the Indian Shore (O&S, no. 295) is based on Parigi's design (see O&S, ii, p. 613, fig. 99) celebrating Vespucci's American landfall. See also Peacock, *Stage Designs of Inigo Jones*, p. 192 and plate 111.

51 Indamora's Headress (O&S, nos 315 and 316) is based on Vecellio's 'African Indian girl' (O&S, ii, p. 624, fig. 102). We should note, however, some similarities between the design of one of the Brachmani's headdresses and an idol shown in Herbert's book.

52 Peacock, *Stage Designs of Inigo Jones*, pp. 239–40.

53 Orgel, 'Plato, the magi, and Caroline politics', 671. *The Temple of Love* is, in fact, highly eclectic, combining classical mythology (Sappho, Homer, Orpheus), Platonic philosophy (Thelema, Sunesis) and even vernacular culture.

54 *Temple of Love*, lines 49–50 in O&S, ii, pp. 600–4. All references are to this edition unless otherwise stated.

55 N. Rothstein, 'Silk in the early modern period, c. 1500–1700', in D. Jenkins (ed.), *The Cambridge History of Western Textiles* (2 vols, Cambridge: Cambridge University Press, 2003), i, pp. 536 (esp. plate 12.5) and 539. One of the Persian coats may also show the outlines of the famous pomegranate design also associated with the east: see Rothstein, 'Silk', p. 531 and O&S, nos 311 and 312.

56 T. Herbert, *Some Yeares Travels into Divers Parts of Asia and Afrique Describing especially the Two Famous Empires, the Persian, and the Great Mogull* (London, 1638), sig. F4r. Like the Druids deployed in the King's masques, the Brahmins in the Queen's provide a parallel mystical authority: see Hugo Grotius, *True Religion* (London, 1632), sig. D9v, who compares them as the 'more civill and tractable kind of people'.

57 'Poligamy is odious among them, in which repose they cease not to villifie *Mahomitans* as people of an impure soule, and stuft with turpitude; yea in this they paralell the *Anticke* Romans ...': see Herbert, *Travels*, sig. F4r.

58 Herbert, *Travels*, sig. G2r.

59 P. Sidney, *A Defence of Poetry*, ed. J. A. van Dorsten (Oxford: Oxford University Press, 1966) p. 37, and L. Hutson, *The Usurer's Daughter* (London: Routledge, 1994), pp. 36–7, 41 and 108–9.

60 Sidney, *Defence of Poetry*, p. 27 (citing Cicero's *Epistles to Quintus*, 1.1.18.); 'Letter to Raleigh', in E. Spenser, *The Faerie Queene*, ed. A. C. Hamilton (Harlow: Longman, 2001), p. 716

61 J. Tatum, *Xenophon's Imperial Fiction: On The Education of Cyrus* (Princeton: Princeton University Press, 1989), p. 190.

62 Hutson, *Usurer's Daughter*, p. 108; Tatum, *Xenophon's Imperial Fiction*, p. 191.

63 Hutson, *Usurer's Daughter*, p. 37.

64 Xenophon, *Cyrupaedia, or the Institution and Life of Cyrus*, trans. P. Holland (London, 1632).

65 C. Nadon, *Xenophon's Prince* (Berkeley: University of California Press, 2001), p. 7 argues that Tatum sees Xenophon and Cyrus as 'ruthless Machaivellians some two thousand years *avant la lettre*' (see also pp. 13–24 for the influence of Xenophon on Machiavelli).

66 A. W. Pollard and G. R. Redgrave (eds), *Short Title Catalogue of Books Printed in England, Scotland and Ireland, 1475–1640, Volume 2, I–Z*, revised W. A. Jackson, F. S. Ferguson and K. F. Pantzer (London: Bibliographical Society, 1976), no. 26068, lists only four copies with the inserted dedication to Lord Holland.

67 A. Griffiths, *The Print in Stuart Britain* (London: British Museum, 1998), no. 103 (pp. 163–4).

68 For instance, Xenophon, *Cyrupaedia*, book 5, ch. 4.

69 L. G. Schwoerer, *'No Standing Armies!' The Anti-Military Ideology in Seventeenth-Century England* (Baltimore: Johns Hopkins University Press, 1974), p. 15. I am grateful to Ian Atherton for this reference.

70 Butler, *Theatre and Crisis*, pp. 29–30. There may only have been three performances of *Temple*, not four (as in Bentley, *Jacobean and Caroline Stage*, iii, pp. 216–18 and vi, p. 96); the evidence for the fourth performance on 14 March is not convincing. It describes a masque of ladies and gives no clear location (*Jacobean and Caroline Stage*, vi, p. 96).

71 M. Butler, 'Reform or reverence? The politics of the Caroline masque', in R. Mulryne and M. Shewring (eds), *Theatre and Government Under the Early Stuarts* (Cambridge: Cambridge University Press, 1993), pp. 118–56, esp. pp. 143–4, responds to Sharpe, *Criticism and Compliment*, and especially the argument (p. 245) that *The Temple of Love* is a critique of the 'sterility and unnaturalness of Platonic love'.

72 E. Denison Ross (ed.), *The Journal of Robert Stodart. Being an Account of his Experiences as*

a Member of Sir Dodmore Cotton's Mission in Persia, 1628–9 (London: Luzac, 1935), pp. 52–3, 78.
73 O&S, ii, p. 491, no. 226.
74 Townshend, *Tempe Restored*, in D. Lindley (ed.), *Court Masques* (Oxford: Oxford University Press, 1995), lines 151, 115 and 161.
75 Veevers, *Images of Love and Religion*, pp. 134–43, suggests a similar connection but as an allegory of Catholic politics (see n. 7 above). Unfortunately, Veevers depends on a loose paraphrase of the text (the youths come to search for love, not to import it as she claims), and as the Persians are fooled by the fleshly allures of the magicians they hardly seem ideal representatives for the Jesuits.
76 W. Prynne, *Histriomastix* (London, 1633), sigs T3v, C2v, 5E3r, 6Dr and G4v. Compare *News from Aleppo* (London, 1628) which describes Catholic worship as 'a mimicall action' (sig. A4r).
77 The phrase 'mystic tribe' (*The Temple of Love*, 231) may also deliberately echo the discourse of puritan prophesyings.
78 See above n. 4 for the French gazette's note of the significance of the date.
79 Letter of Rossingham to Puckering, 31 December 1633, in Thomas Birch (ed.), *The Court and Times of Charles I* (2 vols, London, 1848), ii, p. 228.
80 G. E. Cokayne, *Complete Peerage*, ed. V. Gibbs *et al.* (14 vols in 15, London and Stroud: St Catherine Press and Sutton, 1910–98), v, p. 144 and iv, p. 258: see also S. Poynting, '"In the name of all the sisters": Henrietta Maria's notorious whores', in C. McManus (ed.), *Women and Culture at the Courts of the Stuart Queens* (Basingstoke: Palgrave, 2003), pp. 175–7, and Sanders, 'Caroline salon culture', 452.
81 WRO, CR2017/C2/188, 'A note of such things as are in my lord of denbighs Truncke'.
82 'A lybell called ye health to diuers Lord and Ladies 1636' in BL, Harleian MS 6383, notebook, commonplace book, and parliamentary diary of Gervase Holles, 2nd Earl of Clare, fols 49–50.
83 'The Progresse', sometimes known as 'See what a love there is between', Folger Shakespeare Library, MS Vb 110, 88–90.
84 T. Cogswell, 'Underground verse and the transformation of early Stuart culture', in S. D. Amussen and M. Kishlansky (eds), *Political Culture and Cultural Politics in Early Modern England: Essays Presented to David Underdown* (Manchester: Manchester University Press, 1995), pp. 277–300.
85 Cf. 'Ill news from hell' and 'the sad news ... / ... come from heaven' (lines 166 and 175–6).
86 Puckering writing to Rossingham in 1636 commented on the recent selection of sheriffs and the King's resolve that 'all shall stand, like the laws of the Medes and Persians irrevocable': see Birch (ed.), *Court and Times of Charles I*, ii, p. 253. The proverbial phrase is ultimately from Daniel, 6.2.
87 BL, Harleian MS 6383, fols 49–50.

Chapter 7

Buried alive: Thomas May's 1631 *Antigone*

Karen Britland

At the start of Act 2, in Thomas May's version of *Antigone*, Argia, the widow of the Theban prince, Polynices, complains to her companions about the edict that is preventing his burial: 'Where can we vent our griefs?' she says, 'What power on earth / Can lend our woes redress?'[1] In the context of 1629 and the end of Charles's early parliaments, this lament has a certain topical resonance. In this essay, I want to consider May's play, which was written in the late 1620s and which was published in 1631, to show how it exemplifies some of the concerns that confronted writers throughout the 1630s.[2]

David Norbrook has pointed out that May's reputation has been conditioned by a disparaging verse satire written after his death in 1650.[3] The poem, possibly by Andrew Marvell, put forward the opinion that May espoused the parliamentary cause during the civil war in a fit of pique when he failed to gain the post of poet laureate on the death of his friend, Ben Jonson. However, both Norbrook and J. G. A. Pocock have recently interrogated this image of him, and have shown that his political affiliations were largely consistent throughout his life. For example, after a detailed examination of the translation history of Lucan's *Pharsalia*, Norbrook comments that May's version, published in 1627, is 'hard to interpret ... as an attempt to ingratiate himself with the court' because of the ways the poem could be used to intimate support for republicanism.[4] Nonetheless, he demonstrates that the poet did, quite successfully, seek royal patronage, noting that, around 1628, May's position became closer to 'the dominant voices of Caroline panegyric'.[5] May dedicated a continuation of his Lucan translation to Charles in 1630, and was rewarded with a commission to write two long historical poems for the King that were published in 1633. He also wrote a highly complimentary new year's poem to Queen Henrietta Maria, a copy of which is to be found in a manuscript book owned by the parliamentarian William Elyott, nephew of Sir Simonds D'Ewes.[6] At the outbreak of the civil wars, though, he espoused the parliamentary side, and wrote an official *History of Parliament*, published in 1647.

Although May's name appears relatively often in literary contexts in the seventeenth century, his work has been largely forgotten by modern critics.[7] Nonetheless, his plays speak to their historical moment in fascinating ways, not only manifesting general domestic concerns, but also engaging with a broader European context. An investigation into his *Antigone* provides further evidence that his adoption of the parliamentary cause at the outbreak of hostilities was consistent with his previous allegiances and not the result of a petulant whim. While, like many other writers of his generation, he sought patronage from the court and those associated with it, Norbrook suggests that he admired the idea of 'a politically independent nobility', and adds that in the late 1620s and early 1630s, the belief in such independence was not 'necessarily incompatible with monarchy'.[8] May's success at attracting patronage from Charles indicates his understanding of, and ability to play to, the system. His situation also exemplifies that of many artists and courtiers who found that the beliefs and allegiances they held in the 1620s led them further and further from agreement with the King's policies at the end of the 1630s. Perhaps most interestingly, it also indicates that the early Caroline court was more accommodating of divergent political positions than is sometimes deemed to be the case.

At no point, therefore, can May's *Antigone* be considered a polemical criticism of Charles's methods of government. While the play certainly provides strong reasons for eschewing autocracy, it also furnishes its readers with the image of a just ruler in the character of Theseus, and is a fascinating document that reveals the predicament of many of the writers of May's time.[9] It offered its audience several perspectives on monarchy, and, through its dedication to the courtier Endymion Porter, was just as much a bid for patronage as it was a criticism of Caroline rule.

Porter was a member of the King's bedchamber, and was known as a generous patron of the arts, receiving grateful dedications and poems from such men as William Davenant, Robert Herrick and Thomas Dekker. His own career had been greatly facilitated by the patronage of the Duke of Buckingham and he had become one of the King's closest companions, employed both as a foreign emissary and as an agent who purchased sculpture and painting. Brought up in Spain, he was a cosmopolitan figure, friendly with the leading artists of the day, and known for his ability to influence Caroline cultural fashion.[10] May's dedication can, therefore, be regarded as a reasonably successful bid for recognition from the heart of the court, and his play shows a consummate awareness of the directions in which courtly taste was moving.

May's *Antigone* picks up the famous narrative after Oedipus's fall and just before the deaths of Eteocles and Polynices, the heroine's rival brothers. By the end of Act 1, the brothers have slain each other in single combat, and Creon, Antigone's uncle, succeeds to the throne of Thebes. He immediately forbids Polynices' burial because of his association with the invading Argive army, and Antigone subsequently swears to resist this tyrannical prohibition and to bury her brother's body. She is caught in the act in the company of Argia, Polynices' widow, and is then incarcerated alive by Creon.

Unlike the Sophoclean version of the story, there is no real ambiguity to be found in May's adaptation: the watchwords of virtue and piety run firmly through the text of the play, and serve as an indicator of who is to be considered good, and who bad. Antigone is incontrovertibly virtuous and Creon tyrannical. Indeed, Edward Lautner, whose 1970 doctoral dissertation was a critical edition of the play, remarked disparagingly that 'May has robbed us of the grandeur and nobility of ... Sophocles' art', and notes that the playwright was content rather 'to mention "virtue" and "tyrant" many times hoping by [the] reiteration of a term to give dimension and substance to a concept'.[11]

In contrast to Lautner, I would like to see May's play, not as an inadequate translation of Sophocles, but as the adaptation of a pertinent story in the light of its author's awareness of contemporary politics and an emergent theatrical fashion. In the play's dedication to Porter, May defends his choice of the tragic genre with the assertion that 'saddnesse doth usually afford the best straines of writing', and notes that 'love itself (the usual argument of our new Comedy) is there best written where it is most distressed' (sig. A5). His *Antigone* is a self-declared tragic love story that is meant to appeal to contemporary dramatic taste, and its reiteration of a term such as 'virtue' is part and parcel of that fact. Moreover, in the context of King Charles's promotion of decorum at court, and his presentation of himself as a British hero whose virtue guaranteed national peace, the use of the terms 'virtue' and 'piety' have a topical, if not fashionable, effect.

Lautner also complained that May's heroine was not as headstrong and determined as her Sophoclean predecessor, grumbling that the author was 'content to portray endlessly a long-suffering, virtuous, pure Antigone' whose betrothed, Aemon, was 'the courtly lover worshipping the object of his love'.[12] I would argue that this is exactly the point: Antigone becomes a chaste and virginal heroine, whose familial piety directs her actions and leads her to a saint-like martyrdom. While the play retains its force as an interrogation of bad leadership in the figure of the tyrannical Creon, Antigone's power resides less in her ability to stand as a symbol of individual resistance and more in the way she inspires admiration and pity in her associates. She has more in common with a martyred medieval saint than with her Grecian namesake.

This serves to align her with an alternative type of heroism; one that values the Christian virtues of suffering and forbearance, and which provides an appropriate dramatic model for a tragic female character. Cleansed of any subversive implications that might accrue to her as a woman who stands against the state, May's play locates her firmly within a familial context, in effect domesticating her story.

Furthermore, in a radical departure from the Greek version of the play, the figure of Argia, the dead Polynices' widow, becomes as significant as Antigone herself within May's text. The two women meet over Polynices' body, each with the intention of performing his funeral rites. When they are captured, it is Argia who admits that she defied Creon's edict against the burial of her husband, and Antigone who, in Lautner's words, just says 'me too'.[13] The Sophoclean story is therefore transformed from a sisterly relation (with Antigone declaring that she will bury her brother, and Ismene, her sister, refusing to aid her), to a relation which privileges heterosexual coupling and the married state. Polynices' funeral rites become overwhelmingly the concern of his wife, while Antigone's part in the story focuses predominantly on the tragic impediments that forestall her marriage to Aemon.

This transformation, while again appearing to strip Antigone's character of any subversive implications, also serves to locate it very firmly in a Caroline tradition of romance predicated upon the idea of King Charles and Henrietta Maria's chaste and harmonious love for each other. For example, the first meeting the audience witnesses between Aemon and Antigone occurs in 'unfrequented woods' that are described by Aemon as a 'sad and solitary place' that 'suites with [his] thoughts'. Aemon declares his love to Antigone, asking if she will,

> ... give me leave but to confess my flame,
> Which never can be hid; a better fire
> More chast, more true, and full of constancy,
> (I dare maintain it) warmes no breast on earth.
> No earthly power but sweet Antigone
> Can sentence me to bliss or endless woe. (Act 1, sig. B3v)

The measured rhythms and quasi-religious vocabulary here contribute to the sense that Aemon's intentions are pure and untainted by physical lust. Indeed, his lament invokes a discourse of refined ardour and the mutual exchange of souls that draws heavily on Henrietta Maria's predilection for Neo-Platonism, already being promoted on the Caroline court stage.

In 1626, the Queen herself took part in a version of *Les Bergeries*, a pastoral play written by the French courtier Honorat de Bueil, Sieur de Racan, and applauded by Parisian high society for the nobility of its language. It drew its influences from fashionable romances such as Guarini's *Il pastor fido* and

Montemayor's *Diana*, and owed a particular debt to Honoré d'Urfé's *L'Astrée*, putting forward refined notions of social relations between men and women that privileged fidelity, discretion, marriage, and control over the passions.[14] May's play seems to draw on this pastoral precedent, engaging with the new Caroline fashion, and it comes as no surprise to discover that standing behind *Antigone*, or rather, standing between May's play and that of Sophocles, is a sixteenth-century French version of the tragedy.

In 1580, Robert Garnier, a supremely successful playwright in France, published his version of *Antigone* (significantly subtitled, *La Piété*), with its own development of the Antigone/Aemon love plot. There are enough similarities between the two plays to be able to assert confidently that May's text was influenced by its French predecessor. For example, setting aside for a moment the insistent emphasis on Antigone as a figure of piety, May's opening scene (which depicts Antigone guiding the blind Oedipus, and which was connected by Lautner to a similar moment in Seneca's *Phoenissae*) is clearly a truncated version of the opening scene of Garnier's tragedy.

May's decision to echo Garnier is interesting in several ways. Firstly, and most superficially, the new English Queen was French, and Garnier's plays, which had enjoyed celebrity at the Valois court, were still in popular circulation under the Bourbons. Indeed, in 1611, Princess Elizabeth, Henrietta Maria's eldest sister, mounted an amateur production of Garnier's *Bradamante* at Saint Germain-en-Laye, the country home of the royal offspring.[15] In addition, members of the Garnier family were employed in Henrietta Maria's household, and a certain Claude Garnier wrote a panegyric poem to her on her betrothal in 1624.[16] By adapting a Garnier tragedy and dedicating it to one of King Charles's close associates, May was on extremely safe, and potentially profitable ground.

However, Garnier's play can also be shown to have provided material for a subtle critique of the English political climate in the 1630s. The French *Antigone* was written in the aftermath of the 1572 Saint Bartholomew Day's massacre and, as Gillian Jondorf has noted, contains references to the horrors of civil war and to the dangers of the Huguenots' solicitation of foreign aid in their struggle.[17] Although Garnier was a staunch Catholic, an officer of the Crown, and a man indebted to the ruling house of the Valois, he was not a flatterer, and never a courtier. In effect, his position as a writer in France was similar to May's own in that he was dependent on the system of courtly patronage, yet did not always concur with the direction of royal policy. Taking Garnier's play as a model, May's version of the story interrogates the prevailing political climate, even as it participates in the fashionable genre of romance promoted by the Caroline court.[18] Most significantly, the end of his play, with its motif of Theseus handing the government of Thebes back into the hands of the Thebans, investigates the concept of monarchical autocracy at a time when Charles was in the process of recalling what would be the last of his early parliaments.

Martin Butler has noted of Ben Jonson's 1629 play, *The New Inn*, that it was, in part, a response to the expectations of the moment, figuring a notion of rapprochement and accommodation, rather than confrontation.[19] Interestingly, both Jonson's play and May's were published in octavo by the printer Thomas Harper in 1631; an indication, perhaps, of the two playwrights' close association at this time.[20] The end of May's *Antigone* certainly has a reconciliatory agenda similar to that of *The New Inn*, tempering the image of Creon's tyranny with Antigone's filial piety and with the sword of justice wielded by Theseus. Nonetheless, his version of *Antigone* frequently foregrounds the problems of interrupted or unheard speech in a manner which resounds disturbingly with the historical situation.

In Act 2 of May's play, as I have already mentioned, the widowed Argia complains to her companions about the edict that is preventing the burial of her husband, Polynices: 'Where can we vent our griefs?' she says, 'What power on earth / Can lend our woes redress?' At the end of the same Act, the Theban Chorus enquires: 'What shall we do to cure this fatal stain / Upon our nation? Nothing but complain' (sig. C3v). A sort of quasi-public lamenting is the only course open both to the chorus of native Thebans and to Argia, who is informed by her companion Ornitus that,

> no tears, nor prayers can move
> The ruthless tyrant's mind; an impious oath
> Hath bound his cruelty. (Act 2, sig. B8)

The notion of impiety here is significant, and is the means through which May's apparently domesticated tragedy takes on its political force.

We first encounter the notion at the very start of the play in the first words that Antigone addresses to Oedipus, her father. He has urged her to leave him to his banishment, and she responds:

> Never, never Sir.
> While you are here, Cythaeron's craggy mount
> Is my abode, and far preferr'd before
> ... the towers
> Of wealthy Thebes, for which my brothers strive.
> ... what but impiety,
> And brothers' hatred shall I there behold? (Act 1, sig. B1v)

Piety, which traditionally means to us a reverence and obedience to God, also has the older connotation of 'faithfulness to the duties naturally owed to parents and relatives' (*OED*, piety II. 3). Indeed, it is glossed as such in Cesare Ripa's famous Renaissance emblem book, the *Iconologia*, which asserts that piety 'is the discharge of duty to God, to parents, or those in superior relation'.[21] The notion of impiety invoked here by Antigone is closely linked with the notion of fraternal hatred, and contrasted with the filial piety that she proffers to Oedipus in refusing to abandon him in his banishment. Indeed, the equation is made specific at the end of Act 1, when the Theban Chorus specifically terms the brothers' hate 'impious'.

Not only does May's play condemn Polynices and Eteocles for this sort of impious neglect, it is a criticism, as I have mentioned, that is also levelled at Creon. Creon's first act on acceding to the throne after the deaths of the rival brothers is to forbid the burials of Polynices and his invading Argive warriors. Honouring the dead is, in the economy of this play, a divinely established injunction, and those who disobey it are found to be doubly guilty because they also invariably neglect to honour the living. By seeking to punish the impious brothers in this way, Creon becomes equally impious because he neither respects his relations nor his duty to God. Nonetheless, he is confident that his edict is justified because of his status as a prince.

The differences between these two views of monarchical authority are given explicit expression at the start of Act 4 just after Antigone's capture. Creon accuses her of disloyalty, and tells her that, as a Theban, she is bound to obey his crown and laws. She refuses to excuse her behaviour because, she says, she acted 'by direction from the gods themselves'. Creon counters: 'Is disobedience merit? / Or do the gods command subjects to breake / The lawes of Princes?', and Antigone replies:

> Yes, their wicked lawes,
> Which thwart the will of heauen, the rule of nature,
> And those pure principles, which human breasts
> Did at their first original deriue
> From that Celestiall essence. (Act 4, sig. D5)

Creon appears to believe that princes' laws carry an automatic divine sanction, while Antigone suggests that both subjects and princes are bound by the same divine laws, and that a prince's word may therefore be resisted if it thwarts 'the will of heaven'.

The lawfulness of a royal edict was a particularly pertinent topic in the late 1620s because of popular discontent over what many considered to be illegal taxes levied by the King. In 1628, this came to a head with the parliamentary impeachment of Roger Maynwaring, Charles's chaplain. In 1627, Maynwaring had published two sermons under the title *Religion and Alegiance*, which maintained that the king was within his rights to impose taxes without the agreement of parliament, and that those who refused obedience transgressed the laws of God. Reporting for parliament, John Pym contended that his book was 'a plot and attempt of overthrowing the whole fabric of the government of the kingdom', and that it taught that the king had absolute power, and obliged subjects to submit to illegal commands against their conscience.[22] May's *Antigone* might therefore be said to speak to its historical moment as well as to an established theme within Renaissance tragedy when it implicitly poses the question: 'when does it become lawful for the subject to resist?'[23] The Creon/Antigone dialogue reflects aspects of both sides of the debate about the monarch's power and his position in relation to the law. However, it leaves little room for disagreement that Creon is a tyrant.

Creon's edict against the Argive burials is also shown in the play to be incontrovertibly dangerous for Theban security. At several points, it is made clear that his lack of respect for the corpses will bring foreign displeasure down on Thebes. For example, at the end of Act 2, the Theban Chorus lament:

> Unhappy Creon, thwarting Nature's law
> Upon thyself and fatal Thebes to draw
> The hate and curse of nations, who will make
> The quarrel theirs. (Act 2, sig. C2v)

The fear of foreign invasion in May's version of the play is reiterated on several occasions. Strangely, however, it is precisely this feared foreign intervention (which manifests itself in the figure of Theseus) that finally brings peace to a beleaguered Thebes. This introduces a kind of chiasmic relation into the play's structure, that, I think, is precisely the result of the negotiations a playwright had to undertake in order to write this type of political allegory. On the one hand, Creon's impious actions are subject to condemnation and stand as a warning publicly to observe one's duty to one's dependents or to run the risk of retribution and conflict. On the other, foreign intervention itself is presented as an act of piety, a duty to one's beleaguered brethren. And here again, I would argue, a certain historical analogy can be drawn.

In the context of the late 1620s, the siege of Thebes by Polynices and his Argive army resounds with the conflict at the Ile de Rhé and La Rochelle that began to affect England in 1627 and was concluded with the Treaty of Susa in 1629. While I am loath to draw a direct analogy between the play's significations and the La Rochelle conflict, it is perhaps enough to note that delays in England's preparations of a fleet left the Rochellois stranded and besieged by the French, suffering from thirst and starvation. The sense of abandonment, of a lack of responsibility to the French Protestants, is certainly similar to the lack of respect offered the Argive corpses by Creon. Furthermore, the play makes it clear that there is little distinction to be drawn between the two armies who are fighting each other on the sides of two brothers in what amounts to a civil war. The same could be said of the La Rochelle conflict in each of two ways. On one hand, Charles's support of the French Huguenots opposed him to Louis XIII, his new brother-in-law, in a manner that disrupted a marital alliance that had been conceived, in part, as a defence against the threat of Spain. On the other hand, by aligning himself with, and then failing to come to the relief of, international Protestantism, Charles could be said to be neglecting his responsibilities to his French brethren.[24] May's decision to adapt the Antigone story at this particular historical moment cannot be seen as anything but apposite.

In its figures of the autocratic Creon and the just Theseus, the play therefore presents the two extremes of leadership, offering, I would argue, a criticism and an example of the possibilities of Caroline rule. It also, superlatively, turns the domestic ideal of the Caroline romance back upon itself in its reformulation of the idea that, at its roots, national politics is predicated upon notions of familial responsibility. Despite apparently buying into the fashion for romance drama being promoted at court, and even while it turns Antigone into a heroine worthy of one of the Queen's pastorals, the play does not subscribe to the vision of the Caroline couple's union as the source of all national and international harmony. Instead it promotes a version of piety and love based on active familial responsibility that it then offers up as the basis for good and honourable leadership. The idea of the family put forward here is very different from that of the quasi-magical Caroline marriage presented in official court masques that was imagined to spread harmony out to the nation simply by example.

The play's notions of honour and responsibility are strongly linked with the character of Theseus, who arrives at the end of the action to liberate Thebes for the Thebans with the words:

> ... let Thebes be govern'd by her own;
> 'Twas not our war's intention to enthrall
> Your land, but free it from a tyrant's yoke;
> And to preserve the conquer'd, not destroy them.
> We drew the sword of justice, not of conquest. (Act 5, sig. E5v)

This is a complete departure from the Sophoclean *Antigone*, and significantly introduces into the play both the image of a peace-loving ruler opposed to tyranny, and the notion of government being placed into the hands of the nation – a pertinent topic in the late 1620s. May's Theseus is a ruler who takes care of the unfortunate and impoverished over and above the rich and noble, and whose care for his subjects makes him tantamount to being the guardian of world peace.[25]

In his city of Athens, we are told, there stands,

> A gratious altar, where white mercy dwells,
> The poor man's goddesse ...
> No Frankincense, nor rich Arabian fumes
> Do feed that altar: sighs, and floods of tears

>   Are all that goddess craues; no gold adornes
>   Her humble roofes, as those proud temples rais'd
>   By happy Monarchs, and great conquerers. (Act 2, sig. B8r–v)

This altar is striking in its austerity, and again as an innovation in May's text, seems to have a significance beyond its immediate impact on the development of the story. In the context of the charges made by parliament in 1628 that the English church was threatened by Arminianism and popery, this altar has a very old-school Protestant bias.[26] Furthermore, as a locus to which the exiled and impoverished have recourse, it positions Theseus as the champion of beleaguered underdogs everywhere. If May's additions to the *Antigone* story are to be read quasi-allegorically it seems difficult not to see Theseus as a model of the heroic ruler and champion of international Protestantism that many in England were hoping first Prince Henry, and then Charles himself, would turn out to be.

The plain style of the Athenian altar is also carried over into the play's ideas about language, and stands against courtly luxury and unnecessary excess. In May's play, the notion of an intricate, flattering language is connected explicitly and significantly with the court. Rebuking Aemon for his compliments and protestations of love, Antigone remarks:

>   You come from Court, and speak as that has taught you.
>   This place knows no such language. (Act 1, sig. B3v)

Aemon protests that he 'was never tax'd of flattery' and proceeds to address Antigone in Neo-Platonic metaphors that she subsequently leaves unchallenged. At first glance, this appears to validate the fashionable discourse of Neo-Platonism expounded in Queen Henrietta Maria's pastorals because, expressed between the play's two most virtuous characters, the exchange has to be interpreted as sincere and genuine. However, while Aemon's praise might be true in the singular case of Antigone, her rebuke indicates that the discourse exists at court in a perverted form. In a way, therefore, May's play renovates the idea of Neo-Platonism, stripping it of courtly affectation and giving it back a personal and spiritual signification more in tune with the earlier sentiments of a Sidney or a Spenser. The play's measured iambic pentameters, and its reformation of Neo-Platonism into a discourse that does not lie, contribute to a sense that it is proposing a form of behaviour, and perhaps language and theatre, that is of a spirit with Theseus's Athenian altar. Rather than being ostentatious and superficial, this way of life is built on truth, humility and devotion.

Writing about the Countess of Pembroke's translation of Garnier's *Marc Antoine*, Victor Skretkowicz has suggested that it consciously employed an 'unpretentious' rhetoric that bore witness to the translator's views about 'democracy, republicanism and linguistic purity'.[27] The idea of a plain language deliberately chosen to stand against linguistic excess is attractive, and may even be associated with Ben Jonson's famous views in *Timber, or Discoveries*:

> Wheresoever, manners, and fashions are corrupted, Language is. It imitates the publicke riot. The excesse of feasts, and apparell, are the notes of a sick State; and the wantonnesse of language, of a sick mind.[28]

May, who was a close friend of Jonson's, appears to have held similar views. For example, in a commendatory poem to Joseph Rutter on the publication of the latter's *Shepherd's Holy-day* (1635), he praised his friend's 'elegantly plaine' style, noting that plays and pastorals 'should not perplexe, but recreate the braines'.[29] There is perhaps a coded reference here to Henrietta Maria's infamously convoluted pastoral, *The Shepherds' Paradise*, performed in 1633 and described by a contemporary as lasting seven or eight hours.[30] In contrast to this exposition of the complexities of Neo-Platonic love, May advocates a simple style that does not obscure meaning, and yet he despairs that a reader's 'unjust ignorance' will privilege the obscure because those of 'weake sence' always prefer what they don't understand. *Antigone*'s description of Theseus and his austere altar participates in this idea of plainness, creating an image of a ruler who stands against the ignorant, the unjust and the flamboyant.

This advocation of religious and linguistic austerity is, perhaps, an odd thing to find in a play dedicated to Endymion Porter, a career courtier with known Catholic associations. However, Porter's 'modesty' is honoured in May's dedication, and connected with a desire to see 'the King blest with moe such seruants as you are' (A5v–6r). Conventional flattery aside, this vocabulary links the choice of dedicatee to the play's motifs about counsel, praising Porter as someone who is 'worthy to stand ... in the presence of a King' and implicitly encouraging him to be a good advisor. In the late 1620s, because of his Spanish connections, Porter was involved in the negotiations for an Anglo-Spanish peace that renewed Protestant hopes for the restoration of the Palatinate. The notion of good counsel was therefore extremely pertinent to his position at the time, and May's dedication, prefacing a play that places a profound emphasis upon familial and national responsibility, plays to this moment.

The play also resounds with events after the killing of Buckingham, Porter's chief benefactor, and it is tempting to wonder whether it was written partly as a response to the execution of the murderer John Felton, whose corpse was refused due burial by the King and hung on public display. Norbrook has described how, in certain quarters, because of a popular dislike of Buckingham, Felton's actions provoked a 'chorus of praise for his valour'.[31] One particularly fine epitaph, he says, 'described Felton's corpse hanging in chains', and was concluded in one manuscript version by a quotation from Lucan: *Coelo tegitur qui non habet urnam* ('He is covered by the heavens who has no sepulchral urn'). This, Norbrook notes, comes from the *Pharsalia* and occurs after Caesar's defeat of Pompey and his refusal to bury the corpses that litter the battlefield.

The lament of the Theban Chorus at the end of Act 2 in *Antigone* is taken in large part, and often word for word, from this moment in May's own translation of the *Pharsalia*.[32] Creon is informed that his anger is ultimately fruitless as 'all to natures bosome goe', and that in spite of his actions, the Argives' bodies will be burned 'when earth and seas to flames are turned' (Act 2, sig. C3). It is possible that May simply found this section of the *Pharsalia* appropriate to the *Antigone* theme, yet, given the very public nature of Felton's punishment, it is tempting to read it as a direct comment upon this specific event. Although May's play in no way excuses the actions of the invading Argive army whose corpses litter the battlefield, it makes no bones about the fact that it sees Creon's edict as unnatural, impious and dangerous.

The Chorus subsequently informs us that Creon's land will be 'claim'd by Pluto as his monarchy' and rendered useless to its living residents. In other words, the stain of the ruler's edict will pollute the country, rendering it barren and uninhabitable. However, *Antigone* takes place at a moment characterised by a change of government and Creon's autocratic order soon gives way to Theseus's democratic rationality. In a way, the play's dedication to Porter locates him as the kind of advisor who might promote this latter type of government. Furthermore, as one of Buckingham's former adherents, he was perhaps the most appropriate person to heal discord and to advocate a notion of justice based on respect and responsibility.

Nonetheless, as I have noted, the play registers an anxiety about appropriate counsel through numerous instances where complaints go unheeded or unheard. This anxiety is particularly evident in the second significant addition that May makes to the Sophoclean story in which King Creon ventures out at night on to the pestilential battlefield and receives a prophecy from a reanimated corpse. This moment in the play is again borrowed from May's own translation of Lucan's *Pharsalia* where, at the end of Book 6, the would-be usurper Sextus Pompey entreats a prophecy from Erictho, the Thessalian witch, out of a cowardly fear for what his future holds.[33] In a very similar manner, Creon, disregarding the misgivings of his companion Ianthus, causes three hags to reanimate a corpse which prophesies that his future holds his death. It is a fascinating addition to the plot, and is one that at once panders to a vogue for theatrical witchery, while at the same time intersecting closely with the play's representations of appropriate rule.

On a very obvious level, this scene makes it clear that Creon is pathologically misguided in his choice of counsellors. Ianthus begs him not to consult the witches, but to solicit a prognostication from Tiresias, Thebes's officially sanctioned seer. Creon's impiety in consulting the witches is underlined by Ianthus's opinion that Tiresias uses a magic 'more divine and pure', and that he has been 'taught from the wisdom of the gods above'. Nonetheless, I would also argue that this moment draws together all the moments in the play when characters lament their inabilities to get their complaints heard, crystallising a discourse about good counsel and a ruler's responsibility.

The notion of responsibility etymologically carries with it a notion of responding (from its Latin root, *respondere*), implying a two-way discourse, and consideration for another. Creon blocks this reciprocal motion by refusing to acknowledge the complaints of his subjects, effectively condemning those subjects to silence, and also failing in his own role as a ruler who should respond. The episode with the hags therefore demonstrates Creon's impiety, his bad choice of counsellors, and his neglect of his true subjects' right of reply. Furthermore, even though he is insistent in soliciting such an infernal prophecy, Creon then refuses to acknowledge the future that is foreseen. The baleful reanimated corpse utters only prognostications of death which Creon refuses to accept – even with this counsellor, therefore, there is no right of reply, no question of acceptance.

The episode with the hags can also be taken to stand as a motif for the silenced subject *per se*, for the unpatronised poet, for the counsellor whose advice goes unheard. May's hags place a great deal of emphasis on the majority of the corpses' inability to prophesy because they are too far gone in death, the carcasses yielding only 'cold dead tongues' (sig. C8). This image links the Argive bodies into the play's economy of silences, locating them alongside the Argive widows who are seeking a new idiom in which to lament. Here, as before, there is a blockage in discourse, and a sense that the corpses' language (which, when it amounts to anything at all, comes down to 'broken yells' and 'dismal hizzings'), stands outside the bounds of what Creon (and the witches) recognise as comprehensible. Just as Aemon's apparent flattery was incomprehensible to the virtuous Antigone in her self-imposed exile, so the cold dead tongues of the Argive corpses appear to be unable to speak in any language that Creon is prepared to understand.

Furthermore, when the hags finally command a fresh carcass to speak, it speaks with an authority that is not its own, acting under the constraint of witchcraft and uttering its prophecy of what fate has in store for Creon. The corpse speaks from the same boundary of death in life that will be occupied by Antigone in the closing moments of the play, when she is buried alive at Creon's command. I would like to argue that, on some level, these two moments come to stand, on the one hand, for the writer who must speak in a language that is not entirely his own (who is writing for a patron, or doing lip-service to a politics), and, on the other, for the writer whose visions are unpalatable to the general feeling of the time, who must therefore speak from the margins of life, figuratively dead to influence, in a language that is nearly incomprehensible within the prevailing system.

May's play, I think, registers some deep anxieties about the trend in Caroline politics at the dawn of the 1630s, juxtaposing notions of tyrannical rule against an ideal of leadership based upon monarchical responsibility and dialogue with the people. I think it is not inconsequential that the voices raised against Creon in this play are predominantly female, and express a sense of impotence against the unhearing machinery of state. Joan Landes has noted that, under a divine-right monarch, 'all subjects, male and female, shared a subordinate posture'.[34] The effect of the king's supremacy, she says, was 'to "domesticate", even un-man, those who ought to have been his peers'. In the light of this comment, May's decision to adapt *Antigone* is fascinating. Adopting the courtly fashion for romance, he nonetheless takes up a potentially oppositional position, ventriloquising female discourse in a manner that both accords his female characters a political voice, and yet also gestures towards his own and his peers' sense of impotence under an increasingly autocratic monarchical regime. Nonetheless, in its dedication to Endymion Porter, *Antigone* placed its author as a player within the system of courtly patronage, demonstrating how people whose political positions would diverge wildly by the end of the decade were working together at its start.

May is an extremely accomplished writer who deserves more consideration than he has received, and whose early work bears witness to the political tendencies that were to lead him to espouse the parliamentary cause during the civil war. In the likely absence of a parliament, I think that, in his *Antigone*, it is writing itself that is proposed as a forum for debate. Argia's question, 'Where shall we vent our griefs?', is answered by the very fact of the play's existence. However, it is an answer that remains contingent, grounded in an awareness of the constraints of patronage, and the possibility that a writer, like the figure of Antigone herself (or indeed, like May's own literary reputation), could be banished into silence, could be buried alive.

NOTES

1 Thomas May, *The Tragedy of Antigone, The Theban Princesse* (London, 1631), sig. B7v.

2 See Edward Lautner for a detailed discussion of the date of the play's composition. Lautner follows Allan Chester who believes that May's tragedies were written around the time of his Lucan translations; that is *c*. 1627. Mary Ransom Burke, however, believes that the plays were all written in the 1630s. My own feeling, for reasons explained in this essay, is that *Antigone* should be dated to 1629-30: Edward John Lautner, 'A modern-spelling edition of Thomas May's "The tragedy of Antigone, the Theban Princesse"' (unpublished doctoral dissertation, Case Western Reserve University, 1970), pp. xii–xiii; Allan Griffith Chester, 'Thomas May: Man of Letters, 1595–1650' (unpublished dissertation, University of Pennsylvania, 1932), pp. 97–9, 116–30; Mary

Ransom Burke, 'The tragedy of "Cleopatra, Queen of Aegypt" by Thomas May' (unpublished doctoral dissertation, Fordham University, 1943).

3   David Norbrook, 'Lucan, Thomas May, and the creation of a republican literary culture', in Kevin Sharpe and Peter Lake (eds), *Culture and Politics in Early Stuart England* (Basingstoke: Macmillan, 1994), p. 45.

4   Norbrook, 'Lucan', pp. 50–7.

5   Norbrook, 'Lucan', pp. 57–61. For J. G. A. Pocock's views, see 'Thomas May and the narrative of civil war', in Derek Hirst and Richard Strier (eds), *Writing and Political Engagement in Seventeenth-Century England* (Cambridge: Cambridge University Press, 1999), pp. 112–44.

6   See Bodl., MS Rawl. poet 116, fols 48v–9v.

7   For example, May wrote dedicatory verses to books published by Philip Massinger, James Shirley, and Joseph Rutter. His name is mentioned in Thomas Heywood's poem 'The hierarchie of the blessed angels', and (as 'Lucan's translator') in John Suckling's 'A session of the poets'. It also occurs in *Wit's Recreations* (1640) in a poem 'To Mr. Thomas May'; in the sixth sestiad of Samuel Sheppard's 'The times displayed'; and in William Heminges's 'Elegy on Randolph's finger'. See also, Mathew Stevenson, 'In honorem poetarum', and Aston Cockain, 'To my mistress before Mr Mayes Lucan that I sent her'.

8   Norbrook, 'Lucan', p. 62.

9   I use the term 'readers' deliberately because the play was almost certainly not performed.

10 See *Dictionary of National Biography*, sub. Endymion Porter.

11 Lautner, 'Antigone', p. xxxv.

12 *Ibid.*, p. xlvi.

13 See *ibid.*, p. xlvi.

14 See [Honorat de Bueil, Sieur de Racan], *Artenice* (London, [1626]).

15 Louis Batiffol, *Marie de Médicis and the French Court*, trans. Mary King (London: Chatto and Windus, 1908), p. 156.

16 See Eugène Griselle, *État de la maison du roi Louis XIII* (Paris: Paul Catin, 1912), pp. 83, 85; and Claude Garnier, *Le Bouquet de Lys et de la Rose au nom de l'alliance de France et d'Angleterre* (Paris, 1624). A certain François Garnier, who signed himself 'Procureur General de la Reine de la Grande Bretagne', translated portions of the 1601 edition of John Stow's *Annals* in 1628 (University of Leeds, Brotherton Library, Special Collections, MS 97).

17 Gillian Jondorf, *Robert Garnier and the Themes of Political Tragedy in the Sixteenth Century* (Cambridge: Cambridge University Press, 1969), p. 39.

18 Some of Garnier's plays were already available in English. Thomas Kyd translated his Senecan drama, *Cornélie*, in 1594, and Mary, Countess of Pembroke, famously based her *Tragedie of Antonie* on Garnier's *Marc Antoine*.

19 Martin Butler, 'Late Jonson', in Gordon McMullan and Jonathan Hope (eds), *The Politics of Tragicomedy: Shakespeare and After* (London: Routledge, 1992), p. 172.

20 May and Jonson are reputed to have been good friends. See Julie Sanders (ed.), *The New Inn*, in *The Cambridge Edition of the Works of Ben Jonson* (Cambridge, forthcoming,

2006), for Jonson's association with Harper, and for more information about the printer's output in the years between 1628 and 1632. Harper subsequently published May's *The Tragedie of Cleopatra* (1639), and was involved in the publication of the second Jonson folio.

21 See Cesare Ripa, *Iconologia*, ed. George Richardson (2 vols, London, 1779), ii, p. 110.

22 See J. F. Larkin and P. L. Hughes (eds), *Stuart Royal Proclamations* (2 vols, Oxford: Clarendon Press, 1973–83), ii, pp. 197–9. See also Roger Maynwaring, *Religion and Alegiance* (London, 1627). Maynwaring's book was eventually suppressed by royal decree for 'trenching upon the Lawes of this Land, & proceedings of Parliaments, whereof hee was ignorant'.

23 The phrase is Diane Purkiss's and is used in a discussion of the Countess of Pembroke's *Antonie*. See Purkiss, 'Blood, sacrifice, marriage: why Iphigenia and Mariam have to die', *Women's Writing*, 6:1 (1999), 37.

24 Behind all this, of course, there is also the shadow of the restoration of the Palatinate to Charles's brother-in-law, Frederick V.

25 The character of Theseus does not figure in Garnier's tragedy either. However, May might have been influenced by the opening moments of Shakespeare and Fletcher's *The Two Noble Kinsmen* which show Theseus petitioned by the widows of unburied Argive warriors.

26 See Kevin Sharpe, *The Personal Rule of Charles I* (New Haven and London: Yale University Press, 1992), p. 280.

27 Victor Skretkowicz, 'Mary Sidney Herbert's *Antonius*, English Philhellenism and the Protestant cause', *Women's Writing*, 6:1 (1999), 14, 22. Skretkowicz also points to a family resemblance when he notes that Sir Philip Sidney's *Defence of Poetry* attacked 'the exceptionally pretentious and artificially florid English-Greek styles ... preserved by writers of the euphuist school such as Lyly, Greene and Pettie' (p. 14).

28 C. H. Herford and Percy and Evelyn Simpson (eds), *Ben Jonson* (11 vols, Oxford: Clarendon Press, 1925–52), viii, p. 593. Jonson is obviously advocating a straightforward language as opposed to a copious, and implicitly courtly, idiom. For a discussion of Jonson's use of plain language, see Wesley A. Trimpi, *Ben Jonson's Poems: A Study of the Plain Style* (Stanford: Stanford University Press, 1962); and Ian Donaldson, 'Jonson's poetry', in Richard Harp and Stanley Stewart (eds), *The Cambridge Companion to Ben Jonson* (Cambridge: Cambridge University Press, 2000), pp. 119–39. See also, Kenneth J. E. Graham, *The Performance of Conviction: Plainness and Rhetoric in the Early English Renaissance* (Ithaca: Cornell University Press, 1994).

29 Joseph Rutter, *The Shepheards Holy-day* (London, 1635), sig. A3v. Ben Jonson also contributed a commendatory verse to this volume.

30 Beaulieu to Puckering, 10 January 1633, in Thomas Birch (ed.), *The Court and Times of Charles I* (2 vols, London, 1848), ii, p. 216.

31 Norbrook, 'Lucan', p. 55.

32 Cf. May, *Antigone*, sig. C3, and May, *Lucan's Pharsalia* (London, 1627), Book 7, sigs N7–8.

33 May, *Lucan's Pharsalia*, sigs L1–7.

34 Joan B. Landes, *Women and the Public Sphere* (London: Cornell University Press, 1988), p. 21.

Chapter 8

Placing Caroline politics on the professional comic stage

Matthew Steggle

In the last quarter of a century, there has been almost a complete *volte-face* in scholarly perceptions of 1630s drama. Long considered as apolitical or even anti-political, this drama is now increasingly seen as engaged in the politics of the time, and this essay will survey the current state of play in this area, and suggest that yet more remains to be done on the political engagement of drama of this period. In particular, three main topics will be taken as examples: the court as an institution; foreign policy in the shape of the Thirty Years' War; and the state of the nation as a whole.

As recently as the mid-1980s, the dominant critical paradigm for considering theatre of this period was still that of Alfred Harbage's 1936 book, *Cavalier Drama*, in which, as the title suggests, it is read largely in terms of the civil war to come, and firmly aligned with the royalists in that war. This paradigm influenced even the best of subsequent writing on 1630s drama, such as R. J. Kaufmann's 1961 study of the quintessential Caroline playwright, Richard Brome. For Kaufmann, as for many of his predecessors, Caroline drama was of no great intrinsic merit, being mainly interesting as 'the road between the worlds of Jonson and Congreve': while the 'Jacobean masters' and the practitioners of Restoration drama were touched by literary genius, the dramatists of Charles's era were not, as they worked through the last years of the Shakespearean stage. Insofar as Caroline drama was of interest, it was often read as a symptom of the moral and intellectual weakening of the country in the lead-up to the civil war, and its tone was interpreted as habitually nostalgic, fatalistic, and even elegiac. This interpretation certainly prevailed into the 1980s: for example, David Farley-Hills's influential reading of Brome's *A Jovial Crew* sees that play as unequivocally 'cavalier' in its attitudes and sympathies in the face of an increasingly recalcitrant populace.[1]

But such a reading grants 1630s dramatists a remarkable degree not just of foresight, but also of hindsight, in their presupposed instinctive understanding of their place in history, and is clearly untenable. In his seminal study of Caroline drama *Theatre and Crisis 1632–1642*, published in 1984, Martin Butler argues that the plays of this period can be seen as politically engaged, energetic and dangerous.[2] For Butler, theatres formed one of the few arenas for public debate and foci for public opposition during Charles's Personal Rule. Brome's work, in Butler's account, is a central example of a popular, politically radical drama that did not shrink from confronting the raw issues of the day. This marks a major departure from the political interpretation offered by Kaufmann, in which Brome's plays, like 1630s drama in general, are naturally conservative, pro-hierarchical, and indeed reactionary. Butler's book sparked an overdue debate about the wider terms of reference of Caroline professional drama in general.

Since 1984, subsequent work on Caroline drama has continued to explore the field in the light of Butler's arguments. Such work includes two book-length overviews of the field – Ira Clark's *Professional Playwrights: Massinger, Ford, Shirley, and Brome*, and Julie Sanders's *Caroline Drama: The Plays of Massinger, Ford, Shirley and Brome*.[3] More specific work has followed on each of the four authors named in these book titles.[4] In addition to them, Ben Jonson's Caroline work has been growing in importance within the Jonson canon in recent years, while those playwrights broadly labelled 'courtier' – a disparate group including Davenant, Cartwright, Carlell and Suckling – are also attracting scholarly attention in their own right.[5] Scholars are increasingly willing to move beyond the professional theatre, to encompass Caroline court masque, or the amateur pastoral drama associated with the circle of Henrietta Maria, or indeed the regional drama of which the best-known example is John Milton's *Masque at Ludlow Castle* (perf. 1634).[6]

Thus, many recent readings of the tragedies and tragicomedies of the period view them in terms of politics, and in particular in terms of what can usefully be termed 'high politics' – affairs of state and government, religious affiliation and international alliances. In addition, these readings often assume a strongly monarch-centred model of Caroline politics in action. Thus, a typical politicised reading of a 1630s play, were such a thing to exist, might take one of the many tragedies or tragicomedies set in a safely unreal foreign or historical court. It would look at the ways that the fictional ruler reflects (or pointedly differs from) Charles himself (or from Henrietta Maria, in the light of growing interest in Henrietta's own court as a separate power centre, an interest pursued in this collection in Caroline Hibbard's essay, Chapter 5). In such readings Charles and Henrietta Maria are placed at the centre of the nature of Caroline high politics in all its forms. This is a perfectly valid paradigm to use in the context of the Stuart monarchy, especially since it was certainly a paradigm favoured by Charles himself.[7] But, in what follows, it will be argued that 1630s drama can still address matters of high politics without being personally centred upon Charles or Henrietta Maria. In particular, this essay will focus on the sub-variant of London-set city comedy known as 'place-realism', which makes extensive and important use of particular locations around the capital. It is no surprise that such comedy, with its very specific local topography, addresses matters of local political importance. But in addition, rather more surprisingly, there is often direct reference to high politics – both to the high micropolitics of the court, considered as a set of cultural practices without direct reference to its king, and to the high macropolitics of matters of government and foreign policy.

First of all, it is useful to survey what Caroline 'place-realism' comedy is. As defined in an influential article by Theodore Miles, it consists of a short-lived theatrical vogue marked by six comedies all written in the early 1630s. All of them are set in the particular area of London commemorated in their title or subtitle: Shakerley Marmion's *Holland's Leaguer* (perf. 1631), set in a brothel on the South Bank; James Shirley's *Hyde Park* (perf. 1632), set, as the title suggests, in the eponymous park; Thomas Nabbes's *Covent Garden* (perf. 1633) and Richard Brome's *The Weeding of Covent Garden* (perf. 1633), both reporting on the Earl of Bedford's new building development in West London; and two other Brome plays, *The Sparagus Garden* (perf. 1635) and *The New Academy* (perf. 1636), which dramatise, respectively, a pleasure-garden in Lambeth, and the New Exchange in the Strand. In each of these cases, the location is very specifically referred to in the dialogue and the action.[8]

The usual critical interpretation is that this genre represents a short-lived theatrical fashion, a novelty which was almost outmoded by 1635. As such, the plays are deemed interesting for their almost 'photographic realism' in portraying real London locations, and the manner in which they prefigure Restoration theatrical practice evident in a range of plays from Sedley's *The Mulberry Garden* (perf. 1668) to Wycherley's *The Country Wife* (perf. 1675), which use specific London places as settings. However, for earlier critics, the action of 1630s place-realism plays is not really integrated with their locations. Rather, the plays are considered interesting in terms of social history, for their documentation of a static backdrop as a by-product of their participation in a stylistic 'fad'.[9]

In fact, this analysis is suspect on two counts. Formally, these comedies are much less innovative than such an account suggests, since the technique of place-realism is fundamental to much Elizabethan and Jacobean city comedy. Rather, what develops in the 1630s is a growing interest in using such place-realism to offer commentary on national politics. Place-realism, as a technique, can be traced back to Elizabethan examples such as Ben Jonson's *Every Man Out of His Humour* (perf. 1599), with scenes set in Paul's Walk and in the Mitre Tavern. The Jacobean developments within the sub-genre include a number of city comedies which emphasise their place-realism through their titles, including Lording Barry's *Ram Alley* (perf. 1608), Thomas Middleton's *A Chaste Maid in Cheapside* (perf. 1613), and Jonson's *Bartholomew Fair* (perf. 1614).[10] Jonson's first Caroline play, *The Staple of News* (perf. 1626), sets scenes in the Apollo Room of the Devil Tavern in Fleet Street, a room of particular significance to Jonson since it was at the centre of his personal literary network and the meeting-place of his literary circle. Two subsequent Jonson comedies use suburban, rather than urban, locations – Barnet in *The New Inn* (perf. 1629), and Totten Court in *A Tale of a Tub* (perf. 1633) – but share the precision of reference in their creation of a sense of place.[11] *The Magnetic Lady* (perf. 1632) even goes so far as to specify the London parish in which it is set, St Bartholomew by the Exchange: a fact which enables the audience to identify the particular Laudian vicar it mocks, Dr John Grant. This fact, as Julie Maxwell has argued, makes the play an intervention not just in a local but also a national debate about ecclesiastical politics: in this respect, I would argue, it is typical of the growing interest in the 1630s in using place-realism to comment on national politics.[12]

Miles's list of place-realism comedies can be extended to encompass other comedies of the 1630s and early 1640s. Jonson's successor Brome uses place-realism settings from the start of the 1630s all the way through the decade, writing city comedies with scenes set in identifiable places including Charles's Presence Chamber in *The City Wit* (perf. c. 1629–31), the Devil Tavern in *The English Moor* (perf. 1638), the Temple Walks in *The Damoiselle* (perf. 1638), where the location serves as an emblematic representation of the legal system as a whole, and Ram Alley in *A Mad Couple Well Match'd* (perf. 1639). Indeed, Brome's most successful play, *The Antipodes* (perf. 1638), offers a parody of 'place-realism' drama in which its techniques – deictic announcements of location, appeal to familiar detail, and use of extras to add colour – are used to deceive one character into believing he is in a flagrantly fantastic location: 'This, Sir, is anti-London.'[13]

Brome is not the only practitioner of place-realism in the later part of Charles's reign. In the years leading up to 1642 William Cavendish, first Earl of Newcastle, sets a scene of his comedy *The Country Captain* in the Apollo Room of the Devil Tavern. As noted above, this room was associated above all with Jonson: and since Cavendish was Jonson's major patron at this time this restaging of Jonson's favourite tavern constitutes a self-conscious appropriation of a literary tradition.[14] However, as this survey shows, Cavendish's choice of place-realism technique itself in the late 1630s is not a stylistic throwback, but a use of a current theatrical mode. Place-realism is one of the defining techniques of early modern city comedy in general, and it is still a current mode in the 1630s.

It is not surprising to find Caroline comic drama addressing questions of local politics. *The Weeding of Covent Garden* is a classic example, describing as it does the problems of tavern-licensing and local authority attendant upon the new building development of Covent Garden. But *The Weeding of Covent Garden* is intensely aware, not just of the local problems of Covent Garden, but of the national political context of which it forms part. It is indeed 'larded with references to the intensified royal paternalism of 1632–4', in the form of references to such contemporary issues as Charles's controversial issuing of monopolies on the manufacture of soap; the Proclamation of Restraint, in which Charles sought to restrict the movements of the aristocracy to and from the city; and his reissue of the *Book of Sports* in 1633, a document which asserted the right of country-dwellers to engage in traditional festivals. Hence, Martin Butler reads the play as a critique of Charles's absolutist rule, of his programme of governing without parliament, and of his imposition of arbitrary monopolies, laws and taxes. In this sense, the play constitutes an intervention in national, as well as local, politics; similar analysis has already been extended to other specimens of the place-realism group, including *The Sparagus Garden* and *Hyde Park*.[15]

But high political comment informs other Caroline place-realism drama, touching on the nature of the court system; the wars in Holland; and the state of the nation. The main examples deployed in the argument that follows are three place-realism comedies: Brome's *The City Wit* (perf. c. 1629–31); Marmion's *Holland's Leaguer* (perf. 1631); and Thomas Jordan's *The Walks of Islington and Hogsden* (perf. 1641). Collectively, these plays epitomise the difficulties inherent in gaining a clear overview of 1630s drama. The exact date of Brome's play is uncertain, while *Holland's Leaguer* survives in a 'reformed' version, which therefore does not entirely reflect what was performed on the stage. An analysis of 1630s drama as a strict chronological entity is made additionally difficult by the long plague closures, most notably the eighteen-month closure of 1636–38, and the fragmentary surviving evidence: hence the relevance of Jordan's text from 1641, although, as will be seen, even that is complicated by an apparent anachronism associated with its first publication in 1657. Nonetheless, despite these difficulties, these plays develop a picture of 1630s drama engaged with high politics and inventive in its methods of political representation.

Richard Brome's *The City Wit* innovates by using place-realism to represent the court itself as a physical and cultural space. Within Renaissance drama generally, the conventional way of commenting on the court is within a genre which can represent either a historical or geographically remote court: the best-known examples of this in 1630s drama are perhaps the tragedies of Ford. But Brome's *The City Wit* uses another mode to represent the court, putting it on stage as a place-realism location within what ought to be, generically speaking, a citizen comedy.[16] *The City Wit* features an honest and trusting merchant, named Crasy, who is now bankrupt, thanks in part to unscrupulous courtiers who have failed to pay him for jewellery he has sold to them. From early on in the play, as Crasy is working out what to do, there is a string of references to specific London streets and locations, establishing an atmosphere of urban realism. This proves particularly interesting when the action turns to describing an unnamed 'palace', because the context makes it unambiguous that this palace, too, is in London. Crasy has tricked one of his creditors into thinking he has been invited to the court. Mr Sneakup, one of Crasy's dupes, prepares for the occasion in anxious dialogue with his wife Pyannet:

> PYANNET: Now mark. I will instruct you: When you come at the Court gate, you may neither knocke nor pisse. Do you mark? You go through the Hall cover'd; through the great Chamber cover'd; through the Presence bare; through the Lobby cover'd; through the Privy Chamber bare; through the Privy Lobby cover'd; to the Prince bare.
> SNEAKUP: I'le doe't I warrant you. Let me see. At the Court gate neither knock nor make water. May not a man break wind?
> PYANNET: Umh, yes: but (like the Exchequer payment) somewhat abated.
> SNEAKUP: Through the great Chamber bare.
> PYANNET: Cover'd.
> SNEAKUP: Cover'd? Well: Through the Presence cover'd.
> PYANNET: Bare.
> SNEAKUP: Bare? I will put all downe in my Table-book, and con it by the way.
>
> (i, p. 323)

Displaying a reticence thrown into sharp relief by the specificity of other aspects of the play, Brome stops short of explicitly naming the palace or the royal person involved, although from the context the only possible candidate for the latter is Charles I. In that light, several topical references become apparent. Aside from incorporating a sly remark about Charles's budgetary difficulties in the Exchequer in the late 1620s and early 1630s, this exchange makes comic profit out of the increasing codification and ritualisation of court etiquette. According to Kevin Sharpe, 'Charles's impact upon the style of the court had been felt within days of his accession', but the years around 1630 seem to have seen a further tightening of the behaviour he wished to see there, influenced perhaps by the 'grave ceremonial' of the rituals he had seen at the Spanish court in 1623. A document, probably dating from 1630, prescribes regulations governing 'behaviour at court and qualifications for admission from the entrance gate through the public rooms to the innermost sanctum of the royal bedchambers'.[17] Another protocol introduced by Charles was the use of triple bowing at mealtimes; this is satirised in *The City Wit* when Sneakup is shown practising the details of the interview and how 'to make my three legs' (i, p. 323), while his wife helps him by performing the role of the king. By writing citizen comedy about citizens who go to court, Brome is able to translate royal ritual directly into an opportunity for broad physical comedy.

So far, this is political satire but not of a mode specifically wedded to place-realism. Act 3 Scene 4 of the play, however, is set in the Presence Chamber itself: 'This is the presence.' This scene is therefore deep inside the palace system, which in the case of Charles's main palace at Whitehall comprised an estimated 2,000 rooms and hundreds of staff.[18] Brome continues the satire of the carefully organised protocols. They are depicted reducing those involved to nervous wrecks, rendering them vulnerable to exploitation: indeed, it is Mr Sneakup's fear of these protocols which permits Crasy, disguised as a court officer, to trick him into giving over his jewels. In this way the geographical location is not mere incidental colour but worked directly into the plot. In staging the presence room, where 'the throne represented the majesty of the monarch even in his absence', Brome gets as close as may be to putting the reigning monarch on stage.[19] One may conclude that this city comedy represents and satirises royal micropolitics in precise, and non-allegorical, detail. Although the absently present king is not explicitly mocked, the corrupt courtiers over whom he presides most certainly are. Much of the rest of the play is devoted to an analysis of the economic food web by which courtiers prey on and are themselves prey to citizens, and an attack on the dishonesty institutionalised within such a system. A member of the audience might well be invited to conclude that the abuses depicted in the play need to be addressed by more than just the individual: they might need the attention of the monarch whose Presence is conjured up, in a pointedly incomplete fashion, by the scene at the centre of the play.

Thus, place-realism provides Brome with a way of talking about royal politics without talking directly about the king. A similar sleight-of-hand permits Shakerley Marmion to talk in *Holland's Leaguer* about the wars in Holland without direct reference to any monarch. Representations of these wars within Caroline drama are usually wrapped up either in a history-play context, or in a geographically allegorical manner which avoids the word 'Holland': but *Holland's Leaguer* comes up with another approach.[20] Marmion's play, hugely successful when staged in December 1631, but surviving only in a printed version in which Sir Henry Herbert, Master of the Revels, ordered 'reformacons', still offers an allegorical mode of political engagement.[21]

Holland's Leaguer was a notorious brothel, run by one Elizabeth Holland, whose career has been documented in a short account by Dean Stanton Barnard, and in a much longer and rather contentious account by E. J. Burford.[22] Clearly, it was a fashionable and successful establishment, based in a moated manor house in Bankside. Although the precise sequence of events is not clear, the brothel became famous for apparently resisting a siege by the forces of law and order, and by early 1632 Mistress Holland had left London, seemingly for good.

The story of Holland's Leaguer touched a nerve in Caroline culture, since it was celebrated in numerous texts, including three eponymous ones: Marmion's play, a prose pamphlet by Nicholas Goodman, *Hollands Leaguer* (1632) which offers a mock-biography of Mistress Holland, and a broadside ballad written by Lawrence Price, *News from Holland's Leaguer* (1632). It also features as a location, in place-realism style, in J. D.'s little-known comedy *The Knave in Grain*, so that Marmion's *Holland's Leaguer* is not the only Caroline play which depicts the brothel as a location.[23] Marmion's comedy describes the activities of a group of gallants who visit the Leaguer, which provides the location for Act 4 of the play. The brothel is portrayed as a place of flagrant sin, apparently immune from the efforts of the authorities to control it; in this way the play poses questions about local authority, licensing and control in the liberties of London. To that extent, its 'place-realism' is certainly a commentary on local politics.

More generally, *Holland's Leaguer* reflects an interest in ideas of establishing a private space within the orbit of the city, ideas which are often framed – in a way that Julie Sanders has identified as typical of Marmion's mentor Ben Jonson – within the language of republicanism associated with the Netherlands.[24] For instance, one of the whores at Holland's Leaguer says they will 'carry [their profit] so cunningly away, / Beyond the reach of Iustice, and of all / The iurisdiction in our owne hand, / Like a free state.'[25] But this general theoretical interest in republicanism is given a specific international dimension, in that one of the central puns of the play is that the name of Mistress Holland is also that of a European country.

Instead of a tedious catalogue of all the puns that are made on this through the play, it will suffice to discuss one example:

TRIMALCHIO: Came you from *Holland*?
AUTOLYCUS: Yes, very lately.
TRIMALCHIO: Pray what newes from *Holland*?
AUTOLYCUS: *Holland*'s beleaguer'd.
TRIMALCHIO: What all *Holland* beleaguer'd?
AUTOLYCUS: And wil hold out as long as *Busse* or *Bulloign*.
 They haue their Mote and Draw-bridge, I haue giuen them
 Besides, a draft of a fortification,
 Will hold them play this twelvemonth, for they keepe
 Their passage open, and want no supplies,
 For whosoeuer comes, they pay them soundly:
 The French have made many onflats upon them,
 And still beene foyld.
TRIMALCHIO: Is there such hot service there? (D2v)

Like a well-developed allegory, this simile mixes at least three levels of reference: one on which Autolycus is purporting to describe the country of

Holland; another on which he is describing the moated brothel on the South Bank; and one on which he is describing the bodies of the whores who work there, complete with the threat from 'the French' – syphilis. For all that *Holland's Leaguer* has a specifically local frame of reference, the continued slippage between the brothel and the 'free state' in Europe gives the whole play a 'macropolitical' frame of reference.

Given the name of the institution, it is inevitably true of all the Holland's Leaguer texts that they engage with an international reading to some extent – Goodman's pamphlet, for instance, names its heroine 'Dona Britannica Hollandia', and recounts a fictionalised version of her life, including so much anti-Catholic reference that the whole text has been taken (wrongly, I believe) as an allegory of the progress of the English church.[26] However, in Marmion's play, the international reference is more than just an incidental effect; the story of the Leaguer is intercut with the story of the self-loving Lord Philautus, who undergoes a form of religious conversion after meeting, and failing to seduce, the beautiful Faustina. Abashed, Philautus resolves to make amends by becoming a soldier. In a central scene, he invites the other gallants to join him in going off to 'the warre', from where he shall be heard of 'By the next Caranto' (H1r, H1v). The implication is that these wars are the wars in Holland, in which Marmion himself is known to have served: but the other gallants refuse the invitation, and depart on their own expedition to Holland's Leaguer instead.[27]

In Act 5 Philautus returns from the wars, covered in glory, in contrast to the sorry state of the gallants whose adventure at Holland's Leaguer has ended in their arrest. Faustina celebrates his return:

> Now let mee bid you welcome from the warres,
> Laden with conquest, and the golden fleece
> Of honour, which like *Iason*, you have brought
> T'inrich your Country, now indebted to you. (K1r)

Indeed, it is Philautus who uses his wealth to resolve the predicaments in which the other characters find themselves, ensuring a happy ending to the play.

At first glance, then, a clear political message might be discerned: Marmion's play seems to give support to British involvement in the wars in Holland, which is both personally rewarding for the participants, and productive of honour to the country. However, one might hesitate to reduce the play so easily to a pat solution. Like all comparisons, that between Holland's Leaguer and the wars is double-edged, since it is hard to take Philautus seriously even after his conversion. (This is a man who has attempted to seduce his own sister: not from any incestuous desire, nor because she has adopted a disguise, but because he has simply failed to recognise her, even when she tells him her name.) From another angle, the message of *Holland's Leaguer* is the similarity between the two forms of 'hot service' that the play displays: it could easily be read as a satire in which, as in *Troilus and Cressida*, war and lechery seem strangely similar propositions. Nor is it necessary now to make a choice between these two readings of the play with regard to the wars in Holland, or to speculate on the nature of the unspecified reformations insisted on by Herbert before he would permit the play to be printed. In the form we have it, *Holland's Leaguer* is a text within which the wars in the Netherlands can be directly and indirectly discussed.

As the decade goes on, specific analysis of particular political institutions and issues, of the sort represented by *The City Wit* and *Holland's Leaguer*, seems to shade into an interrogation of the whole idea of the state. For instance, a number of plays from the later 1630s and early 1640s discuss the concept of the commonwealth by means of the device of an alternative society. Examples include Brome's *The Antipodes*, which creates the upside-down society of anti-London; and, as Julie Sanders has noted, Suckling's *The Goblins*, Shirley's *The Sisters* and Brome's *A Jovial Crew*, all display 'alternative' woodland societies of the disempowered as a way of interrogating the political state of Britain as a whole.[28] Once again, there is a specific place-realism twist to this, in the form of Thomas Jordan's 1641 comedy *The Walks of Islington and Hogsden*.

Jordan's play concerns a group of gallants going on an extended drinking spree around the inns of Islington. Interwoven loosely into this story are various love-intrigues, which lead several of the characters, in Act 4, to imprisonment in the Wood Street Compter. Act 5 describes the means by which the characters are released from this imprisonment, culminating in that staple of Caroline tragicomedy, a funeral in which the corpse in the coffin is not in fact dead at all. In the process, the play makes detailed reference to the Compter, one of London's most notorious prisons. Under the older critical paradigm for reading place-realism, it is possible to mine the play for vivid social detail about Caroline prison life:

> Instead of Chambers hung with Tapestry,
> Arras, and Attick pictures, the dark walls
> Are easly beautifi'd with Chalk and Cole,
> According to the melancholly fancy
> Of the sad Prisoners, where the numerous beds
> Shew like so many Graves in a Churchyard,
> With the men rising out ...[29]

A reading of the play in terms of local colour would explore the allusions which hint that some of the characters in the play are representatives of particular living individuals: for instance, the Prologue's claim that Jordan 'hath invented / Persons that you'll all know when they'r presented', or the wicked sergeant's complaint that 'The Players brought me oth' Stage once I thank them in a Play call'd the *Roaring Girle, or The Catchpole.*'³⁰ The play certainly contains reportage of the experience of being in prison, and satire of the way the prison system is abused. However, as in *The City Wit* and *Holland's Leaguer,* this local satire is combined with, indeed resonates with, a broader, macropolitical, frame of reference.

A running joke of the play is the phenomenon of Englishmen running away to France: something which appears, at first, to allude to prominent public figures such as Suckling, Finch, Windebank and Dr Roan, all of whom fled to France for various reasons in the course of the years 1640 and 1641. Numerous jokes are made about such escapes: for instance, Jones, the quibbling cobbler, warns that 'I'le tell you Sir, the sad report goes that most of the English Gentlemen in *France* must return to England agen I am sorry for't'; while the comic Frenchman, seeing English people run away, comments that 'Begar me never saw sush a frisk in my life; Vas dis de skip de Angleteire?'³¹ However, the joke has an intra-diegetic reference, since at the end of the play at least three of the characters turn out to be English people who have fled to France and who have now returned *incognito*. This plot device is a staple of 1630s comedy – featuring in such plays as Brome's *The New Academy, The English Moor* and *The Damoiselle* – but Jordan uses it unusually extensively, and makes it chime with the wider macropolitical picture.

The most extensive reference to high politics comes in the prison scenes themselves, where a number of the characters find that inside the prison there exists an entire alternative society, a carnivalesque version of the world outside. On the one hand, this connects Jordan's play into a tradition of prison writing of which the most relevant prior example is William Fennor's narrative of his experiences in the same prison, *The Compters Comon-wealth, or a Voiage made to an Infernall Iland,* first published in 1617 and frequently reprinted.³² As his title suggests, a central conceit of Fennor's narrative is that the prison constitutes a society within itself, each section of it being 'as a little City in a Commonwealth' (79). In particular Fennor describes the system whereby the inmates manage their internal affairs through a council of senior prisoners. Jordan's play expands upon this idea, creating a form of alternative society: as one of the prisoners says, 'we have suffered under the terrour of Authority, and now we have got the Law in our own hands' (F2r).

But running alongside this idea of the prison as a miniature state is the idea that it is specifically a miniature of England. This is demonstrated most clearly in the scene depicting the arrival of the prisoners in 'ith' King's Ward; tis termed the Hole' (F2r). In Jordan's play, the prisoners in the King's Ward administer their own affairs by council, as in Fennor; but Jordan stages a custom not documented by Fennor whereby at the arrival of a new prisoner this council stages 'a Scaene of mirth, where one is Judge, / And sits a tryal upon life and death' (F2r). Thus, the prisoners hold, in effect, a mock-trial of the newcomer, a page named Wildfire. The most interesting contribution to the chaotic scene that follows is the speech of Lord Lows-Proof:

> Gentlemen of the Kings Ward let us consult upon the business, 'tis for the good of the Hole, and of the whole House; let us for once be wiser and honester then e'r we have been, there may come much mischief by this Wildfire, if he stay long he will consume us, and every creeping thing about us, our beds being all straw is very combustible; the very blowing on's nose blows a bed up. (F2v)

Clearly, the joke here lies in the fact that Lows-Proof is borrowing parliamentary language, describing 'the good ... of the whole House' in terminology that parliament might use to describe itself. Indeed, Lows-Proof's reference to the blowing up of the house chimes with reference elsewhere in the play to the 'Gunpowder-Treason' forty years earlier (E2r), and creates further parallels between this body of prisoners and parliament.

The confusing picture of a mock 'House' which is also a trial court is a highly topical one, ripe for application to a House of Commons which had already organised the trial and beheading of Thomas Wentworth, first Earl of Strafford (March–May 1641) and which had also voted for the impeachment of Archbishop Laud in February of that year. This is where Jordan's play differentiates itself from Fennor and other prison writing, since the usual trope in such narratives is to imagine society inside the prison as resembling the society in the commonwealth outside. In Jordan's hands, the resemblances are so extensive that the trope is made to cut both ways. The play not merely represents the prison government as a version of English government, but also English government as a version of the prison government.

Jordan's technique defies extended allegorical application in this respect, but it does not need extended allegory: like the prison itself, it is already full of satirical squibs simply waiting to be ignited. For instance, the Frenchman Sir Reverence wears an unusual costume in the prison, as Wildfire comments:

> WILDFIRE: Here comes my white Knight in his Lawn Sleeves, now if a Quaker saw him he would take his shirt for a Surpless, and condemn it for a Babylonish Garment, or in good sooth and verily a wicked and superstitious remnant of that foul slaps the whore of Babylon.
> SIR REVERENCE: Begar dat whore of Babylon be one of me aunts. (F1v)

Partly the joke here is at the expense of militant Protestants, for overreacting to the lawn sleeves; however, Sir Reverence's reply turns the joke on its head, since it justifies the Protestant paranoia. In the process, the exchange activates the language of militant English Protestantism in the phrase 'whore of Babylon', and perhaps, in the phrase 'white knight', the nationalist discourse of Middleton's hugely influential allegorical play of 1624, *A Game at Chess*.

But in the satirical literature of this part of Charles's reign, 'lawn sleeves' have an almost iconographical significance as an attribute of bishops in general and in particular of Archbishop Laud. By putting a figure wearing them into a prison, and indeed into a setting which is already, independently, satirising Laud's impeachment by its mock-trial within the prison, Jordan further complicates any sense of political allegory even while redoubling the political satire.[33] Jordan's play is littered with the grand symbols that ought to signify English national identity, debased and misapplied. Saint George is reduced to a simile for a pissing Frenchman; Redcross is merely the name of a street that adjoins the prison. Flylove swears, 'I fly to my colours, red and white, I'm a right English-man', but the colours in question are not the cross of St George but the complexion of Bellaflora. This comedy of 'riotous vulgarity', as G. E. Bentley called it, is, in its own unsubtle way, questioning the nature of English identity; and at the centre of that identity, in this play, is a prison.[34]

At the same time, the very passage under discussion raises a caveat about the methodology of the 'historical moment' implied in such political readings. Wildfire's use of the word 'Quaker' seems impossible in a text of 1641, since the word is not attested until 1647 at the earliest, so that the passage raises the alarming likelihood of at least some post-performance interpolation. It is a reminder that the text of the play as we have it is first known from a printing in 1657, and that all the evidence concerning it – even the statements concerning the date and circumstances of its original performance – derive from this publication. Jordan, of course, had no scruples about historical veracity when it came to ensuring that his publications earned money.[35] Not merely is political allegory always potentially double-edged, then, but the evidence of the 'occasional' content of all early modern plays is always mediated by the second occasion of their publication in written form. This is particularly important in the case of Caroline drama, performed before and often published long after the watershed events of 1642.

In spite of these difficulties of interpretation, it is clear that 1630s drama is, as Butler contended, a strongly political form. Place-realism, which informs, in various ways, *The City Wit*, *Holland's Leaguer* and *The Walks of Islington and Hogsden*, proves a useful touchstone, because it grounds high political commentary, of several different sorts, in known and knowable London locations. All three of the plays central to this essay are concerned with the 'local politics' of the social management of specific spaces: palace rooms, brothels and prisons. In each case the play establishes, in effect, a synecdochic relation between the 'real' place and the national issue – the court system, the wars in Holland, the state of the nation. The fidelity to verifiable details in the representation of the location appears to offer a guarantee of intellectual neutrality and veracity to the picture of national politics which is constructed around it, and it is perhaps this ambition to talk about national politics which is distinctive about 1630s

Caroline politics on the professional comic stage

place-realism: together with a tendency to represent national politics not solely as a function of the personality of the king, but rather as a process in which the king sometimes appears almost a marginal figure. In an impressive feat, these comedies describe an absolute monarchy without allegorically figuring the king or queen. In this respect they differ markedly from the better-known tragedies and tragicomedies of the decade. Nonetheless, they need to be seen – like other 1630s drama – in the context of a diverse and controversial theatre, 'highly political' in both senses of the phrase.

NOTES

1 Alfred Harbage, *Cavalier Drama: An Historical and Critical Supplement to the Study of the Elizabethan and Restoration Stage* (New York: Russell and Russell, 1936); R. J. Kaufmann, *Richard Brome, Caroline Dramatist* (Columbia: Columbia University Press, 1961), p. 7; David Farley-Hills, *The Comic in Renaissance Comedy* (London: Macmillan, 1981), pp. 147–60.

2 Martin Butler, *Theatre and Crisis 1632–42* (Cambridge: Cambridge University Press, 1984).

3 Ira Clark, *Professional Playwrights: Massinger, Ford, Shirley, and Brome* (Lexington: Kentucky University Press, 1992); Julie Sanders, *Caroline Drama: The Plays of Massinger, Ford, Shirley and Brome* (Plymouth: Northcote House, 1999); James C. Bulman's article 'Caroline drama', in A. R. Braunmuller and Michael Hattaway (eds), *The Cambridge Companion to English Renaissance Drama* (Cambridge: Cambridge University Press, 1990), pp. 353–80, is also still a very good survey; developing interest in the field is evidenced, for instance, by the session devoted to Caroline drama at the 2004 meeting of the Shakespeare Association of America.

4 e.g. Sandra A. Burner, *James Shirley: A Study of Literary Coteries and Patronage in Seventeenth-Century England* (Lanham and London: University Press of America, 1988); Ira Clark, *The Moral Art of Philip Massinger* (Lewisburg: Bucknell University Press, 1992); Lisa Hopkins, *John Ford's Political Theatre* (Manchester: Manchester University Press, 1994); Matthew Steggle, *Richard Brome: Place and Politics on the Caroline Stage* (Manchester: Manchester University Press, 2004).

5 Recent work on Cartwright's political contexts includes Jane Farnsworth, 'Defending the king in Cartwright's *The Lady-Errant* (1636–37)', *Studies in English Literature 1500–1900*, 42 (2002), 381–98; Scott Gordon, 'The cultural politics of William Cartwright's *Royal Slave*', in Thomas Moisan and Douglas Bruster (eds), *In the Company of Shakespeare: Essays in English Renaissance Literature in Honour of G. Blakemore Evans* (Madison: Farleigh Dickinson University Press, 2002), pp. 251–69; on Davenant's, Lesel Dawson, '"New sects of love": Neoplatonism and constructions of gender in Davenant's *The Temple of Love* and *The Platonick Lovers*', *Early Modern Literary Studies*, 8:1 (2002), 4.1–36 <http://purl.oclc.org/emls/08-1/dawsnew.htm>; and on Suckling's, Julie Sanders, 'Beggars' commonwealths and the pre-civil war stage: Suckling's *The Goblins*, Richard Brome's *A Jovial Crew*, and James Shirley's *The Sisters*', *Modern Language Review*, 97 (2002), 1–14.

6 See, for instance, Erica Veevers, *Images of Love and Religion: Queen Henrietta Maria and*

Court Entertainments (Cambridge: Cambridge University Press, 1989); Karen Britland, '"All emulation cease, and jars": political possibilities in Chloridia, Queen Henrietta Maria's masque of 1631', Ben Jonson Journal, 9 (2002), 87–108; Karen Britland, 'Florimène: the author and the occasion', Review of English Studies, 53 (2002), 475–83; Walter Montagu, The Shepherd's Paradise, ed. Sarah Poynting (Oxford: Malone Society, 1997); Sophie Eliza Tomlinson, 'Too theatrical? Female subjectivity in Caroline and Interregnum drama', Women's Writing, 6 (1999), 65–80. On Milton's Masque as regional drama, see Philip Schwyzer, 'Purity and danger on the west bank of the Severn: the cultural geography of A Masque Presented at Ludlow Castle, 1634', Representations, 60 (1997), 22–48.

7 On the political charge of Caroline tragicomedy in particular, see Gordon McMullan and Jonathan Hope (eds), The Politics of Tragicomedy: Shakespeare and After (London: Routledge, 1992).

8 Richard H. Perkinson, 'Topographical comedy in the seventeenth century', English Literary History, 3 (1936), 270–90; Theodore Miles, 'Place-realism in a group of Caroline plays', Review of English Studies, 18 (1942), 428–40; Paul W. Miller, 'The historical moment of Caroline topographical comedy', Texas Studies in Literature and Language, 32 (1990), 345–74 adds Nabbes's Tottenham Court (perf. 1634), but dismisses Holland's Leaguer as 'obscure, unreal, allegorical' (350); Sanders, Caroline Drama, pp. 43–55.

9 Kaufmann, Richard Brome, p. 54; Miles, 'Place-realism', 433.

10 Further examples include Jonson's The Alchemist (perf. 1610), precisely located in Blackfriars; for a discussion of space and place in drama of this earlier period, see Janette Dillon, Theatre, Court and City, 1595–1610: Drama and Social Space in London (Cambridge: Cambridge University Press, 2000).

11 See, for instance, Martin Butler, 'Stuart politics in Jonson's A Tale of a Tub', Modern Language Review, 85 (1990), 12–28; Julie Sanders, Ben Jonson's Theatrical Republics (Basingstoke: Macmillan, 1998); and Catherine Rockwood, 'Topicality and dissent in Jonson's A Tale of A Tub', Ben Jonson Journal, 10 (2003), 77–100.

12 Julie Maxwell, 'Ben Jonson among the vicars: cliché, ecclesiastical politics, and the invention of "parish comedy"', Ben Jonson Journal, 9 (2002), 37–68.

13 Richard Brome, The Antipodes, ed. David Scott Kastan and Richard Proudfoot (London: Nick Hern Books, 2000), 2.2.38.

14 See William Cavendish, The Country Captain, ed. Anthony Jonson (Oxford: Malone Society, 1999); Nick Rowe, '"My best patron": William Cavendish and Jonson's Caroline drama', in Timothy Raylor (ed.), The Cavendish Circle, a special issue of The Seventeenth Century, 9:2 (1994), 197–212, esp. 207–9; Timothy Raylor, 'Newcastle's ghosts: Robert Payne, Ben Jonson, and the "Cavendish circle"', in Claude J. Summers and Ted-Larry Pebworth (eds), Literary Circles and Cultural Communities in Renaissance England (Columbia: Missouri University Press, 2000), pp. 92–114.

15 Kaufmann, Richard Brome, pp. 57–61, 67–87; Butler, Theatre and Crisis, pp. 148–57, quotation from p. 148; Miller, 'Historical moment', 345–74 discusses The Weeding of Covent Garden mainly in terms of its relationship to national politics, but also notes the international dimension enabled by references to 'plantations' and tobacco; Sanders, Caroline Drama, pp. 50–2. On The Sparagus Garden, see ch. 3 of Steggle, Richard Brome.

16 On Ford's courts, see Sanders, Caroline Drama, pp. 16–29; on anti-court drama as a

phenomenon, see Albert H. Tricomi, *Anticourt Drama in England 1603–1642* (Charlottesville: Virginia University Press, 1989); on the genre of citizen comedy, see Alexander Leggatt, *Citizen Comedy in the Age of Shakespeare* (Toronto: Toronto University Press, 1973). Discussions of *The City Wit* include Kaufmann, *Richard Brome*, pp. 47–52; Catherine M. Shaw, *Richard Brome* (Boston: Twayne, 1980), pp. 62–8; quotations are from *The Dramatic Works of Richard Brome*, ed. John Pearson (3 vols, 1873; New York: AMS Press, 1966).

17 Brome, *Dramatic Works*, i, pp. 323, 328, 330; Kevin Sharpe, *The Personal Rule of Charles I* (New Haven and London: Yale University Press, 1992), pp. 105–11, 210–11; Kevin Sharpe, 'The image of virtue: the court and household of Charles I', in David Starkey (ed.), *The English Court from the Wars of the Roses to the Civil War* (London: Longman, 1987), pp. 226–60, quotations from pp. 227, 230.

18 Brome, *Dramatic Works*, i, p. 328; Sharpe, 'Image of virtue', pp. 227–30.

19 Sharpe, *Personal Rule of Charles I*, p. 213.

20 Butler, *Theatre and Crisis*, pp. 235–6, discusses Caroline plays about Holland including Glapthorne's comedy *The Hollander* and the lost Brome/Heywood collaboration *The Life and Death of Sir Martin Skink*; cf. also Hans Werner, 'An unambiguous allusion to the Dutch in Massinger's *Believe As You List*', *Notes and Queries*, 46 (1999), 255–6, showing that Massinger's play does indeed have allegorical reference to Holland hardly submerged within its literal setting in the classical world.

21 See N. W. Bawcutt, *The Control and Censorship of Caroline Drama: The Records of Sir Henry Herbert, Master of the Revels 1623–73* (Oxford: Clarendon Press, 1996), p. 317; G. E. Bentley, *The Jacobean and Caroline Stage* (7 vols, Oxford: Clarendon Press, 1941–68), iv, p. 736.

22 Nicholas Goodman, *Hollands Leaguer: A Critical Edition*, ed. Dean Stanton Barnard (The Hague: Mouton, 1970); E. J. Burford, *Queen of the Bawds: or the True Story of Madame Britannica Hollandia and her House of Obsenitie, Holland's Leaguer* (London: Neville Spearman, 1973), who proposes, on very flimsy evidence, that her clients included Shakespeare, Jonson and Alberic Gentilis.

23 J. D., *The Knave in Grain New Vampt (1640)*, ed. R. C. Bald and Arthur Brown (Oxford: Clarendon Press, 1961), esp. Introduction, p. ix.

24 Sanders, *Ben Jonson's Theatrical Republics*.

25 Shakerley Marmion, *Holland's Leaguer. An Excellent Comedy* (London, 1632), sig. H2v; Bulman, 'Caroline drama', pp. 369–70; Allan P. Green, 'Shakerley Marmion', in Fredson Bowers (ed.), *Dictionary of Literary Biography, Vol. 58: Jacobean and Caroline Dramatists* (Detroit: Gale Research, 1987), pp. 133–5 on this play.

26 Dean Stanton Barnard, 'Introduction', in Goodman, *Hollands Leaguer*, ed. Barnard, p. 15.

27 Green, 'Shakerley Marmion', pp. 131–8.

28 Sanders, 'Beggars' Commonwealths', 1–14; see also Rosemary Gaby, 'Of vagabonds and commonwealths: *Beggars' Bush*, *A Jovial Crew* and *The Sisters*', *Studies in English Literature 1500–1900*, 34 (1994), 401–24.

29 Thomas Jordan, *The Walks of Islington and Hogsden, with The Humours of Woodstreet-Compter* (London, 1657), sig. H1v.

30   Jordan, *Walks of Islington and Hogsden*, sigs A3v, E3r; cf. Bentley, *Jacobean and Caroline Stage*, v, pp. 1401–2.

31   Jordan, *Walks of Islington and Hogsden*, sigs C4v, D2r.

32   William Fennor, *The Compters Comon-Wealth, or a Voiage made to an Infernall Iland* (London, 1617); reprinted under variant titles including *A True Description of the Lawes, Iustice, and Equity of a Compter* (1629); a later description of the prison, possibly influenced by the play, is *Wonderfull Strange Newes from Woodstreet Counter* (London, 1642); a text coeval with this play, the semi-dramatic pamphlet *The Counters Discourse with it's Varlets Dictovery* ([London], 1641), calls on the new parliament to effect reform of the system of debtors' prisons.

33   Butler, *Theatre and Crisis*, p. 242, quotes from a description of the bishops going to war: 'Take your Miter to the field, / Let it serve you for a shield ... Let Lawn-sleeves serve instead of Buffe.' For another theatrical allusion to Laud's downfall, one could compare Shirley's *The Cardinal*, licensed 25 November 1641 (Butler, *Theatre and Crisis*, p. 236).

34   Jordan, *Walks of Islington and Hogsden*, sigs C4r, E2r, F3v; Bentley, *Jacobean and Caroline Stage*, iv, pp. 688–90.

35   *Oxford English Dictionary*, s.v. 'Quaker'; on Jordan's unscrupulous publications see, for instance, Patricia A. Pinsent, 'Plagiarism by Thomas Jordan', *Notes and Queries*, 14 (1967), 336–7.

Chapter 9

Stigmatizing Prynne: seditious libel, political satire and the construction of opposition

Andrew McRae

At the close of the 1637 Star Chamber trial of John Bastwick, Henry Burton and William Prynne, the judges conceived an elaborate display of authority:

> The Lord Cottingtons Censure.
> I Condemne these three men to loose their eares in the Pallaceyard at *Westminster*; to be fined five thousand pounds a man to his Majestie: And to perpetuall prisonment in three remote places of the Kingdome, namely, the Castles of *Carnarvon, Cornwall,* and *Lancaster*.
> The Lord Finch added to this Censure.
> Mr. Prynne to be stigmatized in the Cheekes with two Letters (*S & L*) for a Seditious Libeller. To which all the Lord agreed.[1]

Prynne was perhaps singled out for stigmatisation because he had been before the Star Chamber three years earlier, for the publication of *Histriomastix*. On that occasion he had been sentenced 'to stand on the pillorye att Westminster and Cheape side, to loose an eare att eyther place', and to wear 'a paper placed in his hatt', identifying him 'as a sedicious person'.[2] The subsequent judgement thus sought not only to complete the state's apparently unfinished business with his ears, but also to render onto the face of the offender an identification previously inscribed only on paper. Prynne, however, pointedly resisted the state's meaning, reinterpreting the letters 'S. L.' as 'Stigmata Laudis', or 'Laud's Scars'. In a poem circulated after the punishment, he proclaimed:

> Triumphant I returne, my face discryes
> Laud's scorching Scarrs,
> God's gratefull sacrifice.[3]

An exercise of inversion, which typifies the actions of the men and their supporters, the poem translates authorised marks of sedition into unauthorised signs of salvation. It claims for Prynne the status of a martyr, while instead isolating William Laud, Archbishop of Canterbury, as the principal agent of tyranny in the nation. Hence, like so many other details from the careers of these three men, it evidences a state losing control of the semiotics of loyalty and criminality. As Thomas Fuller recalled, 'so various were men's fancies in reading the same letters, imprinted in his face, that some made them to spell the guiltiness of the sufferer, but others the cruelty of the imposer'.[4]

Bastwick, Burton and Prynne published a range of tracts attacking the structures of episcopacy and the policies of the Caroline church. They came from different backgrounds – Bastwick was a physician, Burton a minister and former courtier, Prynne a lawyer – and there is little evidence of contact between them until their trial in 1637. They never saw themselves as forming a coherent 'party', and their arguments and styles of writing differed widely: at the extremes, from Prynne's tendency towards a prolix and legalistic construction of argument, to Bastwick's populism and scurrility. They were united, however, by a commitment to forms of writing and levels of criticism that would stretch the boundaries of the acceptable and the authorised. Moreover, after the failure of Prynne's defence of *Histriomastix* on the grounds that it had been properly licensed, they were increasingly united also by their rejection of the licensing system and their adoption of clandestine methods of publication. (By 1637 links between puritan authors and Dutch printers, in particular, were well established.)[5] Consequently, it was becoming commonplace even before the trial for commentators to link the three men, as a 'puritan triumvirate'. Their eventual punishment, which received wide publicity, aimed to identify them incontrovertibly as figures of illicit opposition: seditious libellers.

In this essay, I want to attend to such struggles over meaning, exploring especially the use of satire in the works of Bastwick, Burton and Prynne. As a mode of discrimination and stigmatisation, satire underpinned at once bitter attacks on the Laudian regime, and subtle explorations of the boundaries between orthodoxy and heterodoxy, loyalty and sedition. As Prynne demonstrated in his verse on the letters 'S. L.', it can be a potent tool for subverting authorised meanings, and positing rival versions of the truth. The sections below consider the construction of opposition in two contexts: firstly, in the texts written by the three men; and secondly, in discourse surrounding their trial and punishment. After early efforts to speak as loyal subjects, I suggest, the puritan triumvirate ultimately did more than anybody in these late Caroline years to define the terms of political conflict.[6]

I

By the mid-1630s, all three of the puritan writers had experienced surveillance and suppression at the hands of the church and state, and the strains were increasingly informing their works. For Bastwick, writing from imprisonment in the Gatehouse in the months preceding the Star Chamber trial, the pressure was palpable; Laud, he commented, 'hath a long time beene nibling at my eares'.[7] Crucially, the three men were struggling at this time to reconcile their habitual professions of loyalty with a sense that whatever they said would be construed as dissent. Burton's *An Apology of an Appeale* (Amsterdam, 1636), for example, is framed as a direct complaint to Charles. He argues, however, that the collapse of a system of counsel at court has severed any line of contact between subjects and their king, so he has been forced to 'give forth [printed] copies' of his text, in the hope that 'some well minded man' will 'dare to doe you so much worthie service, in bringing a Copie to your Majesties hand' (sig. (a)3v). And, however disingenuous the statement may seem, it underpins a subtle perception about the construction of opposition:

> Againe, what censures may I expect of them, who cannot indure to have their deeds brought to the open light? They will be readie to charge me with Popularity, Faction, Sedition, and what not, and all for thus bringing their actions upon the open stage. (sig. (a)4r)

For Burton, under conditions of constraint the voice of a loyal critic, bringing 'actions upon the open stage', becomes perforce the voice of seditious libel. In the year before he would lose his ears and his liberty, embracing his fate with the passion of a martyr, he uneasily accommodates himself to the inevitability of this role.

As evidenced by the teasing play of humility and insurgency in Burton's address to the King, the resources of satire were instrumental to the process through which opposition was created. Satire offered the puritans a model for authorised criticism, a vehicle for unauthorised confrontation, and strategies for evading clear lines of demarcation between the licit and illicit. From native traditions of satire they adopted, when appropriate, the persona of a 'plain-dealing English-man', or 'poore Outcast' observer.[8] If his style seemed 'sharper then usuall', this could be attributed to an excess of passion: 'Zeale and Fidelitie for God and for Your Majestie', as Burton would have it. Burton further invoked the rhetorical figure of *parrhesia*: 'this liberty, and freedome of speech', which 'Sometimes ... showes it selfe in meeknesse and mildnesse, sometimes in a greater measure of zeale, and roughnesse'.[9] *Parrhesia* offered an antidote to 'the cowardise of our times', and legitimised the intrusion of 'the meanest subjects hand' into the business of state.[10] Moreover, under conditions of censorship it might justify illicit pamphlets, such as Bastwick's successive parts of his *Letany*, written in prison and printed on the continent, or *Newes from Ipswich*, which may have been written by any or all of the triumvirate.[11] As the *Newes* proclaims in its opening paragraph, the 'presses formerly open only to *Trueth* and *Piety*, are closed up against them both of late, and patent for the most part, to nought but *errour superstition, and profane-*

nesse'. The true news, therefore, must be disseminated perforce in an unauthorised 'Coranto'.[12]

The verbal dexterity exhibited in such texts underpins a sophisticated attention to the powers and trickeries of language itself. Prynne, though typically dry and methodical, occasionally quotes classical satirists, and also seeks models in the Bible. The title page of a tract designed to refute the arguments of Giles Widdowes, for example, invokes the Proverbs alongside Horace: 'Answer a Foole according to his folly, lest he be wise in his owne conceit ... O major tandem parcas insane minori' (Proverbs 26.35; *Satires*, II.iii.326).[13] Bastwick was still more insistent in his commitment to invention and subversion. He described his *Letany* pamphlets as 'Limbo Rhetorick', vindicating his 'liberty' and freedom of speech in the face of the evident constraints of 'my Schoole in Limbo Patrum'.[14] In one passage, he claims:

> there is no just cause why any should blame mee for mingling *ioca seriis et seria iocis*; all scurrility and prophanesse being avoyded. For there wants not presidents of this kind in sacred writ: that in the most grave and waightiest matters it pleased the Prophets of old to use ironicall speeches, yea the holy Scriptures are full of them.[15]

A text which sets forth the truth 'something merrily' is thus not only more likely to 'please mens phantasies', but may also prove more skilful in identifying the verbal ploys of the enemies of truth. For Bastwick's project, perhaps more clearly than that of either Burton or Prynne, is the demystification of the episcopal authorities' discourse.

At stake in these pamphlets is the very definition of orthodoxy, and the weapons in the battle were the names used to identify the threat of forces and ideas perceived as dangerous. Labels such as 'puritan', 'papist', 'Calvinist', 'Arminian' and 'Laudian', which could be so useful in polemical discourse, were all coined as terms of abuse. Many observers were justifiably anxious about this practice. At the end of the 1620s, George Wither surveyed a religious culture fracturing into, among other categories, '*Papists*', '*Semi-puritans*', '*Anabaptists*', 'Some ... term'd *Arminians*', others 'termed *Puritans*', 'And some, that no man can tell what they be'.[16] The puritans of the 1630s, though expressing similar concerns, committed themselves nonetheless to the controversy. All three men focused on the ways in which they were being 'turned into puritans', arguing that positions considered orthodox in the 1620s were increasingly being labelled as aberrant by the Laudian establishment.[17] Yet while they interrogated the term, they also came to embrace it.[18] Bastwick thus narrates being '*bred*' in his youth '*in as great hatred of Puritans, as any tender yeares was capable of*'; it was only years later that he realised '*that those that were comonly branded with the name of Puritans, were the happiest, and that if any were eternally blessed, they were such of them as squared there lives in sincerity according to their profession*'. He claims that the label is wielded by papists in an effort to marginalise the only forces who oppose their dominance in the English church: 'and therefore they so hate them they stigmatize them with the name of *Puritans*'.[19] Prynne, more earnestly, though with the same intent to reclaim and refashion a term of abuse, devotes a considerable slab of one tract to the definition of true puritanism.[20]

If puritanism was to be aligned with Protestant orthodoxy, the policies and theology espoused by Laud had to be positioned by contrast as innovative. Hence 'novelist' became a word on which the confrontation hinged. This label could inflict considerable damage within a church anxious about its roots, and had been deployed with effect in earlier ecclesiastical controversy.[21] By the 1630s, in debate over the *Book of Sports*, Burton was rebutting claims that those who opposed this contentious Caroline policy were 'factious Sabbatarian Novellists', and claiming instead a sabbatarian tradition which included such pillars of orthodoxy as Richard Hooker and Lancelot Andrewes.[22] In a subsequent text he relentlessly turns the label on his enemies, cataloguing 'innovations' in the church and arguing that,

> these novellers ... are in fact the most dangerous enemies of the King, who under a pretence of honor and love, doe machinate the overthrow of his Kingdome and State, as by altering the State of religion, and by that meanes alienating and unsettling the hearts of his Subjects.[23]

Similarly, Prynne rounded upon 'pur-blinde, squint-eyed, ideal Arminian Novellists', and argued that parliament should 'Strike ... at the roots, as well as the branches of these prevailing Factions'.[24] Both men, it might be noted, wilfully conflate religious and political threats. Obviously enough, for a parliament to purge the realm of 'faction' (a term itself derived from courtly intrigue), the structures of personal rule must first be collapsed.

These strategies, which posit a nexus of religious and political dangers associated with the spectre of Arminianism, evidence the puritans' own skills in the arts of stigmatisation. In the 1620s, when popery was almost universally constructed as 'an anti-religion, a perfectly symmetrical negative image of true Christianity', anti-papist discourse served to define and unite the early Stuart church.[25] In the subsequent decade, by comparison, puritan writers turned the conventions of anti-popery on their opponents *within* the English church. While Laud himself referred to the 'great bugbear called Arminianism', those stigmatised as puritans were increasingly willing to label Laud and the episcopate as Arminians, and to dismiss the doctrine as 'in truth meere Popery'.[26] This was an act of opportunism – as John Selden commented, 'Wee charge the praticall Clergie with popery to make them odious though wee know they are guilty of no such thing' – but it was unquestionably effective.[27] In turn, the vague yet compelling equations of Laudian innovation with Arminianism, and Arminianism with popery, also underpinned easy suppositions about threats posed to the subject's liberties.[28] Bastwick thus identified a political threat when he described Arminians as 'spaniolized', and 'affect[ing] Romanality'.[29] In another tract, he commented wryly that it had in fact become impossible to write traditional anti-papist tracts, since 'such correspondency there is now between the Pope and the *Prelats*, that one cannot write against [the pope], but the *Prelats* say by and by that they are meant by it'.[30]

The political charge carried by such attacks was underlined by the extent to which the writers interwove strands of anti-court discourse with their ecclesiastical polemic. In Jacobean England, popery was consistently associated with a nexus of courtly sins, including 'the notion of evil counsel'.[31] By the 1630s, in the absence of a feared and dominant statesman such as George Villiers, Duke of Buckingham, and at a time when parliaments were an aspiration rather than an actuality, Arminian prelates were newly figured as the greatest threat to the relationship between the king and his subjects. Burton even offered a character sketch, adapting a literary model used countless times against the puritans. The Arminian, he writes,

> is no lesse ambitious of head-ship over men, then his Religion is of copartnership (at least) with God, in His glory. Secondly, as his Religion flatters him, so he men; very officious in soothlesse soothings, the Spaniels, that finde his ambition game.[32]

Arminianism, that is, becomes the doctrine of the courtier. The representation of the man's ambition, and his discourse of 'soothlesse soothings', simply appropriates an existing model from anti-court discourse. Moreover, according to Prynne the 'chiefe practise' of the prelates has

> allwayes beene to alienate subjects affections from their Kings, by putting them upon unjust Taxes, exaction, Projects, Monopolies, oppressions, Innovations; by giving them evill counsell, by stopping the course of lawes, of common Right and Justice, of the preaching power and progresse of the Gospell, by advancing Idolatry, Popery, Superstition, with their owne intollerable Hierarchie and Lordly jurisdiction, by fathering all their unjust proceedings upon Kings, &c. and on the contrary to estrange the Kings hearts from their Subjects, by false Calumnies, by sedicious Court-Sermons and by infusing jealousies and discontents into their heads and hearts against their best and loyallest Subjects without a cause.[33]

Characteristically exhaustive, the statement declares a notional loyalty while nonetheless challenging a swathe of Caroline secular and ecclesiastical policies. Although the most extensive study of Prynne argues that in the 1630s he avoided constitutional issues and resisted a forthrightly oppositional stance, Laud could hardly be blamed for perceiving such attacks on prelates as politically inflected.[34] Indeed the image of corrupt prelates 'fathering all their unjust proceedings upon Kings' (used similarly by Burton),[35] with its underlying assumption that at least the name of the king may be unreliable, lurches towards a justification of popular dissent.

The pre-eminent target of such attacks, of course, was Laud. He was figured as the great 'Politician' of the decade, and was besieged by what he saw as *'the undeserved Calumny of those men, whose mouthes are speares and arrowes, and their Tongues a sharpe sword'*.[36] Bastwick, more than any other, approached this calumny in a tradition of scurrilous libel. He repeatedly draws attention to the Archbishop's body, setting the splendour of his office against an alleged corruption within:

> if you should meet him, coming dayly from the starchamber, and see what pompe grandeur and magnificence he goeth in; the whole multitude standing bare where ever he passeth, having also a great number of Gentlemen, and other servants waiting on him, al uncovered, some of them cariyng up his tayle, for the better breaking and venting of his wind & easing of his holy body (for it is full of holes).[37]

Subsequently, he ironically writes Laud into a letter requesting that his jailer approach the Archbishop on the author's behalf, since his wife is on the point of giving birth and has been left devoid of friends. 'I say she desirs', Bastwick writes, that Laud and William Juxon, Bishop of London, should act as godfathers to the child:

> And if you can obtain this favour at their hands, in her behalfe, that as they *ex officio* ruined her poor husbend; so they would likewise *ex officio mero* do this good as to gratify here in yeelding to, and granting her supplication, (by which, she shall pretily well be provided for of GODFATHERS) *I am most confident I shall procure the WHORE OF BABILON, their old Mistris, to be* GODMOTHER, *with whom they have so long committed fornication.*[38]

Like a further suggestion that Laud might consider inviting Bastwick to live with him, the passage juxtaposes assumptions of Christian charity against a reality of discord and oppression.[39] It seeks to demolish, through the resources of satiric wit, the elaborate edifices of authority which Laud, and indeed the entire episcopal structure, had created.

Such assaults carry a serious intent, and it is not surprising that this passage was pinpointed in the Star Chamber document of information against Bastwick, Burton and Prynne.[40] Crucially, these strategies signify that, to the extent that the writers' professions of loyalty may be believed, they are at the same time fashioning a different concept of the Christian nation than that upheld by Laud, or even Charles. In a barbed letter to Laud, Prynne produced an anagram on his name, 'I made Will Lau', in which the elevation of 'will' above 'law' typifies a perception of individual desires undermining established liberties.[41] Similarly, Burton revises images of the body politic, asking, 'are not the lawes of the Kingdome the ligaments, which fasten and unite the Head and members, the King & his people together?'[42] Elsewhere, like Bastwick and Prynne, he focuses more specifically on the 1628 Petition of Right, which is perceived as a definitive statement of the relation between 'the Kings

Prerogative, his just lawes, & the Peoples liberties'.[43] The potential for a reader to dwell on the adjective 'just' invokes ongoing debates which 'brought to centre stage claims that a fundamental law, guaranteeing to each free man security and due process of law in his lands and goods, shaped the polity of which the king was only a part'.[44] The call for the protection of 'liberties' thus sprawls pointedly outward from a religious context, and into a more fundamentally political debate. Moreover, it may remind the reader of the suppression of parliament; as Burton claimed later, the true culprits of this era were those who 'divided the King from the Parliament'.[45]

The King himself, for all the puritans' claims to be defending the royal prerogative from the unconstitutional incursions of the episcopacy, is represented at telling moments as remarkably fallible. Burton, in a passage that one of his critics found to be so 'execrably scandalous' that he could 'not so much as mention it', hints that James I's publication of the *Book of Sports* may have been influenced by his personal circumstances.[46] Indeed he was, on his progress into Scotland in 1617, 'more then ordinarily merily disposed'.[47] Helpfully unpacking the satire, a more forthright critic asks Burton: 'Good Sir, your meaning. Dare you conceive a base and disloyall thought, and not speake it out, for all that *Parrhesia* which you so commend against Kings and Princes.'[48] For Burton, however, the contemplation of a tipsy monarch was not necessarily an act of disloyalty. As he seeks to demonstrate in *A Divine Tragedie Lately Acted*, the higher 'judgements' of God 'upon Sabbath-breakers and other like libertines, in their unlawfull Sports' may be observed in a pattern of providential punishment evident throughout the realm.[49] By comparison, the king is bound 'in Conscience' to enforce 'his just Lawes'.[50] A pointed analogy demonstrates this duty:

> If any will take upon him to coyne money, by counterfeting the Kings stampe and name: his act is treason: how then shall they escape, if presume to coyne what time they please for Gods solemne worship, though they set the counterfeit stampe of God upon it. Now the Sabbath day is of the Lords owne making and stamping, and therefore called the Lords day.[51]

As his readers would have been well aware, the *Book of Sports* was issued in the form of a royal proclamation in 1618 and 1633, clearly bearing 'the Kings stampe and name'.[52] The effect of Burton's analogy is thus no less than to suggest that the royal prerogative may itself project an illegal affront to both God and the subject. It may, therefore, perform an unholy act of 'counterfeit'.

Burton was unquestionably the most politically engaged of the puritan triumvirate in the 1630s. Nonetheless, even he would not necessarily have become an overtly oppositional figure if the state had not determined to confront him, in print as well as in the courts. Annabel Patterson has argued that the (first) trial of William Prynne marks a signal instance of a rupture in 'a highly sophisticated system of oblique communication, of unwritten rules whereby writers could communicate with readers or audiences ... without producing a direct confrontation'.[53] This phenomenon, however, is equally evident in a series of tracts published against the puritans, concerned to mark a clear boundary between authorised and unauthorised discourse. Most notably, Peter Heylyn, Christopher Dow and Francis White wrote in response to Burton, all evidently mobilised by the hierarchies of church and state: '*commanded* by *authority*', in the words of Heylyn, to rebut a 'Lawlesse, and unlicensed Pamphlet'.[54] Heylyn admitted a legitimate concern that, 'should the State thinke fit, that every libell of yours ... should have a solemne Answer to it, you would advance your heads too high, and thinke you had done something more then ordinary'.[55] Equally, such acts of controversialism served to clarify emergent polarities in the nation, prefiguring the Star Chamber trial in their relentless translation of religious invective into political opposition.

Burton's critics performed this act of interpretation by employing similar strategies to those used by the puritans themselves. Hence, while the texts examined above repeatedly charge that the episcopacy is misrepresenting puritanism, White claims similarly that if anyone challenges Burton, 'Hee forth-with stigmatizeth them in print'.[56] More significantly, while the puritan writers argue that the bishops are appropriating and subverting the name of the king, Heylyn charges that Burton's choice of title, *For God, and the King*, is employed 'as *Rebells* doe most commonly in their *insurrections* [pretending] the safety of the King, and the preservation of Religion, when as they doe intend to destroy them both'.[57] Criticism of the bishops might thus be interpreted as veiled attacks on the King himself: 'If men may, at their liberty, Father the *Kings* acts upon whom they favour not, and then rayle at them at their pleasure ... his Majesty will ere long be faine to stand to his subjects courtesie for obedience to his royall commands.'[58] As seen above, the same image of 'fathering' was employed by Prynne, to represent the prelates' abuse of the king's name. Like any satiric tactic, however, this was always potentially reversible. Consequently, whatever the intentions of Bastwick, Burton and Prynne, their works are rendered oppositional; in White's words, their goal is 'to usher in rebellion and sedition, in the Church and State'.[59] The outcome of their trial, therefore, was virtually inevitable.

II

None of the three controversialists was new to the legal system. Bastwick wrote his *Letany* pamphlets from the Gatehouse, where he was being kept until such time as he should 'recant his errors'; Burton had a history of examination dating back to the late 1620s; while what remained of Prynne's ears after his visit to the Star Chamber in 1634 inspired jokes of recognition from his judges three years later.[60] The 1637 trial, however, exponentially raised the profiles of the men and their texts. Even Kevin Sharpe, despite arguing that the judges went to great lengths to ensure fairness, concludes that the hearing and subsequent punishment marked a turning point in relations between the state and its subjects.[61] The trial and punishment took three outspoken yet relatively powerless individuals, and constructed around them a coherent and threatening opposition movement.

The trial itself was characterised by a complete lack of engagement between the defendants and their judges. Eventually the court proceeded *pro confesso*, since none of the men demonstrated any willingness to answer the charges in a legitimate manner. Instead, Bastwick, Burton and Prynne concentrated their attention on procedural matters, in an effort to undermine the authority claimed by the Star Chamber. Prynne focused immediately on the confusion between secular and ecclesiastical authority in the Chamber, arguing that no bishops should be involved in judging the trial: it 'being no way agreeable with equity or reason that they, who are our Adversaries, should bee our Judges'. The predictable failure of his plea – dismissed as 'libellous' – merely served to reinforce a perception that the prelates were appropriating to themselves the machinery of state.[62] All three also argued that a lack of proper access to legal counsel, and the censorship of their prepared statements, had eroded the 'free liberties of speech' to which a defendant is entitled.[63] Hence what may appear to historians as a wilfully obstructive approach was presented to the public as a denial of natural justice.[64] As a sympathetic account of the case stated,

> the sole charge against them, and the ground of their censures was a supposed *contemptuous refusall to answer*, when as the Offence, and contempt was on the contrary side, in refusing to accept of their answers tendred, and ordering Counsell not to signe their answers.[65]

Their principal response was in fact presented in the form of a cross bill against the prelates. Though dismissed by a newswriter as 'a bold presumption of wretched men', the significance of the cross bill lay in its effort to imagine the process of justice being inverted.[66] The cross bill rehearses and expands upon many of the anti-episcopal arguments the men had previously published, and turns against the bishops the exact charges that they were facing themselves. It is thus the bishops who are of 'schismaticall ambition, & seditious humor', and it is Laud whose actions and speeches 'are of very dangerous consequence contrary to the common lawes, customes, & statutes of this kingdome'.[67] As fanciful as it may be within a legal context, the document projects to the nation a deft act of polarisation: setting charge against counter-charge, and one identifiable group against another.

The men's judges effectively endorsed this plot. Laud, whose speech was published soon after the trial and who made perhaps the most concerted effort to refute the alleged libels, denies at the outset the puritans' claims to be concerned only with religion. For Laud, 'of all *Libels*, they are most *odious* which pretend *Religion*'. Instead, he categorically translates attacks on bishops into political terms, arguing that 'no man can *Libell* against our *Calling* (as these men doe) bee it in *Pulpit, Print*, or otherwise, but he *Libels* against the *King* and the *State*'.[68] The relation between monarchy and episcopacy was one of the great debates of the early seventeenth century. The traditional declaration, 'No bishops, no king', which James I was held to have invoked at the 1604 Hampton Court conference, was duly echoed by Heylyn in his exchange with Burton, and in turn underpins Laud's own assertion.[69] He warns Charles: "tis not Wee onely, that is; the *Bishops*, that are strucke at, but through our sides, *Your Majesty, Your Honor, Your Safety, Your Religion*, is impeached'.[70] Laud, like his fellow judges in 1637, underscores the fear expressed by Sir Thomas Edmondes in Star Chamber three years earlier; Prynne, Edmondes declared, 'taketh upon him to forme a new kinde of governmente'.[71]

The courtroom polarisation between the puritan writers and their judges spilled over into the theatre of punishment. The sentences, as we have seen, were by no means unanticipated, and it is fair to say that the defendants 'actually sought "puritanical martyrdom" for their cause'.[72] Predictably, the execution of the sentences attracted a large crowd, and the men's performances at the pillory were carefully scrutinised and widely reported. According to one report, Bastwick was characteristically 'witty and pleasant all the tyme', punning that 'they had coller daies in the King's Court, and this was his coller daye in the King's Pallace'.[73] As Alastair Bellany suggests, this is probably an 'allusion to the royal ceremonial surrounding the Order of the Garter', and thus turns 'the wooden collar of the pillory ... into his Garter badge'.[74] Burton, meanwhile, drew a series of comparisons between the present punishments and the suffering of Christ. On his first sight of the pillories he is said to have proclaimed:

> Me thinkes ... I see Mount Calvery, where the three Crosses (one for Christ and the other two for the two theeves) were pitched: And if Christ were numbred among theeves, shall a Christian (for Christs cause) thinke much to be numbred among Rogues, such as wee are condemned to be? Surely, if I be a Rogue, I am Christs Rogue, and no mans.[75]

Although his sense of self-importance verges on blasphemy, Burton deftly reminds his audience of the state's audacious efforts to degrade the three men. Heylyn observed subsequently that it 'was a very great trouble to the spirits of many very moderate and well-meaning men, to see the three most eminent professions ... to be so wretchedly dishonoured'.[76] Burton simply offered such observers an alternative interpretation.

The state's imposition of marks on the bodies of the transgressors was similarly reinterpreted. One judge in 1634, when Prynne ultimately escaped with at least some of his ears intact, mockingly contemplated marking his crime in other ways as well:

> I cannott tell whether I should censure him to be branded like Cain with a visible marke, to have his nose slitt, or a brand on his forehead, & to have his ears cutt. but then it may be he may weare a periwigg to hide his forehead or a couple of lovelocks, which he hath soe much inveighed against to hide his ears.[77]

But this comment fails to grasp the potential significance of such marks to the stigmatised puritan. For men trained in a Calvinist tradition, to seek 'the severall markes and characters whereby [Christians] may infallibly know' whether they are numbered among the elect, the marks imposed by a corrupt court might easily be claimed as signs of a godly triumph.[78] For Burton, they were 'glorious marks of the Lord Jesus'; for Prynne, although his critics felt that he 'should have covered his face like the Leper, and cryed, I am uncleane, I am uncleane', the marks defined his identity of opposition.[79] Curiously, in the months after the punishment the authorities in Chester expended considerable efforts tracing freshly painted portraits of Prynne, which presumably traded on the subject's earless and stigmatised state. In a futile gesture of control, the authorities then proceeded to 'deface' the portraits afresh – and when they found themselves short of portraits for a public burning, they burned the picture-frames instead.[80]

As this anecdote indicates, in the aftermath of the trial the state fought a desperate and overwhelmingly unsuccessful battle to reassert its acts of stigmatisation. The judges presumably believed that by banishing the men to prisons in distant corners of the land they would efface their threat at the centre of the nation. In fact, though, the men's respective journeys away from the capital were transformed into wondrous parodies of a royal progress, as the marked miscreants were followed by crowds and entertained by supporters. Laud, already troubled by the performance at the pillory, wondered aloud why 'there were thousands suffered to be upon the way to take their Leave, and God knows what else'.[81] He worried also about a flood of libellous poems and performances which targeted him in the months after the case.[82] Although only a few of these poems survive, some of the more pointedly successful efforts sought visually to invert the structures of justice and authority upon which the state had relied in the Star Chamber. In one case, the Lord Mayor sent Laud

> a board hung upon the Standard in Cheap, and taken by the watch (the thing, I mean, not the man), a narrow board with my speech in the Star Chamber nailed at one end of it, and singed with fire, the corners cut off instead of the ears, a pillory of ink with my name to look through it, a writing by – 'The man that put the saints of God into a pillory of wood, stands here in a pillory of ink.'[83]

Laud's speech, printed at the 'commaund' of the King, is pilloried.[84] The libellers, whose only weapon was 'ink', asserted in opposition to Laud an unauthorised yet culturally influential version of the trial and punishment. As Thomas Wentworth, Earl of Strafford, commented darkly to Laud (as one future royalist martyr to another): 'a Prince that loseth the Force and Example of his Punishments, loseth withal the greatest Part of his Dominion'.[85]

The release of the men three years later marked a triumph for the unauthorised interpretation of the trial, and no doubt underscored for Laud and Strafford the prescience of the latter's Machiavellian aphorism. In the early weeks of the Long Parliament, the Commons reviewed the trials, set aside the convictions and sentences, and awarded the men damages against their persecutors.[86] Imprisoned by now on the Channel Islands, they returned to London in fresh processions through the country, affirming in the process a national community of the godly. Yet this time they were authorised; for the puritans, the will of God was finally coming into alignment with the lesser political authority of the state. As Burton declared to a woman who welcomed him at Charing Cross, 'my suffering on the pilory was made glorious by an inward spiritual power, and hand of heaven upon my soule', whereas 'this my return from captivity was attended with an externall glory shining forth from humane favour'.[87] They duly exploited this favour by returning to the press, presenting new accounts of their lives, trials and punishments, along with freshly radical political arguments. By comparison, Laud was troubled at this time by a fresh wave of libels, which he felt unable to stop. At the time of his trial in 1644, he would lament that 'never man hath ... been made so notorious a subject for ridiculous pamphlets and ballads'.[88] Laud had lost control of the fashioning of his own identity, and was executed in due course as a scapegoat for the perceived failures of the Caroline regime.

By the 1640s, then, the trial and punishment of Bastwick, Burton and Prynne had been incontrovertibly politicised. Although the men's aims had initially been religious, their writings through the 1630s increasingly assumed political significance, while their trial and its aftermath clarified their status as figures of opposition. The resistant stance they adopted in the Star Chamber resonated through the following years, and helped to fashion the myth of this court as an agent of oppression. For Burton, in his 1643 autobiography, the role of parliament in these years was crucial; describing the experience of receiving news of his own imminent release, he comments, 'Blessed tidings indeed, and the more, because it came from a Parliament'.[89] Although he does not call directly for the overthrow of the monarch, Burton is nonetheless decisive in his political sympathies. In an image that pointedly undercuts the authority of monarchical insignia, he declares that he will bear 'what wounds I receive from the adversaries ... as *crownes* upon me'.[90]

Analysis of the works and experiences of these three men thus helps to elucidate the interconnections between religion and politics on the eve of the civil war. In many respects it is simply futile to try to separate religion and politics; the discourses of each were too closely intertwined, and contemporaries too adept at manipulating their relationship. Close attention to language and texts, however, helps to identify vital shifts. Therefore, while it is perhaps an overstatement to argue that 'religious resistance *was* constitutional resistance', an analysis of the careers of Bastwick, Burton and Prynne certainly demonstrates the ways in which religious resistance could be *translated into* constitutional resistance.[91] As we have seen, this construction of opposition was achieved partly through the men's writing, with its artful strategies of subversion and confrontation, and partly also through the state's own miscalculated efforts at stigmatisation. Their works increasingly gathered political significance, and the state itself helped to clarify that significance.

Consequently this essay, like a number of others in the volume, illuminates some of the ways in which political meanings were transformed in the 1630s. This is not a sudden event; as I have argued elsewhere, developments in political discourse over the preceding decades were equally important.[92] Nor was it in any sense inevitable; indeed the works and lives of Bastwick, Burton and Prynne reveal nothing so much as the complexity and uncertainty of religious and political alignments in this decade. And yet those alignments unquestionably took shape, and these men helped to give them shape. Despite their manifold differences and their lack of a coherent political doctrine, these men therefore demand recognition in any narrative of the emergence of opposition in early Stuart England. For, if conflict is to become a reality, it must first be capable of representation. In other words, individuals must be able to identify with ideals and discourses, and these must be defined against other ideals and discourses. Within this context, Bastwick, Burton and Prynne emerge as pivotal figures. While they did not set out to oppose the king and foment civil war, they helped to create the cultural conditions in which conflict became almost inevitable.

NOTES

1 [John Bastwick], *A Briefe Relation of Certaine Speciall and Most Materiall Passages, and Speeches in the Starre-Chamber* ([?Amsterdam], 1638), p. 17.

2 S. R. Gardiner (ed.), *Documents Relating to the Proceedings against William Prynne in 1634 and 1637* (Camden Society, 2nd series, 18, 1877), p. 17; Bodl., MS Douce 173, fol. 7v.

3 Gardiner (ed.), *Documents Relating to the Proceedings*, p. 90. The verse, however, may have been written by a supporter of Prynne rather than by the man himself: [William Prynne], *A New Discovery of the Prelates Tyranny* (London, 1641), pp. 65–6.

4 Thomas Fuller, *The Church History of Britain* (1655), book II, 153–4; quoted in David

Cressy, *Travesties and Transgressions in Tudor and Stuart England: Tales of Discord and Dissension* (Oxford: Oxford University Press, 2000), p. 224.

5   See S. Foster, *Notes from the Caroline Underground: Alexander Leighton, the Puritan Triumvirate, and the Laudian Reaction to Nonconformity* (Hamden, Conn.: Archon Books, 1978), esp. pp. 58–61.

6   Cf. two recent analyses of Bastwick, Burton and Prynne, which have similarly situated the events and discourse surrounding them as pivotal in the emergence of political conflict: Alastair Bellany, 'Libels in action: ritual, subversion and the English literary underground, 1603–42', in Tim Harris (ed.), *The Politics of the Excluded, c.1500–1850* (Basingstoke: Palgrave, 2001), pp. 99–124; and Cressy, *Travesties and Transgressions*, pp. 213–33.

7   *The Letany of John Bastwick* (Leiden, 1637), p. 5.

8   William Prynne, *A Quench-Coale. Or A Briefe Disquisition and Inquirie, in what Place of the Church or Chancell the Lords-Table ought to be Situated* (Amsterdam, 1637), p. 1; Henry Burton, *The Baiting of the Popes Bull* (London, 1627), sig. ¶1v.

9   Henry Burton, *For God, and the King* ([London], 1636), sig. (a)4r, p. 27; on *parrhesia*, see D. Colclough, 'Parrhesia: the rhetoric of free speech in early modern England', *Rhetorica*, 17 (1999), 177–212.

10 Burton, *For God, and the King*, p. 27; John Bastwick, *A More Full Answer* (Leiden, 1637), p. 4.

11 On the authorship and printing of *Newes from Ipswich*, see Foster, *Notes from the Caroline Underground*, pp. 73–4; and W. M. Lamont, *Marginal Prynne 1600–1669* (London: Routledge & Kegan Paul, 1963), pp. 38–9.

12 *Newes from Ipswich* (n.p., 1636), sigs A2r, B1v.

13 William Prynne, *Lame Giles His Haultings* ([?London], 1630). ('O greater one, spare, I pray, the lesser madman.')

14 Bastwick, *Letany*, p. 10.

15 *The Letany of John Bastwick [the Second Part]* (Leiden, 1637), sig. A2r.

16 George Wither, *Britain's Remembrancer* ([London], 1628), fols 246v–7r. Cf. Kevin Sharpe, *The Personal Rule of Charles I* (New Haven and London: Yale University Press, 1992), p. 362.

17 Patrick Collinson, *The Puritan Character: Polemics and Polarities in Early Seventeenth-Century English Culture* (Los Angeles: William Andrews Clark Memorial Library, 1989), pp. 14–15; cf. Nicholas Tyacke's argument that in the early 1630s Arminianism 'almost overnight ... rechristened' Calvinism as puritanism: *Anti-Calvinists: The Rise of English Arminianism* (Oxford: Oxford University Press, 1987), p. 81.

18 Cf. my discussion of *The Interpreter* (1622), probably by Alexander Leighton, in *Literature, Satire and the Early Stuart State* (Cambridge: Cambridge University Press, 2004), pp. 130–2. This poem presents one of the earliest and most impressive efforts to refashion the term 'puritan' as a positive sign of religious integrity.

19 Bastwick, *Letany [Second Part]*, sigs A3v–A4, C3r.

20 William Prynne, *The Perpetuitie of a Regenerate Mans Estate* (London, 1627), sigs **1v–**6v.

21 See, for example, Sir John Harington's early seventeenth-century attack on 'fantasticall Novellists': *A Briefe View of the State of the Church of England* (London, 1653), p. 13.

22 Henry Burton, *A Brief Answer to a Late Treatise of the Sabbath Day* ([?Amsterdam], 1635), p. 13.

23 Burton, *For God, and the King*, p. 99.

24 William Prynne, *Anti-Arminianisme* (London, 1630), sigs a3r, b2v.

25 Peter Lake, 'Anti-popery: the structure of a prejudice', in Richard Cust and Ann Hughes (eds), *Conflict in Early Stuart England* (London: Longman, 1989), p. 73.

26 Quoted in Collinson, *The Puritan Character*, p. 26; Prynne, *Anti-Arminianisme*, sig. 2π3r; cf. J. P. Sommerville, *Royalists and Patriots: Politics and Ideology in England 1603–1640* (2nd edn, London and New York: Longman, 1999), p. 211.

27 *Table Talk of John Selden*, ed. F. Pollock (London: Quaritch, 1927), p. 99; quoted in Sommerville, *Royalists and Patriots*, p. 181.

28 Lake, 'Anti-popery', p. 90.

29 J. Bastwick, *The Vanity and Mischeife of the Old Letany [the Third Part of the Letany]* (Leiden, 1637), p. 19.

30 Bastwick, *Letany [Second Part]*, sig. B1r.

31 A. Bellany, *The Politics of Court Scandal in Early Modern England: News Culture and the Overbury Affair, 1603–1660* (Cambridge: Cambridge University Press, 2002), pp. 141–3; Lake, 'Anti-popery', p. 88.

32 Henry Burton, *A Plea to an Appeale* (London, 1626), sig. a1v.

33 William Prynne, *A Looking-Glasse for all Lordly Prelates* (London?, 1636), p. 25.

34 Lamont, *Marginal Prynne*; cf. Sommerville's critique of this argument, *Royalists and Patriots*, p. 205.

35 Burton, *For God, and the King*, p. 72.

36 [Prynne], *New Discovery*, p. 4; William Laud, *A Speech Delivered in the Starre-Chamber* (Dublin, 1637), sig. A2v (invoking Psalm 57.4).

37 Bastwick, *Letany*, p. 6.

38 Ibid., p. 11.

39 Ibid., p. 13.

40 Bodl., MS Tanner 299, fol. 147r.

41 Gardiner (ed.), *Documents Relating to the Proceedings*, p. 55.

42 Henry Burton, *Apology of an Appeale* (n.p., 1636), p. 29.

43 Ibid., p. 28.

44 L. L. Peck, 'Kingship, counsel and law in early Stuart Britain', in J. G. A. Pocock (ed.), *The Varieties of British Political Thought, 1500–1800* (Cambridge: Cambridge University Press, 1993), p. 105.

45 Henry Burton, *A Narration of the Life of Mr. Henry Burton* (London, 1643), p. 8.

46 Christopher Dow, *Innovations Unjustly Charged upon the Present Church and State* (London, 1637), p. 74.

47 Burton, *For God, and the King*, p. 58.
48 Peter Heylyn, *Briefe and Moderate Answer* (London, 1637), pp. 51–2.
49 Henry Burton, *A Divine Tragedie Lately Acted* (Amsterdam, 1636), title page.
50 Burton, *For God, and the King*, p. 39.
51 Burton, *Brief Answer*, p. 11.
52 *The Kings Majesties Declaration to His Subjects, Concerning Lawfull Sports to be Used* (London, 1618; London, 1633).
53 Annabel Patterson, *Censorship and Interpretation: The Conditions of Writing and Reading in Early Modern England* (Madison: University of Wisconsin Press, 1984), p. 45.
54 Heylyn, *Briefe and Moderate Answer*, sig. d1v; Francis White, *An Examination and Confutation of a Lawless Pamphlet* (London, 1637), sig. A2v.
55 Heylyn, *Briefe and Moderate Answer*, p. 191.
56 White, *Examination and Confutation*, p. 25.
57 Heylyn, *Briefe and Moderate Answer*, p. 24.
58 Dow, *Innovations Unjustly Charged*, pp. 38–9.
59 White, *Examination and Confutation*, p. 133.
60 Sharpe, *Personal Rule of Charles I*, p. 758; *DNB*, sub Bastwick; [Bastwick], *Briefe Relation*, p. 3.
61 Sharpe, *Personal Rule of Charles I*, pp. 758–65.
62 [Bastwick], *Briefe Relation*, p. 4.
63 *Ibid.*, p. 9; see further *DNB*, sub Burton.
64 Cf. Sharpe, *Personal Rule of Charles I*, p. 760.
65 [Prynne], *New Discovery*, p. 40.
66 Quoted in Sharpe, *Personal Rule of Charles I*, p. 761.
67 Bodl., MS Tanner 299, fols 149r, 161r.
68 Laud, *Speech Delivered in the Starre-Chamber*, pp. 1, 4.
69 Heylyn, *Briefe and Moderate Answer*, p. 106. On the debate, see esp. Anthony Milton, *Catholic and Reformed: The Roman and Protestant Churches in English Protestant Thought 1600–1640* (Cambridge: Cambridge University Press, 1995), pp. 454–75; and Sommerville, *Royalists and Patriots*, pp. 196–9.
70 Laud, *Speech Delivered in the Starre-Chamber*, sig. A2v.
71 Gardiner (ed.), *Documents Relating to the Proceedings*, p. 23.
72 Sharpe, *Personal Rule of Charles I*, p. 761.
73 Gardiner (ed.), *Documents Relating to the Proceedings*, p. 87.
74 Bellany, 'Libels in action', p. 112.
75 [Bastwick], *Briefe Relation*, p. 24.
76 Peter Heylyn, *Cyprianus Anglicus or the History of the Life and Death of William Laud* (London, 1668), part 2, p. 313; quoted in Sharpe, *Personal Rule of Charles I*, p. 764.

77 Bodl., MS Tanner 299, fol. 131r.
78 Prynne, *Perpetuitie*, title page.
79 Burton, *Narration of the Life*, p. 45; [Prynne], *New Discovery*, p. 102.
80 Cressy, *Travesties and Transgressions*, p. 228.
81 William Knowler (ed.), *The Earl of Strafforde's Letters and Dispatches* (2 vols, Dublin, 1740), ii, p. 99.
82 See Thomas Cogswell, 'Underground political verse and the transformation of English political culture', in S. D. Amussen and M. A. Kishlansky (eds), *Political Culture and Cultural Politics in Early Modern England: Essays Presented to David Underdown* (Manchester: Manchester University Press, 1995), p. 277.
83 W. Scott and J. Bliss (eds), *The Works of William Laud* (7 vols, Oxford, 1847–60), vii, p. 371.
84 Laud, *Speech Delivered in the Starre-Chamber*, sig. A2r.
85 Knowler (ed.), *Strafforde's Letters*, ii, p. 119.
86 John Morrill, 'The religious context of the English civil war', *Transactions of the Royal Historical Society*, 5th series, 34 (1984), 166.
87 Burton, *Narration of the Life*, p. 42.
88 Quoted in Cogswell, 'Underground political verse', p. 293.
89 Burton, *Narration of the Life*, p. 38.
90 *Ibid.*, p. 46; my italics.
91 Sommerville, *Royalists and Patriots*, p. 214.
92 McRae, *Literature, Satire and the Early Stuart State*.

Chapter 10

Coteries, complications and the question of female agency

Jerome de Groot

> It will not grieve me (friend) though what I write
> Be held no wit at Court.[1]

Coterie culture during the 1630s is a diverse and complicated subject increasingly well served by literary and historical criticism. Work on this subject is still at an early stage, but what is already clear is that our notion of what the jigsaw of connections between public and private culture in the period might look like is in need of some revision. I want to suggest here that a study of the complexities of a single, brief text produced from, and meditating upon, the courtly margins can focus our understanding of the intricate poetic, religious and political interactions of extra- and sub-courtly groups during the mid-1630s; the text appears at a nexus point that permits us to read mid-1630s culture in intriguing directions. Just as Julie Sanders's reclamation of the Countess of Carlisle has revealed a much more nuanced and diverse culture of Platonism at work in public and private, so a consideration of the sub-courtly fringe confirms that our habit of relying upon 'the formulation of Henrietta Maria's circle at court as merely an alternative monolith to Charles's' must be considerably revised.[2] The nexus and network of coteries, factions, relationships (familial, sexual, religious, patronage and political), friendships, and alliances of convenience present in the 1630s court are complex and important. The interaction, interrogation and overlap between these groups complicate our understanding of 1630s culture. Indeed, 'complicate' is a key word here – as Martin Butler, Erica Veevers and Malcolm Smuts amongst others have pointed out, one of the chief characteristics of texts from the 1630s, particularly those which were produced on the relative margins of the court, is an engagement with and sometimes celebration of contradictions and inextricable conflicts; complication is both participant and progenitor during the period.[3]

The rise of Henrietta Maria and her ragtaggle collection of Catholic intelligentsia, discontented courtiers and ambitious Platonists to the point in 1637 at which Laud could worry that 'the party of the queen grows very strong' has been much debated.[4] Laud's presentation of the 'party of the queen' suggests that Henrietta Maria had a programme, and her 'party' a working dynamic, which perhaps ascribes it too much unity and purpose, particularly in the early and mid-1630s. Martin Butler usefully describes the Queen as a 'focus' for discontent, a point of meeting or a symbol to deploy. What this essay does is concentrate on the networks coalescing around the Queen and her court, exploring their relationship with Catholic coterie culture and the poetic circles of the Inns of Court. Of particular interest are the nodal connections and interrelationships between legal circles and coterie Catholic circles. An exploration of these associations, using the facilitating example of a dedicatory poem written by the poet and playwright William Habington, suggests much for and complicates our understanding of court culture, female agency, disguised Catholic dissent and coterie relationships during the decade.

The Inns of Court during the 1620s and 1630s were teeming with energy and were an emblem for 'this polluted age'.[5] Part of what James Grantham Turner calls the 'seething subcultures' of early modern London, they were variously centres for poetry, theatre, debate, loyalty, philosophy, dissidence, resistance, drinking and arguing.[6] They were religiously suspect (Lincoln's and Gray's Inns were particularly Catholic, as Henry and John Donne's experiences testify).[7] The Inns' unique status within the vibrant culture of London at the period lent them a diversity and plurality unattainable elsewhere. Francis Lenton warned in *The Young Gallant's Whirligigg* against the various temptations that a young man might discover in a place where masquing, gaming, poetasting and drinking were such an embedded part of the culture. Lenton's ominous poem warns young men against attending the Inns and illustrates the close link between an emergent youth or gentlemanly 'gallant' culture, the Inner Temples and the court: 'His parents him supply to buy him bookes / As hee pretends: but stead of Cokes Reports, / Hee's fencing, daüncing, or other sports.'[8] Elsewhere Lenton characterised those at the Inns as particularly innocent but prone to mischief; an 'Innes a Court Gentleman' is 'an Infant, newly crept from the Cradle of learning, to the Court of liberty, from logicke to law (both grounded on reason) from his tutor to the Touchstone of wits, where he is now admitted amongst the braue imps of the kingdome, to grow Pillars of their Countrey'.[9]

Francis Lenton is himself an interesting example of the ill-defined figures frequenting the grey areas between Holborn, London Catholic coteries and the Queen's court. He claims in the preface to *The Young Gallant's Whirligigg* to have 'once belonged to the Innes of court', although there is no record of his attending; 'belonged' may be a general term for associating with rather than officially entering chambers.[10] This loose phrasing is characteristic of Lenton who claims to be 'one [or sometimes the only] of Her Majesties poets' in his frontispieces, as heir to Davenant; again, such a position was never made official, but he clearly had some connection to Henrietta Maria, and he celebrated his position as 'scholler in the court of arcadia'.[11] Like the playwright James Shirley and Habington himself, Lenton was deeply involved in the Inns of Court response to *Histriomastix*; his 1634 *The Innes of Court Anagrammatist* commemorated the marshal and students who presented Shirley's *Triumph of Peace* to the King on behalf of the Inns of Court, claiming that the masque 'Shew'd Englands Gallantry, and Noble Spirits'.[12] He also had a life in manuscript, scribally publishing and circulating Neo-Platonic work influenced by Nicolas de Caussin to sympathetic patrons such as Henrietta Maria's chamberlain the Earl of Dorset or Sir Anthony and Lady Cage.[13] He is the kind of cultural synthesiser commonly negotiating between Holborn, the London Catholics and Somerset House. Working on the fringes, through manuscript circulation as well as publication, he maintained a series of important and often invisible patronage connections.

I want to explore the vibrant life of these fringe groups by concentrating on the relationships between three sub-courtly figures: James Shirley, William Habington and Robert Stapleton. All three have clear connections to Henrietta Maria, but also interact with poetic circles in Holborn, Catholic factional groups in London and coteries in the country. They demonstrate the vibrancy of extra-courtly groups in the 1630s, share a sense of alienation, and, as has been argued in depth about Shirley but which I would extend to both Habington and Stapleton, inform our understanding of the status and agency of women during the period. Their immediate connection was through a Gray's Inn literary and legal circle congregating around William Cooke's publishing house in Furnival's Gate, Holborn. Cooke was Shirley's publisher and his shop became the meeting point for a scholarly poetic circle gathering around the playwright. Most of the material Cooke produced was composed by the Shirley circle; as Allan Stevenson points out, thirty-one of thirty-eight books entered by Cooke on the Stationer's Register came from this group.[14] The rest of his oeuvre was legal textbooks. A clear example of the relationships fostered by using the same publisher is that Cooke's only published output in 1634 was Habington's *Castara* and Stapleton's *Dido and Aeneas*.

Like the University volumes published in the 1620s and 1630s, the Inns of Court groups created a public forum in which to advance a corporate poetic identity. Rather than volumes of panegyric praise, however, the groups used dedicatory poems. The volumes are conceived of as complete entities; the dedications work as more than mere praise, combining discourses of friendship and poetic alliance with political and religious assertions in coherent and subtle fashion. They are inherently part of the work itself, rather than ancillary material. The men's friendships were formed in this real and conceptual arena of poetic camaraderie unique to the Inns and their literary output, a situation in which expressions of homosocial bonding became more than rhetorical posturing and took on a variety of distinct and overlapping implications. The Shirley coterie first collaborated in a coherent fashion in 1630 when their manifesto of literary friendship appeared as the commendatory verses prefacing and defending James Shirley's *The Gratefull Servant*.[15] Shirley's friends were defending him from literary attacks by Davenant and his supporters, as well as politically motivated religious denunciation. The prefatory poems – unusual in number and protective tone – were the result of a 'free vote of my friends whom I could not with ciuility refuse'.[16] Stapleton and Habington both contributed verses, as did Charles Aleyn, John Hall, Thomas Randolph, John Fox, Thomas Craford and Philip Massinger (the circle also included Edward Sherburne and Thomas May). The importance of literary and poetic friendship is evident, as is the construction of a conceptual group in clear imitation of the Tribe of Ben. Habington's poem anoints Shirley the heir to Jonson, and as a dramatist whose work will be the 'glory of the stage' and heal political wounds:

> Confesse vs happy since th'ast giuen a name
> To the English Phenix, which by thy great flame
> Will lieu, in spight of malice to delight
> Our Nation, doing art and nature right.[17]

Shirley's verse can make this old world young again, transforming and renewing the troubled nation. The sense of rebirth – and of cyclical poetic inheritance – is combined with politicised terminology of newness, Platonic perfection and 'right'.[18] These writers were fascinated with inheritance, inclusion, authority and agency; the poets writing to Shirley do so to praise him and to sustain an image of themselves as a collective and exclusive club.

Many of the associations within the group were lent edge by religious and specifically Catholic kinship; indeed, *The Gratefull Servant* was dedicated to the powerful Catholic Francis Manners, Earl of Rutland. Shirley and Habington were clearly experimenting with religious language in their early poems, and conducting a literary dialogue at the same time. Kenneth Allot recreates a poetic conversation consisting of manuscript versions of Shirley's 'to E:H: & W:H' and Habington's 'To a Friend, Inviting him to a meeting upon promise'.[19] Both poems playfully conflate sack (Spanish wine) with Catholicism, and celebrate the ritual of religious friendship. Habington's poem specifically attacks William Prynne; he and Shirley were involved in the extensive apologies of the Inns of Court for Prynne's insults to Henrietta Maria in *Histriomastix* in 1634.[20] The two poems, produced within the relative intimacy of manuscript, use their dialogue to create a modulated version of the standard corporate identity of the Inns of Court, nuanced by contemporary political circumstance and the cultural reaction of the legal profession. The dialogue or answer genre created a discourse particular to these poems. This practice is a characteristic feature of the dedications and verses of friendship composed by the Holborn group. The symbiotic relationship between text and dedication, the dynamic dialectic of framing verse contextualising and informing what follows, is characteristic of the ambiguous status of the poems produced by the coterie.

Habington was from a staunchly and proactively Catholic family and circle.[21] He was educated at St Omer and then for a time in Paris, probably at the Jesuit Clermont College. He had a similar religious and educational background to Robert Stapleton, and this lent backbone to their poetical friendship; certainly there is evidence that they dissented together.[22] In addition to the Inns of Court, he was involved with various coteries and literary groups. Habington used his family connections to access court circles and gain entry to Worcester House, where Lord Herbert of Raglan entertained the cream of London Catholic society.[23] In his 1634 collection *Castara* he dedicates poems to such prominent papal enthusiasts as the Earl of Argyll, Endymion Porter and Venetia Digby. His wife Lucy was daughter of William Herbert, Baron Powis, and cousin of Henrietta Maria's favourite the Countess of Carlisle.[24] The volume itself has the motif of a flaming heart circled by laurels as part of the frontispiece. An important dimension to bear in mind, too, is the significance of his religious and political profile on the continent; Habington was Henrietta Maria's papal representative in 1636, his position sponsored by his uncle the Earl of Pembroke. His European education and connections reflect the complexity and reach of Catholic networks at this time. That Habington is of great importance as a connection between various Catholic families and coteries is fast becoming apparent. He was a cultural synthesiser, connector and catalyst, a crucial player in the factional religious and courtly politics of the 1630s. Habington is one of several figures who appear at the fringes of key factions and coteries during the 1630s, connecting widely different groups. He is a figure who extends Smuts's polycentrism beyond the court and into a variety of non-courtly spaces; at and around the court, but not *of* the court. The key characteristic of his work, and that which connects it clearly with that of the sentiments of the Shirley coterie, is the sense of being an outsider, of very firmly asserting a cultural identity at odds with an orthodoxy that is itself slippery to define. Habington is disenfranchised by not being part of any one group, but his very non-conformity gives him membership to a 1630s discourse of dissidence and difference.

The literary circles of the Inns of Court were centred on Holborn, but at times they spread further. Lucy Hutchinson records that her husband, disliking Holborn when he arrived at Lincoln's Inn in May 1636, removed himself to Richmond. She relates that he was persuaded to go due to the proximity to the Prince's courts:

> that if he pleas'd in the meantime to goe to Richmond, where the prince's Court was, ... he might be accomodated, and there was good company and recreations, the King's hawkes being kept neere [...] soe he went to Richmond, where he found a great deale of good young companie, and many ingenuous persons that by reason of the Court, where young princes were bred, entertain'd themselves in that place, and had frequent resort to the house where Mr. Hutchinson tabled.[25]

Richmond attracted many members of the Inns of Court; for instance, John Denham was probably also there at this point.[26] The 'prince's Court' at Richmond referred to by Hutchinson was not that of the Stuart princes but of the Prince Elector of the Palatinate, Charles Louis, and his presence in Richmond the motive for the Middle Templers to visit the area. Culturally, the Inns of Court were strongly linked to Charles Louis; in 1635 they revived their long-dormant revel traditions in his honour.[27] The Middle Temple, and Shirley in particular, venerated both Charles Louis and Henrietta Maria. The relationship to the Palatinate issue and the defence of Prynne instantly politicised the Inns of Court and this is the immediate political context for the Holborn circle, although to argue that they had a common agenda would be disingenuous. Yet their link with the royal courts gained an increasing religio-political dimension; in 1640, for instance, the Earl of Pembroke sponsored the production of Habington's *The Queen of Aragon*, for Martin Butler the apotheosis of sophisticated, complicated 1630s play texts.[28]

The key context for the connections between the Holborn group and the Queen's court is that of the poetic coterie. Poetic coteries depended on contending models of exclusivity and collaboration. On the one hand, copying poems into commonplace books suggested a clear hierarchical relationship between the poet and the owner of the immediate manuscript; on the other, coteries rewrote, retransmitted, reordered and commented upon each other's work. It is not simply straightforward manuscript transcription, and the models for coterie transmission and circulation are different to those for, say, the Universities or the Inns of Court. Of course, these other manuscript forums overlap with and influence coterie development; this article describes an example of one such interaction. Coterie manuscripts, such as those compiled by Constance Aston Fowler (Huntington Library, HM 904) or Sir Henry Cholmley (Houghton Library, Harvard, MS Eng. 703), suggest developing relationships and recreational poetic circulation. Coteries can be familial, religious, political or social; they cross a variety of boundaries, and intersect. They demonstrate a subtle and developing network of local and national contacts and they are also particularly important in showing us a neglected female role in textual transmission.[29] The Tixall coterie, of which Constance

Aston Fowler was one member, had connections to many local Catholic contacts, as well as familial links to the Sadleirs in Hertfordshire, and courtly links through Sir Walter Aston's ambassadorship to the Spanish court during the 1620s and 1630s.

Miscellanies such as Fowler's included poems from a diverse selection of poets, some exclusively and explicitly connected to the family (such as those in her text by Richard Fanshawe), and others more generally related. For instance, William Habington appears in Fowler's notebook.[30] Habington has no clear connection to the Tixall circle other than his religion; whilst his poetry was not widely disseminated in manuscript, it appears to have had some currency amongst Catholic families and circles. The elegy on Venetia Digby he published in *Castara* also appears in a c. 1633–34 manuscript volume of poems on her death, BL, Additional MS 30259. This volume, a presentation manuscript obviously intentionally compiled as a tribute collection, also includes some of Habington's poetic cohort in Thomas May, Thomas Rutter and Thomas Randolph. Peter Beal suggests that Habington's limited circulation in manuscript was intentional, a controlled and specialised way of circumscribing the scope of his audience.[31] This would chime with the coterie and occasional nature of his published verse, with its large number of commendatory and personalised poems – it is notable that one of those poems copied into the Tixall manuscript is a poem to a childhood friend and kinsman of Habington's (George Talbot) who himself wrote the dedicatory poem to *Castara*. The Tixall circle, a clear if complicated religious, familial and literary coterie, involve Habington in their self-presentation and his Platonic, religiously inflected verse was obviously of some currency. The poem to Talbot occasions an answer poem by Katherine Thimelby chiding the poets on their masculine exclusivity: 'S^r, since you are profest to dwell / I'th Heauen of friendship'.[32] This refutation of the homosocial poetic friendships formulated and presented in London is an interesting sidelight onto the gender politics of the Tixall volume, and of family coterie compilation as a whole. Furthermore, the notion articulated in Thimelby's verse of a complex dialogue between text, interlocutor and manuscript present in the answer-poem genre clearly interacts with the multivalent and multi-voiced character of the coterie compilation. These dialogues are ongoing, and the network of connections and interplay is significant to our understanding of the status of manuscript, as well as providing insight into the literary, political and religious culture of the period.

Habington is appropriated by the Tixall group, but their interventions were part of a larger issue of control and a wider network of Catholic relationships. Indeed, his poems are used as part of the creation of poetic communities and consciousnesses even after they are published, as is shown by the commonplace book of Arthur Capell (BL, Harleian MS 3511).[33] A similar use of a poet to give external inflection in this manuscript is the poem 'on John Felton in chains', supposedly composed by Henry Cholmley of Roxby, Yorkshire. This widely transcribed poem lamenting the death of Buckingham was a notable Catholicised addition to undergraduate commonplace books.[34] These University collections tended to be much less sympathetic to courtly Platonism, Catholicism and other concepts that the Inns of Court were more comfortable with. It is striking to find, for instance, in what is otherwise a completely standard University collection (Houghton Library, Harvard, fMS Eng. 626, miscellany of Sir Anthony St John Bletso), 'Ave Maria, or A Hymne in memorie of our Saviours Blessed, Virgin-Mother', and the very rarity of these Catholicised poems presents the compilations as being at once of the University manuscript discourse but importantly interacting with a more familial, recusant coterie tradition. Bletso was part of a Catholic family with clear links to the circles celebrating Platonic and Marian devotion in London; his elder brother, Oliver, was the dedicatee of Francis Lenton's popular London 1631 taxonomy *Characterismi: Or, Lentons Leasures*. Lenton, as described above, was a figure working in the Holborn/Catholic/courtly coterie nexus, and the connection to Bletso and Sir Anthony's commonplace book demonstrates that the categories of manuscript 'environment' or 'scribal communities' which Arthur Marotti and Harold Love describe are more dynamic than formerly argued.[35]

The poem on Felton meant that Cholmley had a 'public' life in manuscript (although the text was never officially ascribed to him); he also encouraged the compilation of a coterie family manuscript, now held in the Houghton Library, Harvard. The Cholmley commonplace book is a fine example of a family coterie compilation. Ranging from probably the late 1620s to the late 1650s, featuring familial poetry and more widely circulated material, the manuscript is a collection in several hands of poems, epitaphs, lists, occasional verses, translations and, notably for a collection of poems like this, answer poetry. Much of the dynamic of 1630s miscellanies lay in the overlapping of answer poetry and the interplay between poets, readers and compiler. Cholmley's commonplace book reflects a standard educated-class determination to anthologise (including standard poems by Carew, Waller, Herrick and Jonson, the most anthologised poets of the period). It is consciously local in scale, too, incorporating poems by Sir Albertus Morton (p. 16), 'by sr Warham St. Leger of Ouldcome als Oucome in Kent' (p. 41), a reply 'To the Author his brother' by Anthony St Leger (p. 42), 'An Epitaph made vpon ye death of ye Lady Hayes first wife to ye now Earle of Carlisle, and daughter to ye Lord Deny made by L.A. by my best Cosen Laurence Ashbournham' (pp. 42–4), 'by my brother Sr Hugh Cholmley' (p. 45), Sir Nicholas Selwin (pp. 105–11), 'Hary Wiat' (pp. 58–60), and Sir Edmund Scory (p. 61). The importance of the domestic dynamic, although obviously and significantly missing female voices, is key to the establishment of a masculinist coterie compilation, transcribed and transmitted between men as part of homosocial bonding and as a continuation of University, Inn or Court, or school dialogues. It is unclear whether any of the compilers were female; certainly the manuscript was prepared for and not all by Henry Cholmley, although he annotates the final version (adding page numbers), and several of the hands are relatively unschooled. However, no overt female voice is heard.

One might appear marginally, however. If Julie Sanders is right and the Tixall group are 'in some ways highly typical, and even representative, of a certain social sphere', then their methods of silent or invisible compilation might be applied here.[36] Certainly female relationships are important in the make-up of the manuscript. There are poems on issues specific to the family which conflate the domestic with the national; on page 89 there appears 'Upon the death of Sir William Twysden, who died the 8th of January 1629'; this is swiftly followed by an 'epitaph on death of Prince of Wales, 1629'. Sir William Twysden was the father of Hugh Cholmley's wife Elizabeth; her brother contributes a poem on Lucy Percy, the Countess of Carlisle in 1639 which is answered by Edmund Waller and then defended.[37] The St Legers of Kent probably come through the Twysden connection, too; the male Cholmleys were from Yorkshire (Sir Hugh being MP for Scarborough and living in Whitby at this point), whereas Elizabeth's family was from Kent. The appearance in the collection of two poems from this family again suggests her influence. The St Legers also allow an early date for the collection; Warham St Leger died in 1631. We can even make a connection with 'Hary Wiat' too, given that Elizabeth was related through her father to Sir Robert Wyatt. Sir Hugh Cholmley, of course, went to Gray's Inn, so was part of the Inns of Court, returning us to that poetic context; he reports that he was introduced to his wife in Hyde Park through a 'Kentis gentleman' from the Inns, suggesting that she might also have some Holborn connection.[38] Certainly the Cholmleys lived in Kent for much of the period between 1622 and 1629, and for summers up to 1639.[39] The various families named in the manuscript do not appear in Hugh Cholmley's *Memoirs*, again suggesting that he was not particularly involved with them – he complains that he was too concerned with business to enjoy much of a life, and that his wife was more sociable than he.[40]

The collection shows us the dynamic and unique mode of poetic compilation that went to construct a domestic, religious and familial character of sorts. Of particular importance are occasional poems, an interrelationship between 'public' and 'domestic' verse, and the creation, through answer poems and dedicatory titles, of a complex dynamic of audience. As we have seen, the deployment of poems in this collective fashion is important to the Holborn circle as part of their attempts to delineate a particularised identity for themselves. More important for my present purposes, however, particularly in the light of the possible involvement of Elizabeth Cholmley in the compilation of the manuscript, is the fact that sometime after 1635 Henry Cholmley married the widow of George Twistleton, Catherine. It is probable that Robert Stapleton came into contact with the Twistletons in 1633–34 when Sir George was in London due to ill-health; he died soon afterwards.

Robert Stapleton had been educated in the Benedictine convent of St Gregory at Douai, becoming a monk of the order in 1625. He returned to England a few years later, becoming attached to the Prince of Wales's court in the 1630s and being knighted by the King in 1642.[41] He submitted to Rome to nullify his profession, apostatising when he was refused.[42] Despite Stapleton's apostasy, he maintained various Catholic connections, primarily through his friendship with William Habington and his connection to the Shirley circle. In late 1634 William Cooke produced a translation by Stapleton based on the fourth book of the *Aeneid*.[43] This volume was dedicated to the then Lady Catherine Twistleton, daughter of Henry Stapleton, Yorkshire relatives of Robert. The dedication to Lady Twistleton directly connects Robert Stapleton, the Holborn group and the provincial Catholic coterie. Furthermore, prefacing the translation there is a prefatory poem 'On DIDO and Æneas, Translated by my much honourd, much lou'd friend, *Robert Stapylton* Esq.', signed by 'W[illiam] HABINGTON'. The poem is not included in modern editions of Habington's work, meaning that the complex and suggestive relationship between the two poets which it reveals has never been analysed. We can use Habington's poem on his friend as a lens to refract our discussion of the extra- and sub-courtly groups during the mid-1630s. His poem conflates different audiences: the provincial nobility, the court, the Queen and Catholic recusant circles. The various contexts already sketched out allow the text and Stapleton's dedication to be inflected in a number of different ways; they appear at a nexus point that permits us to read mid-1630s culture in intriguing directions. Habington's poem, when read in conjunction with Stapleton's dedicatory preface, tells us a great deal about notions of female cultural agency in the 1630s. The contexts for the poem provided here present it as part of a suggestive culture of interaction and interrelation.

The fact that Stapleton dedicated his *Aeneid* to Lady Twistleton indicates that her involvement in cultural production was more important than a passing whimsical preference for Virgil. However, it is relatively clear that the relationship was intellectual and familial rather than financial. As her possible or probable involvement in the Cholmley manuscript suggests, Lady Twistleton was engaged in the common practice of circulating manuscripts, reading and transcribing. The image is not one of prescription but of educated women out of court being involved in manuscript culture, irrespective of gender; agency is more intellectualised and dynamic. Indeed, many of our understandings of the role of women in 'domestic' manuscript work and transmission may be obscured by poor contemporary editing. If Stapleton's actions as a translator are compared with those of his contemporaries, for instance, we can see the

Coteries, complications and female agency

full scope of such female agency. John Denham was also translating Virgil at this point, producing the work that was to become *The Destruction of Troy* in 1656. A transcription of this work exists in a 1630s manuscript miscellany owned by Lucy Apsley (soon to become Hutchinson).[44] The transcript is in her own hand, yet the transmission of the poem is generally cited as the 'fruit of the temporary conjunction of her husband, her brother, and Denham at Lincoln's Inn'.[45] Lucy Apsley has been assigned a passive, scribe's role. Denham was not circulated in manuscript in the 1630s; it is only at the court in exile that he achieves a presence in poetic miscellanies. The appearance of Denham's poem in Apsley's commonplace book indicates some kind of female cultural agency; she would have been sixteen or so when they met, and a keen Latinist. She also copied out extracts from Caussin's *Holy Court*, suggesting further intricacies and interrelationships between the *préciosité* of Henrietta Maria, the Inns of Court – and their manifestation at Richmond, where Apsley lived – and translation of Virgil. Whilst Denham and Apsley probably came into contact in Richmond, there is a clear possibility of her interaction with another poetic circle in Holborn, suggesting once again that this overlapping of groups and families was common.

Poetic and intellectual relationships during the 1630s were not directly dependent upon finance either. Patronage of a monetary kind was becoming to some extent outmoded by the popular market, as is shown by Shirley's dedication of *Changes* to Lady Dorothy Shirley (herself a coterie poet):

> 'Tis not this great man, nor that Prince, whose fame
> Can more advance a Poem, than your name,
> To whose cleere vertue truth is bound, and we,
> That there is so much left for History.
> I doe acknowledge custome, that to men
> Such poems are presented; but my pen
> Is not engag'd nor can allow too farre
> A Salick Law in Poetry, to barre,
> Ladies th'inheritance of wit, whose soule
> Is active, and as able to controule,
> As some 'usurpe the Chaire, which write a stile
> To breath the Reader better than a mile;
> But no such empty titles buy my flame;
> Nor will I sinne so much, to shew their name
> In print: some servile Muses be their drudge,
> That sweat to finde a Patron, not a Iudge.[46]

This Platonic celebration of the accomplished or *honnête* woman grants Dorothy Shirley an entry into society balanced by the example of her virtues. She is an example, an ideal – yet this idealisation complicates the enfranchisement of social involvement. Female intellectual patrons, as Erica Veevers argues, helped to influence society 'by displaying both virtue and attractive grace'.⁴⁷ The key word is 'displaying' – performance and social agency are combined in this enacting of *honnête*. Women are at once freed and constrained: as Kim Walker argues in relation to Shirley's 1633 play *The Bird in a Cage*, a 'degree of female autonomy' is allowed but 'carefully contained'; female agency, in similar fashion to female performance, is seemingly celebrated but only within strict guidelines and under the adoring and constructing gaze of the male writer.⁴⁸ Performance legitimates and contains the female; the presentation of virtue involved in courtly Platonism and intellectual patronage simultaneously circumscribes and enables the transgression of the female. Sophie Tomlinson has argued that the 'performative aspect of the feminocentric court culture disrupted the symbolic ordering of gender'; I would suggest that these printed or public texts are part of a confused masculine reaction concerned with curtailing this disruption.⁴⁹ The newly empowered performative woman – in particular, the Queen, but throughout the 1630s the more intellectually and influentially heavyweight of courtly ladies – was something to celebrate yet simultaneously a source of anxiety that needed to be silenced, marginalised and controlled.

Stapleton's dedication to Lady Twistleton is fulsome in its praise. He has published the work rather than let the copy remain for her in manuscript, he claims, 'my chiefe design, to doe honour to so excellent a Kinswoman: in whose naturall perfections our Family in whose vertues our Time glories'.⁵⁰ Stapleton's dedication asserts that he was moved to translate the work because Lady Twistleton read no Latin. His textual construction of Lady Twistleton suggests that her innate virtues are in some way unsullied by the mark of masculine education, and her lack of education is presented as an index of her virtue. She is projected into the public sphere, objectified as the apotheosis of her family. The volume will be a monument to her purity and beauty, raised to honour her and presented by a faithful servant. However, there is some ambiguity and perhaps anxiety in this, which further complicates our understanding of the presentation of female agency; whilst women may have been at work behind the scenes and in manuscript, they were still problematised within the masculine discourse of print. The panegyrical nature of dedicatory poetry insists that the relationship between poet and patron is delicately nuanced; Stapleton's publishing without her consent rather counterpoints the alleged respect. He begs her indulgence: 'I tooke this Copy for your Ladiship, pardon me that I publish it.'⁵¹ Whilst feigning to foreground her status as a cultural motivator, Stapleton simply reworks a paradigm of subjection into this seemingly newer model of patronage. He had already disclosed an anxious relationship between poet and female subject in his dedicatory poem to *The Gratefull Servant*:

> Thou art too little iealous of thy muse,
> Her beauties seene to free, she doth not use
> To weare a maske or veile, which now a dayes
> Is growne a fashion.[52]

The remainder of the poem presents the play as feminine and slightly dangerous: 'there's witchcraft in thy words' he claims, 'Though to the stage it would be thought blest harme / Might it still bewitch'd which such a charme.'[53] Rather than allow his women words, Stapleton writes them out of the equation, allowing them only a representation defined visually (the frontispiece of the gracefully tragic Dido) or through the masculine author/father: the 'Epistle Dedicatory' defines and frames Twistleton through her male relatives: 'TO MY MOST HONOURED Lady, My Lady TWISTLETON, Daughter of *Henry Stapleton* Esquire, and Wife to Sir GEORGE TWISTLETON, *Baronet*'.[54]

In *Dido and Aeneas*, Stapleton's male voice mediates the relationship between audience and text, using a version of femininity that owes much to the Platonic tropes current at court to assign Lady Twistleton an ill-educated passivity. Stapleton emphasises that

> DIDO fell by her owne hand a Martyr of CHASTITY, not a SACRIFICE to PASSION: but let not this move you to suspect my Authour, as envious to your Noble Sexe, or ambitious to enlarge the ROMAN Conquest in a Ladies fame, farre be it from your apprehension, as from his: he writes a POEM, not a HISTORY, and draweth not the Picture of DIDO but of ART to life.[55]

Stapleton chivalrously protects Dido from an aggressively gendered history and the attentions of a groping Virgil. Lady Twistleton's desire to understand Virgil becomes the site from which Stapleton can launch his poetic career. This relationship is reflected in the text itself, as Dido becomes the foundation for both Stapleton's career (as conceived in Habington's poem) and the imperial adventures of Aeneas. Men continually project their ambition onto Dido and then move on. Again, this suggests that whilst women are key figures behind the scenes, as cultural motivators or intellectual patrons, their status in the forum of print is ambivalent and controlled. The presentation of Dido by Stapleton is complex and anxious. As he asserts, she fell 'a Martyr of CHASTITY, not a SACRIFICE to PASSION'. This perfectly encapsulates the position of the strong female in Stapleton's typology – virtuous and moderate, not destabilising and passionate. She displays her *honnête*, her accomplishments and her stoic example. The engraving on the frontispiece once more emphasises her grace, beauty and significance as an expression of exemplary *préciosité*.

The concept of female power and agency is bound with the portrayal of Dido, and thus perhaps crucially compromised. Habington presents Dido's funeral pyre as the site of Stapleton's poetic triumph and his monument to posterity; she lends him a cultural nexus he can use to further his name and career: 'Euen this Peice will raise / Not subject to times rage, or Enuies spoile, / A Pyramid to thee in Dido's Pile'.[56] The Holborn coterie was extremely concerned about questions of cultural inheritance and agency. They often figured themselves as part of a line of wit, reviving dormant traditions in a cyclical fashion. The notion of poetic legacy being created anew from the ashes of the dying bird (Habington's 'English Phenix') complicates the metaphor of Dido's pile. She is not reborn, Stapleton is; her death enables his rise, he will create from her ashes. Again the emphasis is upon using the female to attain cultural capital and agency, undermining the powerful woman by vampirically stealing her essence for one's own purposes. Where the Holborn poets looked to their poetic ancestors for legitimacy and assurance, Habington here presents Stapleton using Dido as a cultural crutch, easily cast aside when no longer necessary. There is no mention of Aeneas in Habington's poem, and he makes only fleeting appearances in Stapleton's dedication. Dido seems to be centre of power and the cultural motivator, but she is constantly in thrall to male action, either poetic or martial. The attitude to female cultural agency is ambivalent, to say the least. The aroma of the exotic attached to the figure of Dido as a pagan and African Queen, and the 'Pyramid' her ashes will physically support, is both fashionable and ambiguous. Orientalism figured highly in the court of Charles I, and particularly in the entertainments of Henrietta Maria, yet the overlapping notions of conquest and the development of virgin land clearly impact upon the poem's underlying theme of containing the transgressive.

The prime tone of Habington's dedicatory poem is of alienation, and in this it shares concerns with the poems of the Shirley circle and coterie poets generally. There is a suspicion of the court and a quiet celebration of sub- and extra-courtly cultural spaces that are more virtuous, straightforward and less ambiguous. The court is a site where bad poets of 'seeming wit' have their names "mong Ladies glorified'. Again, there is ambivalence and a suspicion of female agency – women are the audience and the power in this court, but their heads are easily turned. The foppish and feminised Sir Whisper makes his jibes for the pleasure of a courtly lady, acting a role in front of his admirers. There is a whiff of intrigue in his quietly conspiratorial comments. The court is effeminate, effeminising and not a place to desire. Habington's connections lend edge to his dismissal of other court poets; he intimates that the mainstream court is no longer culturally valid, that the circles he and Stapleton are involved in are more important and virtuous. The smaller groups and coteries appear to Habington as the proper and real courts – complex, different, vibrant, intellectual. In his poem to Stapleton Habington sets up a distinction between the 'impure' activities of the court, both poetically and spiritually, and the work Stapleton is engaged with. Translation, in Habington's model, is both a distinct poetical action, and a pure and chaste religious activity.

Stapleton's poetics are right and virtuous, in contrast with the falsely mixed culture of the court, the 'ship of fooles'.[57] Habington insists that translation is nobler than the standard imitative models of poetry now prevalent, advising Stapleton not to mind those that claim 'copies want th'Originals art'.[58] He is involved in a virtuous cycle, a continual rebirth or reconfiguration of scientific virtue and exemplary progress.

The jokes about size and scale may refer to the dwarf Jeffrey Hudson and others of the Queen's favourites. They also reflect a concern with physical states outside of 'normal' bounds that echo the ambiguous sexuality of Sir Whisper. Habington figures the foolish courtiers as mere performing dwarves in comparison to Stapleton's true intellectual purpose. Stapleton is prudent and sensible; his work is pure and sustainable, in plain contrast to his critics who have wasted what talents they had: 'prodigally spent / Like riotous youth, only on monies lent'.[59] His translation is based on hard work and scholarliness, rather than hedonism and the conceptualised non-value of credit. He 'Dost onely spend oth'stocke of thy owne wit'; skill is something one has a finite amount of and should be husbanded, not wasted.[60] The purity of Stapleton's approach means that he is 'not forc'd to write / Like the gay Pandar, or smooth Parasite / To win oth'sense of man'.[61] He is not a persuasive mercenary writing for money; his art is not commodity. It has real value, irrespective of fashion and faction. Habington's lines praise Stapleton's chaste and scholarly life, explicitly setting his learning and poetics against a culture of patronage and pseudo-Latin poetry emerging from the court. The implicit dig at versifying hacks emphasises Stapleton's distance from the contemporary practices of the court and privileges his status as a cultural outsider. Habington punningly suggests that the court is not the true index of poetic achievement but that Stapleton will find praise from posterity: 'Court not Opinion, and triumphant bayes / Will follow Vertue.'[62]

Habington echoes the assertions by the poets from the Inns of Court that they are addressing (and creating) a different cultural space with an intentionally different identity and proud independence: this non-conformity contrasts with Laud and Duppa's Oxford which was in thrall to the King and part of the Caroline design. Stapleton would have been exposed to the activities of the Oxford panegyricists due to his attachment to the Prince of Wales's privy court, of which Brian Duppa was also a member; he and Habington differentiate themselves from the more celebratory productions of the Universities by their ambivalent approach to the Caroline project.[63] The University collections are also informed by the educational, masculine discourse of Oxford and Cambridge; work emanating from the nexus of Holborn and the Catholic coteries was less politically inflected, more ambivalent about the status of women and concerned with celebrating difference rather than employing poetry for ideological purposes.

William Habington's poems of 1634-35 (the two slightly different editions of *Castara*) themselves portray various images of sterilised and submissive womanhood. 'A Mistris', he writes, 'sings, but not perpetually, for she knowes, silence in woman is the most perswading oratory'; a wife is 'inquisitive onely of new wayes to please him [her husband], and her wit sayles by no other compasse then that of his direction'.[64] The poems celebrate Platonic chastity and virtue; there are verses 'Upon the mutuall love of their Majesties' and on 'The Perfection of Love'. As Veevers notes, Habington critiques the idolisation of women whilst celebrating the modest and moderate *honnête femme*.[65] The implication that female intellectual agency is a trope of controlling moderation is illustrated in the passivity foisted upon Lady Twistleton by Stapleton's preface. She is an exemplar to be offered gifts, one of the 'Noble Sexe' but not an equal. Similarly, the Oxford panegyrics of the 1630s associate Henrietta Maria with comparable passivity, 'translating' or transferring from the masculine Latin of University disputation to allow her conference with them. The role of the translator, whilst ostensibly supine to both patron and author, is in fact rather more powerful than is at once apparent, the relationships subtly nuanced.

Habington claims that Stapleton's unfashionable work is based upon a Neo-Platonic 'Vertue', contrasted with the debauchery and impiety of the court. Through following the examples of accomplishment, moderation and beauty demonstrated by such women as Lady Twistleton, and by ignoring 'Opinion', timeless and transcendent art will be produced that will monumentalise Stapleton's reputation, 'A Pyramid to thee in Dido's Pile'.[66] Once again the gender dynamics subjectify the exemplary woman as a mere stepping stone for the ambitious man. Stapleton's translation and Habington's dedication, then, articulate a series of positions that complicate our understanding of the literary and political atmosphere of the 1630s. They both illustrate a clear concern with the non-courtly, and the relationship between the outsider and the court; and they both assign the role of poet, writer or translator a clear status, in distinction to the propagandists and parasites at court. Habington presents an image of the author as proudly independent, speaking truth in non-mainstream spaces, almost a dissident voice in the wilderness. The poem presents a jaundiced view of the court written from the fringes. Foreignness, otherness and isolation, such concepts are presented as positives, constructing an identity of difference, of constructive alienation related to virtue. Conversely, however, when applied to gendered agency such terms are deployed in a revisionist fashion, seeking to culturally construct and constrain femininity into a standard and uncomplicated model. Stapleton's text is at the meeting point of several different discourses of the 1630s. It encompasses the construction and transmission of a coterie or group identity and dynamic, the coded celebration of the virtuous female and an attendant complication of the

Coteries, complications and female agency

role and agency of aristocratic and extra-courtly women. Whilst the contexts for the volume seem to tend toward a more complicated and certainly more liberated model of female textuality, particularly with relation to the compilation, composition and transmission of manuscripts, this intellectual and familial agency can be seen to be compromised and contained through authorial and print strategies designed to exemplify and thereby further disenfranchise.

APPENDIX

On DIDO and ÆNEAS, Translated by my much honourd, much lou'd friend, Robert Stapylton Esq;

> Thy life and Verse is such, I dare commend
> Thee and thy labours, and boast thee my friend
> To my advantage: for I good must be
> And knowing, if I praise thy wit and thee.
> Nor can praise swell thee, who nere hop'st to sit
> At the loud-talking helme of seeming wit,
> And steere the ship of fooles; who tak'st no pride
> To haue thy name 'mong Ladies glorified,
> Or Lords like them iudicious: who hast wealth
> Enough to drinke, not mentioning their health.
> Thy soule is liberall: not forc'd to write
> Like the gay Pandar, or smooth Parasite
> To win oth'sense of man. Thy fanci's find
> A vertuous operation in the mind.
> But those hereafter to the World youle show
> By this Translation you now Print we know
> You Latin understand, a Science few
> Haue reacht oth'magnified Poetick crew,
> Who yet perswade the Courtier, Maro's vaine
> Is Pigmey to their owne Gyganticke straine.
> And they who haue the ancient Latins read,
> Or late Italians, will uncrowne thy head
> Of its due Laurel, and sharpe Criticks be
> Not 'gainst thy worke, they cannot, but 'gainst thee
> Who wouldst not their fine cunning imitate,
> Intitling that thy owne, thou didst Translate.
> By this they grew proud minions to fond Fame,
> Thogh like the Moon they shind with borrowd flame
> Cold in themselues: or prodigally spent
> Like riotous youth, only on monies lent.
> While thou, as I, how ere they malice it,
> Dost onely spend oth'stocke of thy owne wit.
> Endeauour nobly still. And should the sport

> Of vs but the gay wonder of the Court,
> The perfum'd Sir Whisper ith'Ladies eare,
> That Dido doth not in thy language beare
> Due state, or copies want th'Originals art,
> Bid him, play with his Fan and Act his part.
> Court not Opinion, and triumphant bayes
> Will follow Vertue. Euen this Peice will raise
> Not Subject to times rage, or Enuies spoile,
> A Pyramid to thee in Dido's Pile.
>
> W. Habington

NOTES

1. William Habington, 'To my honoured friend and kinsman, R. St. Esq', *Castara* (London, 1634), lines 1–2. I am indebted to the Houghton Library, Harvard for a fellowship to work on manuscripts during 2002. This article has benefited hugely and gratefully from the selfless input of James Knowles, Danielle Clarke and particularly Julie Sanders, for which much thanks.

2. Julie Sanders, 'Caroline salon culture and female agency: the Countess of Carlisle, Henrietta Maria, and public theatre', *Theatre Journal*, 52 (2000), 450.

3. Martin Butler, *Theatre and Crisis 1632–42* (Cambridge: Cambridge University Press, 1984); Erica Veevers, *Images of Love and Religion: Queen Henrietta Maria and Court Entertainments* (Cambridge: Cambridge University Press, 1989); R. Malcolm Smuts, *Court Culture and the Origins of a Royalist Tradition in Early Stuart England* (Philadelphia: University of Pennsylvania Press, 1987).

4. Laud to Strafford, quoted in Caroline M. Hibbard, *Charles I and the Popish Plot* (Chapel Hill: University of North Carolina Press, 1983), p. 51. For an overview of the diversity of political and religious opinion cleaving to Henrietta Maria during the 1630s, see R. Malcolm Smuts, 'The puritan followers of Henrietta Maria in the 1630s', *English Historical Review*, 93 (1978), 26–45.

5. Francis Lenton, 'A Fiction by way of Argument on this Booke', *The Young Gallants Whirligigg* (London, 1629), line 2.

6. James Grantham Turner, *Libertines and Radicals in Early Modern London* (Cambridge: Cambridge University Press, 2002), p. xii. On the Inns of Court in general, see Jeremy Maule, 'Donne and the words of the law', in David Colclough (ed.), *John Donne's Professional Lives* (Cambridge: D. S. Brewer, 2003), pp. 19–37, and Martin Butler, '*Love's Sacrifice*: Ford's metatheatrical tragedy', in Michael Neill (ed.), *John Ford: Critical Re-Visions* (Cambridge: Cambridge University Press, 1988), pp. 201–31.

7. John Carey, *John Donne*, (London: Faber & Faber, 1981), pp. 8–12.

8. Lenton, *Young Gallants Whirligigg*, p. 5.

9. Francis Lenton, *Characterismi: Or, Lentons Leasures* (London, 1631), sig. F4r.

10. Lenton, *Young Gallants Whirligigg*, sig. A2v.

11. Beinecke Library, Yale University, Osborn MS b.205, fol. 17v; see also Veevers, *Images of Love and Religion*, pp. 82–3, 146–7.

12 'To the Foure Honourable Societies, and famous Nurseries of Law, the Innes of Court', *The Innes of Court Anagrammatist: Or, The Masquers masque in Anagrammes* (London, 1634), line 14. See Laurence Venuti, 'The politics of allusion: the gentry and Shirley's *The Triumph of Peace*', *English Literary Renaissance*, 16 (1986), 182–205.

13 To Dorset, Beinecke Library, Yale University, Osborn MS b.205; to the Cages, Huntington Library, MS HM 120.

14 See Allan H. Stevenson, 'Shirley's publishers: the partnership of Crooke and Cooke', *The Library*, 4th series, 25 (1945), 140–62. Biographical information on Shirley's residence in Holborn is found in William D. Wolf, 'Some new facts and conclusions about James Shirley', *Notes and Queries*, 227 (1982), 133–4.

15 See Sandra A. Burner, *James Shirley: A Study of Literary Coteries and Patronage in Seventeenth-Century England* (Lanham and London: University Press of America, 1988), pp. 65–7.

16 'The Author to the Reader', *The Gratefull Servant. A Comedie* (London, 1630), sig. A5v, line 2.

17 'To my friend Mr Shirley upon his Comedy', lines 22; 15–18.

18 The trope of the phoenix rising has a complicated history in relation to Catholicism, see John Watkins, '"Out of her ashes may a second phoenix rise": James I and the legacy of Elizabethan anti-Catholicism', in Arthur F. Marotti (ed.), *Catholicism and Anti-Catholicism in Early Modern English Texts* (Basingstoke: Macmillan, 1999), pp. 116–37.

19 Kenneth Allot (ed.), *The Poems of William Habington* (London: University Press of Liverpool at Hodder and Stoughton, 1948), p. 181. The references were 'toned down' for the published versions.

20 Shirley's *Bird in a Cage* also reacts to Prynne, see Kim Walker, '"New prison": representing the female actor in Shirley's *Bird in a Cage*', *English Literary Renaissance*, 21 (1991), 383–400.

21 He sometimes is found as 'Abington'. For the main biographical information see Allot (ed.), *The Poems of William Habington*, pp. xiv–xvii.

22 Burner, *James Shirley*, p. 98.

23 See Hibbard, *Charles I and the Popish Plot*, p. 154. In 1634 rumours of a papist uprising centred on the house and some of the regular visitors, mainly Sir Kenelm Digby and his wife Venetia: Kevin Sharpe, *The Personal Rule of Charles I* (New Haven and London: Yale University Press, 1992), p. 843.

24 Of course, not all of Henrietta Maria's followers were strictly Catholic, or Catholic at all, see Smuts, 'Puritan followers'. For discussion of the ambiguous religious convictions of a particular member of Henrietta Maria's court, see D. L. Smith, 'The fourth Earl of Dorset and the Personal Rule of Charles I', *Journal of British Studies*, 30 (1991), 257–87, and 'Catholic, Anglican or puritan? Edward Sackville, fourth Earl of Dorset, and the ambiguities of religion in early Stuart England', *Transactions of the Royal Historical Society*, 6th series, 2 (1992), 105–24.

25 Lucy Hutchinson, *Memoirs of the Life of Colonel Hutchinson*, ed. with an introduction by James Sutherland (London, Toronto and New York: Oxford University Press, 1973), pp. 27–8.

26 Brendan O Hehir, *Harmony From Discords: A Life of Sir John Denham* (Berkeley and Los Angeles: University of California Press, 1968), p. 12.

27 See Martin Butler, 'Entertaining the Palatine Prince: plays on foreign affairs 1635–37', in Arthur F. Kinney and Dan S. Collins (eds), *Renaissance Historicism: Selections from English Literary Renaissance* (Amherst: University of Massachusetts, 1987), pp. 265–93.

28 See Butler, *Theatre and Crisis*, pp. 28–35.

29 See Julie Sanders, 'Tixall revisited: the coterie writings of the Astons and the Thimelbys in seventeenth-century Staffordshire', *Staffordshire Studies*, 12 (2000), 75–94, and Victoria Burke, 'Women and early seventeenth-century manuscript culture: four miscellanies', *The Seventeenth Century*, 12 (1997), 135–50.

30 'On Castaraes sittinge on Primrose banks', fol. 27v; 'upon Castaries and her sisters goinge A foote in the snow', fol. 28v; 'To the honourable George Talbot', fols 152v–3v.

31 Peter Beal, *Index of Literary Manuscripts, Volume II, Part 1* (London and New York: Mansell Publishing Limited, 1987), pp. 500, 504.

32 'ansure to these uerses Made by Mrs K. T.', Huntington Library, MS HM 904, fols 153v–4v, lines 1–2.

33 See Geoffrey Tillotson, 'The commonplace book of Arthur Capell', *Modern Language Review*, 27:3 (1932), 381–92. Capell copies nine Habington poems on fols 23v, 52v–55v.

34 See for instance copies at BL, Additional MSS 47111 and 15226; Folger Shakespeare Library, MS Vb. 43; Bodl., MSS Ashmole 38, Eng. poet. c. 53 and e. 14, Malone 21 and 23, Rawlinson poet. 84, 147, 160, 199, and Tanner 405. The poem was printed in the miscellany *Wit Restor'd* in 1658.

35 Arthur F. Marotti, *Manuscript, Print and the English Renaissance Lyric* (Ithaca: Cornell University Press, 1995), pp. 44–61; Harold Love, *Scribal Publication in Seventeenth-Century England* (Oxford: Clarendon Press, 1993).

36 Sanders, 'Tixall revisited', p. 81.

37 Houghton Library, Harvard, MS Eng. 703, pp. 148–9; 150–1; 152.

38 Jack Binns (ed.), *The Memoirs and Memorials of Sir Hugh Cholmley* (Woodbridge: Boydell Press, 2000), p. 84.

39 Binns (ed.), *Memoirs of Sir Hugh Cholmley*, pp. 86–99.

40 *Ibid.*, p. 87.

41 He does not, however, figure in the household expenses of the children of Charles I (BL, Harleian MS 7623) compiled in 1638 or 'The Names of all the Servants that attend the Prince his highnes, and the rest of his Mate Royall Children in Chamber, Household and Stable' compiled in 1641 (BL, Harleian MS 3791, fols 108r–16v).

42 Hugh Aveling, *Northern Catholics: the Catholic Recusants of the North Riding of Yorkshire 1558–1790* (London, Dublin, Melbourne: Geoffrey Chapman, 1966), p. 251.

43 *Dido and Aeneas the Fourth Booke of Virgils Aeneis now Englished* by Robert Stapleton Esqr. (London, [1634]). Entered on the Stationer's Register on 11 November 1634.

44 Nottinghamshire Record Office, MS DD/HU1.

45 O Hehir, *Harmony from Discords*, p. 13; Peter Beal perpetuates this narrative in his entry on Denham in *Index of Literary Manuscripts, Volume II, Part 1*, p. 331.

46 James Shirley, 'To Lady Dorothy Shirley', *Changes: Or, Love in a Maze* (London, 1632), lines 16–31.

47 Veevers, *Images of Love and Religion*, p. 27.
48 Walker, '"New prison"', p. 400.
49 Sophie Tomlinson, '"She that plays the king": Henrietta Maria and the threat of the actress in Caroline culture', in Gordon McMullan and Jonathan Hope (eds), *The Politics of Tragicomedy: Shakespeare and After* (London: Routledge, 1992), p. 192.
50 *Dido and Aeneas*, sig. A2v.
51 Ibid., sig. A2v.
52 'To my friend Mr Shirley upon his Comedy', lines 5–8.
53 Ibid., lines 16; 17–18.
54 *Dido and Aeneas*, sig. A2r.
55 Ibid., sig. A2r–v.
56 'On DIDO and ÆNEAS', lines 40–2.
57 Ibid., line 7.
58 Ibid., line 37.
59 Ibid., lines 29–30.
60 Ibid., line 31.
61 Ibid., lines 12–13.
62 Ibid., lines 39–40.
63 See Raymond A. Anselment, 'The Oxford University poets and Caroline panegyric', *John Donne Journal*, 3 (1984), 181–201.
64 'A Mistris', lines 28–30; 'A Wife', lines 34–5.
65 Veevers, *Images of Love and Religion*, p. 47.
66 'On DIDO and ÆNEAS', line 43.

Index

Note: 'n' after a page reference indicates the number of a note on that page.

Abbas, Shah, of Persia 114
Adamson, John 5
agrarian history 14
Alexander, Sir William (later Viscount Stirling) 76
Aleyn, Charles 192
Ali Beg, Naqd 114, 119
Allot, Kenneth 192
Andrewes, Lancelot 36, 175
Anna of Denmark, queen consort to James VI and I 93, 100, 103, 107n.6, 110n.53
Antrim, Randal MacDonnell, 2nd Earl of (previously Viscount Dunluce) 41, 129
Antwerp 16–17
Apethorpe Hall 17
Arden, Elizabeth 105
Arden, Goodeth 105
Argyll, Archibald Campbell, 8th Earl of 41, 43, 193
Arminianism 4, 147, 174, 175–6
 see also Laudianism
Arundel, Alathea Talbot Howard, Countess of 14, 17, 98, 129
Arundel, Thomas Howard, 14th Earl of 14, 24n.70, 33, 41, 81–2, 98, 99, 114–5, 129
Aston, Sir Walter 195
Atherton, Ian 83

Barlow, Thomas 118
Barnard, Dean Stanton 160
Barry, Lording 157
 Ram Alley 157
Bastwick, John 8, 9, 171–88

Beal, Peter 195
Beaumont, Elizabeth 104
Bedford, Francis Russell, 4th Earl of 15, 156
Bellany, Alastair 11, 181
Berwick 40
 Treaty of 87
Bingham 16
Bletso, Sir Anthony St John 196
Bolsover 7, 16, 26n.85
Book of Sports 7, 8, 18, 158, 175, 178
Bordier, Jacques 99
Boucan, Jacques, alias Cordier 100
Britland, Karen 7, 17
Brome, Richard 5, 15, 26n.85, 154, 155
 Antipodes, The 157, 163
 City Wit, The 157, 158–60
 Damoiselle, The 157, 164
 English Moor, The 157, 164
 Jovial Crew, A 154, 163
 Mad Couple Well Match'd, A 157
 New Academy, The 156, 164
 Sparagus Garden, The 156
 Weeding of Covent Garden, The 15, 156, 157
Brotton, Jerry 112
Brown, Cedric 16
Bryson, Anna 37
Buckingham, George Villiers, 1st Duke of 2, 3, 33, 79, 82, 96, 98, 104, 139, 148, 149, 176, 196
Buckingham, Katherine Villiers MacDonnell, Duchess of 129
Bueil, Honorat de, Sieur de Racan 141
Burford, Ephraim John 160
Burgess, Glenn 30

Index

Burton, Henry 8, 9, 171–88
Butler, Martin 15, 122, 143, 155, 158, 166, 189, 190, 194
Byrd, William 18

Cage, Sir Anthony 191
Cahill, Daniel 100
Calvinism 4, 35–6, 174, 182
Campion, Thomas 18
Canny, Nicholas 31
Capell, Arthur 195
Carew, Thomas 3, 5, 7, 13, 125, 196
  Coelum Britannicum 7, 125
Carew, Lady Thomasina 103
Carlell, Lodowick 155
Carlisle 40
Carlisle, Lucy Percy Hay, Countess of 110n.52, 126, 128, 189, 193, 197
Carnarvon, Anne Dormer, Countess of 130
Carnarvon, Robert Dormer, 1st Earl of 130
Cartwright, William 155
Castlehaven, James Touchet, Earl of 11, 126
Catherine de Medici 96
Catherine of Aragon 93
Caussin, Nicholas de 191
Charles I 1, 2, 3, 4, 5, 7, 16, 19, 39, 104, 155–6, 158, 159, 173, 177–8, 181, 189, 202
  artistic patronage 63, 99, 106, 118, 121, 138
  as Prince of Wales 35, 100
  courts and household 12, 94, 121, 140, 157, 159–60
  East India Company and 115, 117
  finance 28, 30, 32, 159
  Henrietta Maria and 2–3, 37–8, 68, 75, 86, 89n.2, 92, 93, 96, 141
  image of 50–69, 121, 122, 127, 140
  military affairs and 3, 4, 8, 30, 32, 34, 39, 41, 42, 43, 121–2, 145–6
  religion and 4, 8, 35, 44, 95–6
  Scottish coronation 7, 8
  writings 9, 74–88
Charles, Prince of Wales (later Charles II) 102, 105, 198, 203
Charles Louis, Elector Palatine 12, 33, 40, 194
Cholmley, Elizabeth 197–8
Cholmley, Sir Henry 194, 196, 197–8
Cholmley, Sir Hugh 197
Cicero 120
Clarendon, Edward Hyde, 1st Earl of 3
Clark, Ira 155
Clifford, Lord Henry 18
Cogswell, Tom 14
Coke, Sir John 74, 75, 77
Con, George 96
Congreve, William 154
Conway, Edward Conway, 1st Viscount 74
Conway, Edward Conway, 2nd Viscount 9, 34, 41
Cooke, William 191, 198
coteries 1, 5, 12, 17, 189–209
Cottington, Francis Cottington, 1st Baron 171
Cotton, Dodmore 114
Courteen, Sir William 115
Coventry, Thomas Coventry, 1st Baron 74
Cowley, Abraham 16
Creaser, John 6
cultural geography 6, 10, 13–14, 16
Cumberland, Francis Clifford, 4th Earl of 18

Davenant, Sir William 24n.70, 38, 111–37, 139, 155, 191, 192
  Britannia Triumphans 55
  Salmacida Spolia 38
  Temple of Love, The 111–37
Davenport, William 11
Davies, Julian 7, 35
Dean, Forest of 11
De Groot, Jerome 7, 12, 17
Dekker, Thomas 139

Index

Denbigh, Susan Feilding, Countess of 103, 104, 105, 118, 130
Denbigh, William Feilding, 1st Earl of 13, 105, 115–18, 126, 130, 133n.26, 134nn.31, 40, 135nn.43, 47
Denham, Sir John 199
Denmark 93
Dering, Richard 100
Desmond, Bridget Feilding, Countess of 126, 130
Desmond, George Feilding, 17th Earl of 126, 130
D'Ewes, Sir Simonds 138
Dieussart, François 99
Digby, John 32
Digby, Lady Venetia 193, 195
Donne Henry 190
Donne, John 190
Dorchester, Dudley Carleton, Viscount 33, 34, 74
Dorset, Edward Sackville, 4th Earl of 8, 30, 129, 191
Dorset, Mary Sackville, Countess of 129
Dover, Henry Carey, 1st Earl of 130
Dover, Mary Carey, Countess of 130
Dow, Christopher 179
Drayton, Michael 17
Dugard, Thomas, 17–18
Duppa, Brian 203
Dupplin, George Hay, Viscount 76
D'Urfé, Honoré 141
   L'Astrée 141

East India Company (Dutch) 113–14
East India Company (English) 113, 114, 115, 117
Edmondes, Sir Thomas 181
Edward I 93
Elizabeth I 92
Elizabeth, Princess (later Queen of Bohemia) 36, 38
Elliott, John Huxtable 112
Elyott, William 138
Essex, Elizabeth, Countess of 126, 129

Essex, Robert Devereux, 2nd Earl of 32–3
Essex, Robert Devereux, 3rd Earl of 126, 129

Falkland, Lucy Cary, Viscountess 105
Fane, Lady Rachel 17
Fanshawe, Sir Richard 17, 195
Farley-Hills, David 154
Felton, John 2, 148–8, 195–6
Fennor, William 164–5
Finch, John, Lord Chief Justice 164, 171
Fletcher, Alan 11
Forced Loan 30
Ford, John 5, 22n.35, 26n.85, 158
Fowler, Constance Aston 194–5
Fox, John 192
France 3, 30, 92–110
Fuller, Thomas 172

Garnier, Françoise 101
Garnier, Robert 142, 147
   Antigone 142
   Bradamante 142
   Marc Antoine 147
Geertz, Clifford 14
Gentileschi, Orazio 98
Gerbier, Balthazar 86
Gibson, William 114
Girouard, Mark 14
Goodman, Nicholas 161
Goring, George Goring, Baron 130
Goring, Mary Goring, Baroness 130
Gough, Melinda 96
Grand Remonstrance 3
Grant, John 157
Greenwich 97, 98
Grynder, Ralph 99
Guarini, Giovanni Battista 141
   Il pastor fido 141
Gustavus II of Sweden 13, 43

Habington, Lucy Herbert 193
Habington, William 191, 192–3, 194, 195, 198, 202–3, 204

Castara 191, 195, 204
Queen of Aragon, The 194
Haddington, Thomas Hamilton, 1st Earl of 76
Hall, John 192
Hamilton, James Hamilton, 3rd Marquis of (later 1st Duke of) 42, 76, 77, 78, 79–80, 82, 85, 86, 87, 104, 129
Hamilton, Mary Hamilton, Marchioness of 115, 129
Hampden, John 9
Harbage, Alfred 154
Harper, Thomas 143
Henrietta Maria, queen consort to Charles I 1, 122, 123, 141, 147, 155–6, 192, 198, 199, 200
  artistic patronage 7, 17, 96–100, 111, 122, 128, 138, 141, 148, 155, 202
  court and household 3, 12, 17, 94–5, 99, 101–6, 142, 189–90, 191, 203
  foreign policy and 3, 100–2
  image of 93–4, 124, 126, 127, 204
  religion 95–6, 98, 193
  see also Charles I
Henry, Prince of Wales 16, 35, 55–6, 59, 68, 147
Herbert, George 5
  Temple, The 5
Herbert, Sir Henry, Master of the Revels 160
Herbert, Thomas 113, 114, 119–20, 123, 125, 133n.23
Herrick, Robert 5, 7, 139, 196
  Hesperides 7
Heylyn, Peter 4, 179, 181
Hibbard, Caroline 2, 13, 17, 39, 155
Holland, Elizabeth 160, 161
Holland, Henry (son of Philemon Holland) 122
Holland, Henry Rich, 1st Earl of 41, 81, 121, 130
Holland, Isabel Rich, Countess of 130
Holland, Philemon 121

Holles, Gervase 126
Hooker, Richard 175
Hopton, Sir Arthur 81
Hudson, Jeffrey 203
Hughes, Ann 17
Hutchinson, Lucy Apsley 64, 193–4, 199
Hutton, Ronald 10

Inns of Court 22n.35, 55, 190, 191–4, 196, 197, 199, 203
  Gray's Inn 190, 191, 197
  Lincoln's Inn 193, 199
  Middle Temple 194
Ireland 2, 10, 11, 12, 30, 31

James VI and I 2, 3, 18, 32, 36, 37, 67, 103, 178, 181
Jondorf, Gillian 142
Jones, Ann Rosalind 115
Jones, Inigo 37, 52, 53, 55–6, 57, 59, 60, 61, 62, 63, 65, 67, 68, 69, 70n.16, 97, 112
Jonson, Ben 7, 11, 15, 18, 67, 68–9, 138, 154, 155, 161, 192, 196
  Alchemist, The 11, 168n.11
  Every Man Out of His Humour 156
  King's Entertainment at Welbeck, The 7
  Love's Triumph through Callipolis 55
  Love's Welcome at Bolsover 7
  Mortimer, His Fall 16
  Oberon, the Fairy Prince 54–5
  Pleasure Reconciled to Virtue 18
  Prince Henry's Barriers 55
  Magnetic Lady, The 157
  New Inn, The 143, 157
  Sad Shepherd, The 16
  Staple of News, The 157
  Tale of a Tub, A 7, 157
  Timber, or Discoveries 148
Jordan, Thomas 15, 158
  Walks of Islington and Hogsden, The 158, 163–6

Index

Kaufmann, Ralph James 154, 155
Kent, Elizabeth Grey, Countess of 129
Kent, Henry Grey, 18th Earl of 129
Killigrew, Anne 103
Killigrew, Elizabeth 193
Knowles, James 12–13
Kynaston, Sir Francis 15
   Corona Minervae 15

Lake, Sir Thomas 32
Langelüddecke, Henrik 4
Lanier, Nicholas 97, 99–100
La Pierre, Simon de 100
Laud, William, Archbishop of Canterbury 4, 8, 40, 44, 75, 80–1, 84, 85, 88, 132n.12, 165, 166, 171–2, 173, 175, 176, 177, 180–1, 182–3, 190, 203
Laudianism 4–5, 9, 37, 157, 174, 175
   see also Arminianism
Lautner, Edward 140, 141
Lee, Maurice 76
Leicester, Robert Sidney, 2nd Earl of 75, 82–3, 86
Lenton, Francis 190–1, 196
Le Sueur, Herbert 99
Lindsey, Elizabeth Bertie, Countess of 130
Lindsey, Robert Bertie, 1st Earl of 130
Lipsius, Justus 29–30, 31, 42, 44, 45
local history 14
London 16, 22n.35, 34, 49, 69, 99, 100, 114, 156–67
   Arundel House 14, 17, 108n.33
   Covent Garden 15, 156–8
   Holborn 190, 191, 193, 194, 197, 198, 199, 202, 203
   Hyde Park 156, 197
   St Bartholomew by the Exchange 157
   St Gregory 8
   St James's Palace 50–1, 98, 109n.35
   St Paul's Cathedral 4, 8, 37, 156
   Somerset House 97, 98, 99, 109n.39
   theatres 9, 11
   Westminster 26n.83, 171
   Whitehall 36–7, 55, 97, 98, 118, 160
   Worcester House 193
   see also Inns of Court
Louis XIII of France 145–6
Love, Harold 196
Lovelace, Richard 16
Lucan 138, 148–9
Ludlow 8, 9, 15, 18, 155

McCullough, Peter 35
Machiavelli, Niccolò 29, 30, 120
Macinnes, Allan 77
Mackay, Donald, 1st Lord Reay 77–8
McRae, Andrew 8
Madagascar 24n.70
Madrid, Treaty of 3
Mar, John Erskine, Earl of 76
Marcus, Leah 7, 8
Margaret of Anjou 95
Marie de Medici, queen consort of Henri IV 97, 102
Marmion, Shakerley 156, 158
   Holland's Leaguer 156, 158, 160–3, 164, 166
Marotti, Arthur 196
Marvell, Andrew 138
masques 5, 13, 19, 35, 37, 50–69, 96, 111–37
Massinger, Philip 18, 192
   New Way to Pay Old Debts, A 18
Maxwell, Julie 157
May, Thomas 17, 138–53, 192, 195
   Antigone 138–53
   translation of Lucan's *Pharsalia* 138, 149
Mayerne, Theodore de 98–9
Maynwaring, Roger 33, 36, 144
Menteith, William Graham, 7th Earl of (later Earl of Strathearn, and of Airth) 76–7, 78, 79, 86, 87–8
Mico, Richard 100
Middleton, Thomas 157, 165
   Chaste Maid in Cheapside, A 157

215

Game at Chess, A 165–6
Miles, Theodore 156, 157
Milton, Anthony 4
Milton, John 8, 9, 11, 15, 18, 45, 155
   *Masque Presented at Ludlow Castle, A
     (Comus)* 8, 9, 11, 15, 18, 155
'Molette, Claude de' 97–8
Monmouth, Elizabeth Carey, Countess
   of 110n.53
Monmouth, Robert Carey, 1st Earl of
   110n.53
Montemayor, Jorge de 142
   Diana 142
Montagu, Walter 7, 148
   Shepherds' Paradise, The 7, 148
Morrill, John 11

Nabbes, Thomas 15, 156
   Covent Garden 156
Neo-Platonism 5, 7, 111, 113, 122, 128,
   146, 148, 189–90, 191, 192,
   204–5
Newcastle, William Cavendish, Earl of
   7, 12, 16–17, 26nn.85–6, 157
   Country Captain, The 157
Newport, Anne Blount, Countess of
   130
Newport, Mountjoy Blount, 1st Earl of
   130
Norbrook, David 138, 148–9
Northumberland, Algernon Percy,
   10th Earl of 3, 35, 41–2

Ochiltree, James Stewart, Earl of 77–8,
   79, 86
Orgel, Stephen 112, 119

Palatinate 3, 8, 36, 39, 84, 148
parliament, English 1–2, 9, 32–4, 43,
   44, 74, 83, 92, 101, 138, 143, 144,
   147, 165, 175, 178, 183
   Long Parliament 29, 42, 88, 93,
     165, 183
   Short Parliament 1, 43, 88
parliament, Irish 2

parliament, Scottish 2
Parr, Anthony 112
Parr, Katherine 93
Parry, Graham 5
Patterson, Annabel 178–9
Peacock, John 6, 13, 16, 19, 97, 119
Pembroke, Anne Clifford, Countess of
   129
Pembroke, Mary Sidney, Countess of
   147
Pembroke, Philip, 4th Earl of 129, 193,
   194
Petition of Right 11, 177–8
Petitot, Jean 99
playhouses 5, 9, 11
Plumb, John 102–3
Pocock, John 29, 138
Porter, Endymion 19, 24n.70, 97, 139,
   140, 148, 149, 151, 193
Portland, Frances Weston, Countess of
   130
Portland, Jerome Weston, 2nd Earl of
   130
Portland, Richard Weston, 1st Earl of
   101
Poynting, Sarah 9
Price, Lawrence 161
Prynne, William 6–7, 8, 40, 124–5,
   126, 171–88, 191, 192
   Histriomastix 6–7, 124, 171, 172, 191
Pym, John 144–5

Randolph, Thomas 192, 195
Reeve, John 2
Restoration drama 154, 156
Richard, Lewis 100
Richelieu, Armand Jean du Plessis de
   30, 101, 102
Richmond 194, 199
Ripa, Cesare 143–4
Roe, Sir Thomas 113–14
Rogers, Malcolm 19
Roxburgh, Jean Kerr, Countess of 103
Rubens, Peter Paul 97
Rupert, Prince 24n.70, 82

Russell, Conrad 2, 84, 90n.24
Rutland, Francis Manners, 6th Earl of 192
Rutter, Joseph 148, 152n.7
  Shepherd's Holy-day 148
Rutter, Thomas 195

Said, Edward 111, 112, 128, 131n.9
St Antoine, Monsieur de 16, 50–3
St Leger, Anthony 196
Sanders, Julie 128, 155, 161, 163, 189, 197
Scory, Sir Edmund 196
Scotland 2, 3, 7, 8, 9, 10, 11, 12, 18, 40, 41, 42–3, 74–91, 103, 178
Scott, Jonathan 28, 29
Scudamore, John Scudamore, 1st Viscount 82
Sedley, Sir Charles 156
  Mulberry Garden, The 156
Selwin, Sir Nicholas 196
Shakespeare, William 68
  Hamlet 68
  Troilus and Cressida 163
Sharpe, Kevin 77, 78, 159, 180
Sherburne, Edward 192
Sherley, Sir Anthony 113
Sherley, Sir Robert 114, 118, 119
Sherley, Lady Teresa 118, 119
Ship Money 5, 9, 34, 35, 39, 43
Shirley, Lady Dorothy 199
Shirley, James 5, 11, 15, 17, 26n.85, 152n.7, 191, 192, 198, 199, 202
  Bird in a Cage, The 200
  Gratefull Servant, The 192, 200
  Hyde Park 156, 158
  St Patrick for Ireland 11
  Sisters, The 163
  Triumph of Peace, The 22n.35, 55, 191
Sidney, Sir Philip 120, 147, 153n.27
Singh, Jyotsna 117
Skipton Castle 18
Skretkowicz, Victor 147
Smuts, Malcolm 4, 6, 10, 15, 189, 193

Smythson, John 14–15
Smythson, Robert 14–15
Somerset, Edward, Lord Herbert of Raglan 193
Sophocles 146
  Antigone 146, 149
Sovereign of the Seas 4, 35
Spain 3, 40, 101, 139, 146, 148
Spenser, Edmund 55, 120, 147
  Faerie Queene, The 55
Spottiswood, John, Archbishop of St Andrews 76, 85
Stallybrass, Peter 115
Stapleton, Robert 191, 192, 198, 200–3
  translation of Virgil's *Dido and Aeneas* 191, 201
Steggle, Matthew 10, 15
Stevenson, Allan 191
Stodart, Robert 123–4, 126
Stoeffken, Dietrich 100
Stoyle, Mark 14
Strong, Roy 14
Strafford, Thomas Wentworth, 1st Earl of 11, 30–2, 34, 40, 41, 42, 43, 44, 45, 83, 84, 85, 87, 88, 126, 165, 183
Suckling, Sir John 5, 155, 163, 164
  Goblins, The 163
Susa, Treaty of 3, 145
Sufi, Shah, of Persia 114, 117

Tacitus 31
Talbot, George 195
Tatham, John 16
  Love Crownes the End 16
Thimelby, Katherine 195
Thirsk, Joan 14
Thirty Years' War 3, 8, 13, 28, 30, 126
Tixall Circle 17
Tomlinson, Sophie 200
Totnes, George Carew, 1st Earl of 74
Townshend, Aurelian 13, 15, 65–9, 124–5
  Albion's Triumph 55, 57, 60, 62–3, 64, 65–9
  Tempe Restored 13, 96, 124–5

Index

Traquair, John Stewart, 1st Earl of 85
Turner, James Grantham 190
Turner, Victor 14
Twistleton, Lady Catherine 198–9, 200, 201, 202, 204
Twistleton, Sir George 198
Tyacke, Nicholas 4

Underdown, David 14

Van Dyck, Sir Anthony 5, 13, 19, 38, 41, 50–5, 97, 109n.34, 115–19
Vane, Sir Henry 33, 34, 43, 79, 86
Veevers, Erica 96, 189, 199–200, 204
Villiers, Eleanor 104–5

Wales 8, 10, 11, 12, 14
Walker, Kim 200
Waller, Edmond 196, 197
Warwick, Robert Rich, 2nd Earl of 129
Warwick, Susan Rich, Countess of 129
Welbeck 7, 16
Werburgh Street Theatre, Dublin 11

White, Francis 179
'Wiat, Hary' 196, 197
Wilford, Nicholas 114–15
Williams, Raymond 10
Williamson, Arthur 35
Wilton House 14
Wimbledon 97, 98
Wimbledon, Edward Cecil, Viscount 130
Wimbledon, Sophia Cecil, Viscountess 130
Windebank, Sir Francis 75, 81–2, 83, 84, 85–6, 88, 101, 164
Wither, George 174
Wood, Jeremy 50
Wyatt, Sir Robert 197
Wycherley, William 156
   Country Wife, The 156

Xenephon 120–2, 125, 126–7
   Cyropaedia 120–2, 125, 126–7

Young, Michael 3

EU authorised representative for GPSR:
Easy Access System Europe, Mustamäe tee 50,
10621 Tallinn, Estonia
gpsr.requests@easproject.com